My Name's Not Robbie Any More

A Modern Novel Laced With Humor

Lea Hope Becker

ISBN: 1500834181
ISBN 13: 9781500834180

MY NAME'S NOT ROBBIE ANY MORE

A Mother's Tale of Losing a Son and Gaining a Daughter

Acknowledgments

In this challenging world we occupy, I don't think anybody can get a successful book published without a big helping of outside intelligence to counter one's gaps in creativity.

I want to thank those people who assisted me with the writing and polishing of this book. On numerous occasions these folks kept me from hitting the wall or leaving town in a funk. My appreciation goes to my Palm Beach County writing group buddies, Barbara Bixon, Pat Williams, Carren Strock, Lee Ravine, Bea Lewis, Charlie Sterbakov, Bunny Shulman and Joe Berardino. My friend from high school, Harriet Baker, provided continuous moral support and offered many suggestions during the evolution of this story. My dear and long-time Chicago friend, Dr. Kiya Immergluck, read the entire manuscript and suggested many helpful revisions because some of the stuff I wrote was bound to make somebody nervous. I know it made both of us nervous. My equally dear friends, Pat Hoppe and her daughter, Chris Hoppe, coached me as I grappled with the cover concept. The result of all this help and wringing of hands is what's in this book.

Dedication

If ever a mother had a supportive group of children as I have had for the last half century, it has to be me.

My daughter, Merle, has believed in my work throughout my writing process. She persisted in her attempts to get me to acquire a website, solving some technical issues as she designed it. I also leaned on her to restore my energy, and even my sanity, as I traveled back and forth from West Palm Beach to Chicago to take care of business. She encouraged me at other times with helpful e-mails and phone conversations. I also benefited by use of her comfy sofa, where Merle and her husband, Jeff, accompanied by Leila, the Cat, comforted me as I vented, caught shuteye and laughed with them until after midnight.

My son, Barry, has been caring and as understanding as possible as I did my best to nurture our long-distance relationship with phone calls that should have been more frequent on my part. His interest and curiosity about my new career as a writer has been exceptionally helpful.

My son, Howard, never wavered in his affectionate acceptance of the many times I had to conclude our phone calls with, "Sorry, Hoz, I'm in the middle of a paragraph," or words to that effect. His "OK, Mom, I'll let you go, Luv Ya!" echoed in my ears more often than the number of rainy days in my neighborhood during the months of July and August, as I finished this book.

To Merle,, Barry and Howard, I dedicate this novel. The story has nothing to do with their lives, but it has everything to do with the caring relationships that a mother and her children need to have and preserve during their time on earth. May they all be as warm as in our foursome.

Lea Hope Becker, the Mom

MY NAME'S NOT ROBBIE ANYMORE

A story that could be true, but isn't, by Lea Hope Becker

Sometimes you sense that an earth-shaking event is about to occur in your life. It might even be lurking on your doorstep. Suppose you opened your front door to discover that a package was being handed to you that would not only turn your day upside down, but would rudely affect your marriage, your social and family life, your goals and your familiar routines. Would you use every tactic and skill you'd ever acquired in order to emerge damage free? Naturally, I'm leading up to something that happened to me which turned out to be a monster kick in the head. It was several days after my Seventieth birthday, maybe a bunch more. I was spreading night cream along the creases in my neck when our eight chime doorbell rang. What happened after that caused even more creases and worry lines to appear.

1

I was in a hurry to work on my skin this morning. The rejuvenating lotion was next on my routine when I heard some hard knocking following what must have been several doorbell rings. My faded plaid bathrobe was untied and my fingers were oily. As I padded in my slippers from my bathroom over to the front door and stood on tiptoes to peer through the peephole, I attempted to wipe my hands clean inside the pockets.

"Just a minute, Joanne," I called through the door, "I'm having trouble turning the doorknob."

"I've got a certified delivery for you."

"Oh, thanks."

I tied my loose belt and coaxed the brass doorknob open by using the robe as a glove. Since it had now become laundry, I did a full scale wipe job down the sides of the fabric. Our friendly mail lady was holding a stack of letters and other paraphernalia.

"Here's your regular first class, Mrs. Sternberg, and I need you to sign for the certified."

"Sure thing. I'm glad your pen is attached to your clipboard."

"Sorry to interrupt your morning. Is that medicine on your neck?

"Sometimes I put night cream on in the daytime."

"I'll be on my way. Your phone is ringing."

I was holding a bulky manila envelope in my hands. The return address was that of my 42-year-old son, Robbie. I closed the front door and tossed the handful of bills and brochures on the dining room table, still clutching my son's envelope. I hadn't heard from him for weeks, and now I sensed it might be him on the phone, calling me and sending mail which would pin my ears back on the same day. That pride and joy son of ours was talented at everything except communication with his mother. I picked up the phone in my cubbyhole of an office and sneezed before saying hello.

"Mom? Or should I say God Bless You?"

"Wait, I just sprayed the whole phone." I grabbed a tissue and wiped my nose and everything else that appeared to be moist.

"Mom, it's me."

"I know it's you. You finally learned how to dial my number -- did your conscience do it?"

"Mom, don't be sarcastic with me -- I have something important to tell you. First of all, is Dad home?"

"No, he went skeet shooting. I didn't even hear him get out of bed."

"Well, I'm glad he's not there. What I'm going to say isn't easy. Are you sitting down?"

"No, I'm standing here like a statue. I already don't like the sound of this -- you're not going to tell me you just proposed to that former stripper with the five-inch long zebra-painted fingernails, are you?"

"Of course not, I've told you she's just a friend -- not a sweetheart."

"Robbie, there's a sort of a falter in your voice. Did you just work out?"

"No, but I just told you that I have something to tell you that's not easy."

"So tell me, what's wrong already. Don't tell me your chronic nosebleeds are back?"

"Well, Mom, uh, like, it's not quite like that -- it's about my recovery."

"You're not on drugs, thank God for that, so what are you recovering from?"

"I've just been released from the hospital."

"Robbie, what's wrong?"

"I'll explain everything, but I have to prepare you."

"Is that why I haven't heard from you, and does that have anything to do with what's in this envelope I'm looking at?"

"I can't see what you're looking at. I'm calling from Ohio. You're in Florida."

"It's got your return address and it's thick and banged up like it came from North Korea, or somewhere."

"Oh, when did it arrive?"

"About one hundred heartbeats ago -- give or take. They were irregular."

"Sorry, I'm guessing you haven't opened it yet."

"That's a splendid guess."

"Good, now here's what I called about."

"Whatever it is, say it slowly."

"I've had to change my name. It's not Robbie any longer."

"Go on, I know you've done something I'm not going to be able to talk about."

"You know what I'm going to tell you?"

"I sort of know. This is all about sex, isn't it? And I was worried about your hanging around with that stripper because she's built like a dike with nuts instead of ovaries."

"STOP TALKING!!!"

I clamped my lips together, determining never to open them again.

"Are you there?"

"MmmmmmMMMM!"

"I've had a sex-change operation, which took three separate surgeries. You're not going to be calling me Robbie any longer. Do you like the name, "Roberta?" Or maybe "Reba?"

I stood by my desk holding the phone, praying that I was dreaming and that the space around me was about to dissolve and I'd be flat on my back in my bed. "Is this real, Robbie? Maybe it's just a test."

"It's real, Mom. Mom? Are you all right?"

"No, I'm not all right. I think I might be having a seizure, but don't worry, it's mild. Don't send the ambulance."

"You were supposed to get the envelope and read it before I called."

I didn't answer. Robbie/Roberta/Reba hadn't hung up, despite my silence. With a hang-up, I would have heard that unwelcome recorded message after a buzz: "If you'd like to make a call---"

"Are you there, Mom?"

"Maybe I'm here. I'm still breathing. You do the talking."

"The operation was very expensive."

"Oh, does the envelope contain a, oh, what, a, bunch of bills?"

"No. It's a medical report. Linda gave me a loan -- a big one. I used up my savings. But there's still about twenty thousand I've got to come up with."

"The operation -- Is it reversible?"

Silence on the wire. Awful, horrifying, nerve-jangling silence. Then a croaked voice response: "It's not like a raincoat."

"Please don't talk to me like I'm still in first grade!"

"You're raising your voice -- please don't do that."

"What about your therapy?"

"I'm still going."

"I guess I have to open the envelope. Will I be having to read all the details of the exchange of your gonads?"

"Uh, huh."

"And of course, I'm the one who has to give this news to Dad."

"Uh, huh."

"Can I call you Robbie until the whole thing sinks in? Maybe I'm not as surprised as all that. It's your father I'm worried about. He'll have an attack -- either his heart or gas -- I'm not sure."

"I had a hunch you figured it all out, Mom. But what was it that actually clued you in?"

"Oh, something Monica said to me a few months ago."

"Monica? Who's Monica?"

"My former hairdresser. She died recently. Anyway, the last time she gave me her special color and cut treatment, I was telling her about our last visit to your apartment in Ohio. I told her about that French doll you had sitting on your bed."

"I thought you kept my private stuff to yourself."

"Well, I did and I still do. Telling my hairdresser was like talking to a priest."

"Mother, we're Jewish!"

"Monica was Catholic, I think. She thought you were most likely a woman in a man's body."

"Just from talking about that doll?"

"No, from some other things I told her. Anyway, nobody else knew what we talked about. She's dead and you're our long distance kid. So who else knows?"

"Just a few of my friends, including the woman you worried about. Linda was with me all the way -- all these last few years. I wouldn't have done it without her encouragement, and, of course, without her financial support."

"I figured that too. My daughter Linda, who's more like a man than a woman, has been your other mother for years. At least it feels that way. You'd better not blame me for having a hard time with this."

"I'm not blaming you."

"If I told this whole story to a script writer to make a soap opera out of it, he'd say it was too off the wall."

"It's out there, Mom, you have no idea."

"I just thought of a title for a new book. How about "Men Who Are Women and the Men Who Are Men Who Love Them."

"Mom, I know you're doing your published writer mom thing with the jokes, but I can't deal with it just right now. Also, I'm still weak and have to get off the phone. Please, open the envelope. There's a letter I wrote in there explaining why I couldn't tell you before I did it."

"I'll open the envelope. I'll read everything. Then I'll make a decision about how and when to tell Henry. He'll go nuts. We've both assumed you were gay and stifling yourself. Henry still does. Then I talked to Monica and began to see the light at the end of your tunnel. Some tunnel! You went into it as a handsome bachelor and came out as a what? A handsome old maid? When will this be public?"

"Not yet, Mom, and don't think of me as an old maid, please. They say I look good, but I'm nowhere near ready to face anyone else in our family, especially Aunt Beth and her upper crust husband. Cousin Cissy might be OK, but not that elite clan she's marrying into. I'm not even comfortable letting Aunt Julie Sue in on it, and definitely none of the younger cousins. I need a lot more time."

"I have to admire your moxie. In fact, I have to admire my own. I'm not dreaming and I'm not having a seizure. I'm not even mad at you -- well I'm mad because you didn't trust me. You're still my child. I know I birthed you because whatever happened about your male, uh, features, you still have my forehead and my eyes. And longer eyelashes than I have -- probably because I fed you so well."

"Mother, I have to hang up now."

"OK, I'll take care of your father if he starts to hyperventilate."

"You'll do fine, Mom, I know you will. But I do need some money from Dad."

"Like right away?"

"No. Take your time."

"You know that I love you, and I always will, but I don't know what the child I love looks like, and now that I'm loving a 42-year-old man who isn't a man any longer, I need to know all about your appearance. I just can't picture you as a six-foot two-inch tall brunette. For now, just tell me about the part that isn't covered up."

"I won't have to shave my face any more. I'm just as tall and a little thinner. My hair is still long and wavy."

"And your, you know?"

"A woman's body, Mom. Almost finished."

"Almost? What part did they leave out?"

"Read what's in the envelope."

"Was it painful?"

"No. They don't let you suffer like it was the Middle Ages. I think I'll be a much happier person."

"Let me think about the name, dear. Is it okay that I call you 'dear?'"

"Sure, Mom. I appreciate that. I love you so very, very, oh, --"

"Are you crying?"

"Sort of."

"Do you have handkerchiefs and not just Kleenex?"

"I think I have what I need."

"I have another question."

"Yes?"

"You didn't call me on my 70th birthday. Linda called me and wished me a happy birthday in your place. Were you still a man on my birthday? I need to know."

"I think I was saying Goodbye about ten minutes ago."

"Don't call here again until I call you. I don't want Dad picking up the phone. And stay off the e-mails and Facebook and Twitter broadcasts to the whole world. Keep it quiet for the time being."

"Of course."

I hung up the phone and realized in that moment that I didn't have any room in my hoard of worries to be concerned about what my neck looked like. Instead I was worried that this news about our son would have a major effect on my health. My right eyelid began to twitch. Did my face know something? I considered calling my internist. But what would I tell the nurse who answered? "Miss, I just found out my son is a daughter and my eyelid is twitching and I'm worried about my heart and my digestion and I think I'm suffering from brain cramps." Would she schedule me for a physical when I had just had one three weeks ago?

I had been standing that whole time during the phone conversation. There were two mirrored medicine cabinets flanking the large mirror over our sinks in the master bath. At the very least I needed to look at my right eye to see what turned on the motor in the eyelid. I walked like an unrecovered alcoholic from my office to the bathroom to look in the mirror. What I saw was a woman who needed work on her neck. At least the eyelid had stopped twitching. I was right in the neighborhood, so, despite my fears, I turned my head both left and right to inspect both side views. Could a phone call like the one I'd just had turn me into a hopeless old crone? I felt that my entire face had fallen from the first floor to the basement.

2

Henry was out having a good time with his shooting buddies and I was riddled with anxiety. He was due home in about an hour, but I needed more than an hour to collect myself after my conversation with Robbie. First of all, he wasn't Robbie any more. Second of all, I couldn't handle the first of all. Recalling some breath training I'd been given earlier in my nervous life, I inhaled deeply several times. The psychologist taught me how to stop before I passed out. We owned a blood pressure kit and I retrieved it from a cupboard in our kitchen. I couldn't get an accurate reading because my pulse was pounding like I'd just run a marathon. Lying down seemed sensible, so I made my way from the kitchen to my bedroom, grabbing the furniture to avoid stumbling. My robe smelled from the night cream, so I took it off and lay on the bed in my pajamas in pondering position. There had to be a safe way to break the news to Henry. How could I paint this picture with a gentle enough stroke? That we might be welcoming someday a new son-in-law at a ceremony where Robbie, or Roberta, or Reba, was to pledge undying love and devotion to a man? Suddenly the woman stripper with excess underarm and facial hair seemed angelic. Would our former son, now a daughter, look for a macho type, like a heavyweight champion, or a bouncer? And would they want to adopt babies and bring them up as girly-boys? I mercifully passed out while still in a state of disbelief.

Had the alarm clock rung? No, the alarm dinger wasn't even set. I heard a beeping noise coming from the kitchen. The double doored refrigerator was calling to report a possible infraction -- somebody hadn't closed it securely. There was danger lurking of soft butter, and maybe worse. Henry still wasn't home. The last thing I needed was a nagging refrigerator, so I got up and limped over to the kitchen to close the one door that always seemed to open itself up by a poltergeist. I knew we had one in our house because food kept disappearing from one of the cabinets. Another clue was that the glass surface of our dining room table had suspiciously recurring fingerprints that didn't match any of ours. On my way back to the bedroom I tried to reconstruct my interrupted dream. A ghostly figure was walking around on somebody's huge front lawn wearing a strange outfit. It might have been a shorty nightgown because its long legs showed. The creature resembled a character from "Night of the Living Dead." I knew the identity of the nightgown-wearing walker because it had Robbie's face, but the body was neither male nor female. It was sexless, like the bottom half of a Barbie or Ken doll. The dream was frightening, but my reality wasn't any better.

I wasn't the type to feel sorry for myself wearing pajamas all day, so I decided to get dressed. After struggling into yesterday's knee-length shorts, baggy tee-shirt, underwear and running shoes, I dealt with my unruly hair. The mirror over the dresser would have been my choice, but I'd left my comb in the bathroom. With a few deft swipes, my windstorm swept look subsided, but I wasn't finished. There was the business of the back of my head and my hand held mirror revealed tangled hairsprayed clumps sticking out in several directions. It was another day to put on the baseball cap. I brushed my teeth and searched in a few places for my watch. It was on my wrist. My back seemed stiffer than usual and I was beginning to feel the type of headache caused by being a parent. I spotted four liberated strands of hair lying in my personal sink basin. Henry's personal sink basin was always free of hair and dotted with bits of shaving soap. My job was to prevent any stray hair strands bearing my color from flying into his space. As I picked each of the four strands off the porcelain, my stomach gave a slight hint of upset followed by a full-fledged cramp. It was a near certainty that my superstition about bearing children was coming true. Any woman who had enjoyed such a quick and easy first child's birth as I had experienced with Robbie was bound to suffer her overdue punishment in the future.

The still unmade bed looked too inviting to ignore. I dove back into it and prayed to the God of Time Travel. *Please, please, make me twenty-two years old again! OK, I'll settle for thirty-two -- that was a pretty good time for me!* I picked up my favorite scientific escape book off the stack on my nightstand. It was Stephen Hawking's "A Brief History of Time." I cracked open the book, scanned the Table of Contents, and tried to read a few pages, but I couldn't find anything regarding age reversal. Nothing helped my mood, so I remained in bed, crabby and still Seventy Years Old. The front door was being opened by an individual who had a key.

3

I could feel a rhythmic thumping in my chest. Despite the wax buildup in my ears, the ticking of the alarm clock seemed louder than ever. Henry had returned home and I was afraid he'd hear my accelerated heartbeat with his stethoscope ears. He'd wonder why I was fully dressed and shuddering in our bed at this hour. I listened to the noises indicating his movements. First came the metallic click-swish as he dead-bolted the inside of our front door. Then there was a discernible plop as he placed his gun box on the floor of the family room. His next move should have been to open the box and remove the shotgun so he could take it to our utility room to begin the gun-cleaning process. I recognized the squeak of the box being opened, but then I heard his footsteps coming toward our bedroom. At first I kept my eyelids closed, but opened them a crack as he entered his personal space. He was the man of the house and he had his own wall.

"Marlene, are you snoozing?"

"Not exactly." I watched in fear as Henry placed his over-under skeet-shooting shotgun atop his chest of drawers.

"Why are you lying there?"

I raised my torso to a sitting position. "OK, I'm through lying down. Well, I needed a nap. I see you've come back from the range. It must be a Friday."

"Honey, don't you know what day it is? Yeah, I have to clean the gun, but it needs a repair. I have to get a part out of my closet."

"Oh, that's nice."

"Why is it nice? It's a damned nuisance. I'm sorry I woke you. Go back to sleep if you wish. I'll be quiet."

"Don't you have to change your sweaty shirt and brush your teeth like you always do when you come back from shooting?"

"I'll close the bathroom door so you can go nighty-nite in the daytime."

"Don't bother. I have something to tell you. It will require several sentences."

"Can it wait?"

"Go change your shirt and brush your teeth, but maybe you should listen to me before you go clean and fix your gun. Did you have lunch?"

"Just peanuts."

"I'll wait here for you on the bed."

The fates had intervened and granted me a small sliver of time to better compose myself. In those precious moments while Henry scrubbed the peanut leavings out of his teeth and changed shirts, I planned how to break the news to him as though I were writing a formal outline. One. Visualize husband's precise reaction upon infecting his routine afternoon. Two. Realize that he deserves peace and quiet after spending several hours in the hot Florida sun attempting to nail clay target birds along with other gun nuts. Three. Get hold of my own emotions because hysteria was contagious and Henry was susceptible. Four. Take comfort in the fact that we've already discussed our son's sexual problems; Henry already knew that Robbie wasn't a chip off the father's block. Five. Be understanding. A man of Henry's nature required a tactful approach from a wife with a revelation.

He emerged from the bathroom and went to his shirt drawer.

"Henry, I have to introduce a topic."

"A topic?" Sounds like you want to read one of your articles to me."

"No, then the word 'topic' is misleading. Actually, it's a revelation."

"Oh, a revelation. That's different."

My hands were shaking and I knew I had to slow my words so that I didn't sound like the world was coming to an end. But I had already made a mistake by not swallowing one of Linda's mood-altering medications. We always kept a bottle for her when she visited.

"Marlene, why are you holding onto the comforter for dear life?"

"I have something to tell you and it's hard."

"Have you gone and done something I won't like?"

"Not quite, Henry, Robbie has, however."

"Robbie? Don't tell me he's knocked up that stripper?"

"Worse than that, Henry. Worse than that."

"He killed her? Well, maybe that's not so bad, so long as he doesn't get caught."

"Henry, I know you're joking, but what I have to say is serious."

"Sorry, dear, you know I sometimes exaggerate. Now, are you going to shock me?"

"You know how Robbie has always been gentle, like a woman almost, even last year, when he sent you that oversized birthday card."

"Oh, the one with the flowery sentiment? I remember. The card had some stinky perfume, but there was a beautiful poem on it that Robbie composed himself. He turned down my offer of a subscription to that wrestling magazine, but he spent money to take a poetry class."

"Your offer happened at least three years ago, dear. Henry, I recommend that you be seated."

"We're in the bedroom. How can I be seated? The cedar chest is so stuffed I can't sit on it. You got rid of that one bedroom chair we used to have so you could buy an extra dresser."

"Sit on the bed, Henry."

"OK, I'm on the bed, what did that son of ours do?"

"He's changed his body."

"Changed it how?"

"He's had an operation."

"What kind?"

"The kind that will drive you to drink, or to the rabbi."

"Will you please be specific?"

"OK, he's gotten rid of his dick and his balls and replaced them with female parts. Was that shocking enough?"

"He's WHAT????????"

"He's had a sex-change operation. It's a done deal. Linda was there for the whole thing. We'll be calling him, I mean her, either Roberta or Reba."

"**He's lost his fucking mind**!"

"I was afraid you wouldn't take it well."

"If you were me, would you take it well?"

"I was worried you'd have an attack, like explode with uncontrollable feelings."

"**<u>I don't explode</u>**!!! Curse loudly, maybe." Henry stared at me the way a prosecutor might stare at a surprise defense witness. "So, now despite our careful upbringing, our son has gone overboard. I was hoping he was merely gay."

"I told you so many times he wasn't gay. Now you know my revelation."

"He called you while I was out?

I nodded.

"Well, I guess I can forget that I have a son."

I began to weep.

"Please don't cry. I hate it when you cry, but this time I . . . Marlene, are you OK?"

"Yes, I'm fine."

"You don't look fine." Henry took me in his arms and hugged me for about a minute. A half hour would have worked out better.

I watched his face for any hint of a sudden breakdown. *He gets it -- he knows I'm not stretching the truth and that I'm giving it to him straight. The color of his skin is changing. This might not be good.* Several dark moments passed and then he turned away from me, and I worried about his health. *A man of seventy-one and a half shouldn't have to deal with this kind of thing. It's bad enough that he has to observe the loose skin area below my chin that's been sagging more and more with each passing day. I keep buying more scarves and lately I've caught myself speaking with my head bowed. Now what's happening?*

"Henry, are you saying some kind of a Hebrew prayer, like a brocha?"

"I don't think they have a brocha for this situation. Don't talk for awhile, OK?"

Several more dark moments passed.

"Marlene, I want you to take this the right way and not as an accusation. I have to ask you this: Did you actually know in advance he was going to do this now? I can't believe you encouraged it."

"I suspected it, Henry, but if you're insinuating I encouraged it, I'd be quite upset. Why the hell would you think that?"

"You've been nagging me about getting a facelift for over a year now. If you're silly enough to think of paying a doctor thousands to make you look two years younger, then how much of a leap is it to suggest that our handsome son with those feminine instincts got his package changed into a ---- oh, don't make me say it!!!"

"Henry, Henry, I knew Robbie was having some hormone treatments, but I was afraid to dig too deeply. He could have been upping his testosterone for all I knew! Did I have the slightest hint he'd be going off the deep end like this? Did I need this kind of grief at the same time I'm crossing the seventy-year-old mark? **What did I do to deserve this**? And why was it such a, a, I think I'm choking, a secret?"

"He didn't want us to talk him out of it. He hid the whole thing from us. I'm sorry I brought up the facelift thing!"

"Linda, plus a few of his friends, those people he trusted. Not us. What he did and why I want a facelift are two completely different things! Lots of women my age get facelifts. Older women do it to get men to love them more. My own sister did it. I don't know too many men who are crazy enough to want to be women. Do you?"

"Oh, just a thought -- maybe you mentioned the face-lift idea to him and it ignited his own body-hating issues. I guess I'm sorry I said that."

"How sorry?"

"Sorry enough. Right now I'd like to take that kid and shake him until his Johnson falls off!"

"Henry, he doesn't have any --------!"

"Don't say it!"

"Henry, it's done already. He wanted to be a complete woman. He has felt for a very long time that he WAS a woman. What else is there to say? He's got different hormones than you have. They're even different than mine! And she's **your** son too!"

"OK, OK, let's get beyond the blame game. Marlene, I can tell when you're upset -- your face is red as a raspberry."

"And your face is the color of a rhubarb -- you'd better calm down, or it'll turn into an eggplant."

"I'm calming down."

"Right now I can only think of the implications for uh, our child. I'm not sure even what name to call him, uh, her."

"Sure, sure, honey, I guess I shouldn't have blamed you. I just lost it."

"I needed a kind thought from you, not a discussion about my face. Can't you see I'm really suffering?"

"I guess so." Henry paused and stared at the rug. I figured he was reflecting on his new status as the father of two girls instead of the father of one of each sex. His lips were moving like a taciturn man going into a verbal windup. When his power of speech returned I was reminded of how he looked on that day the stock market tanked back in the late eighties. *Why can't men deal with their feelings like normal people? Don't they realize that everything shows?*

"I'm, uh, going to bring my gun to the utility room now, but I won't stop to clean it or make a repair. I'll be right back."

"I'll wait, honey. Take your time -- I'll be right here on the bed, maybe for about a week."

As he left the room I continued to sit upright and kept rearranging the pillows behind me so that I could pretend I was a semi-invalid and that someone would attend to my every need. I glanced at the back of my hands to determine if any new veins had popped. When Henry returned, he bore a pensive look, but his skin color seemed to have returned to normal. His eyes had the look of a man who had just invented a new way to experience religion. Then he spoke with a thoughtful air.

"I'm assuming he had the operation at a major hospital in Ohio. Maybe I should be angry with Linda. You said she was there the whole time."

"He sent a full medical report so we'd have all the details. And yes, Henry, she was present and he said she gave him a temporary loan for a big part of it."

"Well, what about the rest of it? We both know that Robbie doesn't have savings worth shit. Does he even have decent health insurance? Wait a minute -- what am I thinking? I'm a former insurance man! Sex change surgery isn't normally covered except for prison inmates! Where the hell is he getting the rest of the money from?"

"Henry, that's another thing I've got to lay on you. Keep sitting on the bed, dear."

4

Was my 37-year-old daughter, Linda, who now lived and worked in Cleveland, something other than a talented woman with mechanical ability? I didn't know of any of our friends in our age group who had a daughter who operated a bus company and frequently repaired the motors of the buses herself. When she wasn't wearing those grease-stained coveralls, she wore such tailored clothes and had been seen smoking little cigars. Henry and I agreed that she came from his side of the family. Some of his brothers never wore anything else but coveralls.

I woke up from my second daytime nap in a pile of sweat. I remembered Henry had gone out again to run some errands. The sun was pouring through the bedroom window and illuminating my 10-carat gold necklace. I had left it sitting on the triple dresser, still awaiting its storage in the jewelry armoire. Since I hadn't died and gone to wherever the Jewish purgatory was located, I wrestled myself free of the summer weight blanket that had become stuck to my bare legs and walked over to the phone in my cubbyhole office to call Linda. If her secretary answered, I had a ready-made message: "Please ask my daughter to call me immediately." Amazingly, perhaps because I hadn't sinned for the past few hours, Linda answered the phone herself.

"Linda, I'm so relieved you actually answered your phone on the first try! I got the news about Robbie this morning! I'm sure you know all about what we spoke about, knowing how interwoven you two are."

"Did you get the whole story?"

"How do I know? It came as such a shock. We knew he wasn't happy about his manhood, but not that unhappy!"

"When was the last time you saw her in person?"

"'HER, YOU SAID 'HER!' So I wasn't dreaming!"

"No, Mom, I've been helping Rob with her transition, not to mention the financial end."

"He, oh, I mean she, sort of mentioned where most of the money for the operation came from. Why did it have to be a secret from us, the parents?"

"I loaned the money for most of the surgeries, but she's paying for the anesthesia plus the hormone treatments. They're quite expensive. She needs even more money and wants you to ask Dad for a loan."

"Stop right there -- why should Dad pay for any of it?"

"Because he can -- we know he still has the first buck he ever earned under a floorboard somewhere. Rob has worked her tail off to come up with a lot of the money."

"Then he really went through a change. I didn't think Robbie had anything saved. So, again I've misjudged your brother, uh, sister."

"You have no idea how hard this decision was. I tried to stay out of it, but Rob was determined. The new name is still up in the air, and for now, I call her Rob."

"Well, I just got through discussing this whole thing with Dad. It was the hardest most frightening conversation we've ever had. He's angry that we weren't involved with Robbie's decision."

"Look, the secrecy part wasn't my idea -- it was her requirement. She didn't trust how Dad would react, to say the least. You know that Dad is mired in his early twentieth century beliefs that being gay or sexually ambiguous is behavioral nuttiness."

"What about me? I can't handle it either!"

"Yes you can, Mom. Look, Robbie called you first, didn't he?"

"You said Robbie! He! You aren't clear either!"

Linda merely coughed and paused at that moment. At least she didn't hang up or give me some cockamamie excuse why she couldn't talk any longer.

"Linda, Robbie said that none of our family knows and that this has been going on for a few years. I'll admit I suspected it months ago."

"Well it isn't public. I and his medical team know, naturally. Oh, there are a few close friends who know, and one fellow at his auto plant who was supportive, and now you and Dad. Rob figured he'd better continue to look and act like a man to hold onto the job, even while he was getting hormone treatments. It was dreadful for him, but he managed it. The hormone stuff began about two and a half years ago. Remember when you two visited Robbie the last couple of times?"

"Yeah, the lights in the apartment were so dim we couldn't see what he really looked like. Dad thought that whole visit was weird, but I don't think he had a clue about what was going on."

"You did, Mom, but you too were afraid to talk to Dad about it. Can you imagine what Rob was feeling? So let me continue, please. The medical team is marveling how well she handled everything. And just like Robbie was a handsome guy, as a woman, she's quite striking. Say, do you like the name 'Roberta?'

"I'm not sure, but when I really get down to it, isn't it kind of old-fashioned? If she really wants to stick with the "R," there's more modern names, like "Redfield," or maybe "Reese," or if you give me time, I can probably come up with a real winner--"

"Mother, I'd like to discuss this further, but right now I'm busy. I have two appointments scheduled soon--"

"Great. We'll discuss the whole thing next year!"

"Don't get mad. It just happens to be a bad time. I've got some critical business decisions brewing."

"Sure, the last time it was good was when I was sixty-nine. At least help me out. How soon can we mention this whole thing to the family?"

"Oh, Cissy's wedding. Well, we talked about that. Let's wait for now. I promise I'll call you back as soon as I can."

"I'm not sure I can keep it all secret. Maybe I can."

"Mom, you can do it. You already got past Dad's reaction. That was the worst part. Rob will be relieved."

"I'm worried that Dad will shut Robbie out of his life."

"All he needs is time. Rob needs time. It will all be OK."

"I'm glad you're so confident."

"I'm proud of you, Mom, but I have to say goodbye. I've got a date with a banker in ten minutes!"

"A banker you're attracted to or a banker for a business matter?"

"Her name is Sally. She runs the investment division where I have my Chicago account."

"I guess I sort of sensed that. I don't even know why such a question comes out of my mouth!"

I said goodbye to Linda feeling like a dope for expecting her to hang on the phone with me like one of my gossipy women friends. Linda was Linda. I wished I knew who Robbie was, or was going to be. Right at that moment I didn't even know how to address him, or her, or what. Didn't my new daughter have to put something on a replacement drivers' license pretty soon? And when would I stop treating my 42-year old child like a youngster who needed a mother to make decisions?

5

My chest was still pounding intermittently. At least I had gotten past the part where my husband was told that his firstborn had incurred considerable expense to have his genitalia redone. And why did I even think to use the term "redone?" It wasn't like he had decided to change the wallpaper and the carpeting in his apartment.

My mind began retracing my entire childbearing life -- the whole 42 plus years of motherhood. *What kind of creature had I been gestating? Back in 1968 I thought a new male baby was a male for life. Oh, surely a certain percentage of humans had discovered that their hormones dictated otherwise, but to do a medical switcheroo?* With tears in my eyes I prayed aloud to the God I had neglected to report to according to my Jewish teaching: "Please, Lord, give me the strength to get through this screwed up period of my life, and I'll be good, I promise." Then I began to rethink the words of my prayer, because God wouldn't appreciate the term "screwed up." Since I was a good self-editing writer, I revised my prayer: "Please, Lord, give me the strength to maintain my love and devotion to and for the child I have borne and give her peace of mind." My tears seemed to dissipate, so perhaps that rephrased prayer had worked. But I couldn't seem to put the brakes on all my mental anguish. I focused on the beginning of Robbie's existence.

All those blue nappies we had received as gifts after his birth had been in vain. He evidently hadn't liked being male for some unknown period, and it must have gone deep, like clear down to that "Y" chromosome. I may have been his birth mother, but Henry was involved too. Where in our respective family genetics did the he and the she DNA get crossed up? And what could I do about it?

It really bothered me that Henry thought I had influenced Robbie. Did Henry actually believe I had actively encouraged the operation? Like being some kind of cheerleader yelling from the sidelines, "You Go, Girl!" Then again, I did howl about wanting a facelift, so I guess Henry equated that driving ambition of mine with our son's actions. But these two different operations weren't even similar. I wanted to look younger, while Robbie wanted to have his body match what her brain dictated! Anyway, I deserved to look better because I wasn't really Seventy Years Old -- that was just a date of my arrival as recorded on the birth certificate. A damned time stamp! Ouch, did I just disprove my own argument? Didn't Robbie want to square his identity with some sex stamp on his birth certificate also?

I was too young to be my age! Society determined the type of behavior for a woman with the number of years I had under my belt. Should a Seventy-year-old mother have to act like she was past her prime? An over-the-hill stereotype not to be taken seriously? Was I someone who bitched and complained? Cranky or even cantankerous? Not me, oh no. I'm mentally about 62! Even Henry wanted me to look lovelier so he could indulge his fantasies. He kept telling me to change my brand of makeup, or leave off the damned makeup altogether. Hey, he didn't flatly refuse to help me pay for a facelift, he just figured it wasn't a priority. He knew other women were getting it done and that there were competent doctors out there who could do it. Ergo, he should have agreed that it was okay for medical practitioners to make women's faces prettier. Why shouldn't I get on the bandwagon! Henry doesn't understand me much and he is nowhere when it comes to understanding Robbie.

I walked over to our entertainment center in the family room and opened one of the drawers. Family photos and a few letters occupied that space. My sister Beth had gotten several face fixings and I had taken a photo of her with my new digital camera. There was the picture I had composed with such mixed emotions. I was so proud of myself for learning how to operate the camera, but so insanely envious of how attractive Beth had turned out. She looked younger and sweeter than she really was. Anyone looking at that picture would have described her as soft-hearted and kind. *Never in a lifetime did I think her looking sweeter was possible. Well,*

Beth was rich and we were -- I don't know -- medium low middle class? Rich people could cheat nature and medium low middle class people could pine forever. Should I have kept my mouth shut altogether? No, fixing my face had become my obsession. I had gone to the mall right after dinner one night. While I was trying on a new jacket I saw my profile in those dressing room triple mirrors. The person in those three panels was a woman who had allowed her face to age faster than her mental attitude. If that was the way I looked to others, something had to be done about it. If doctors had been able to make Beth look younger and more angelic, maybe there was hope for me. It might help my case with Henry if I looked youthful and innocent. Let's see, it was just a few months ago. I think I remember now. I had been procrastinating making the decision to have surgery and then came the day I learned that my beloved hairdresser had died suddenly. That whole day was a turning point, like I needed another turning point. . . .

6

I sauntered from the parking lot over to the front door of the Sunrise Hair Salon. It's not easy for a woman who is sixty-nine and ninety-nine 100ths years old to saunter. There's a bit of a pretense involved. Not even my rugged and bruised Nike sneakers nor my Miami Dolphins tee-shirt could disguise the fact that I wasn't exactly an athlete. Making my way from the car to the destination was simple enough, but easing my bottom from behind the steering wheel to the pavement was often hit and miss. The trick was to never twist my left knee at a certain angle. Knees were the second thing to go bad, right after the names of one's best friends. Sometimes I spoke to my leg and back muscles: "OK, folks, check to see where the ground is --do it gracefully -- that's good." When I knew that I had landed safely on terra firma, every cell in my body relaxed, as if they all said, "Aaahhh."

I paused in my step and exhaled with a sigh, but then hitched up my motivation and allowed my denial to take over. *Age denial -- that was my theme -- the driving force which kept me from wallowing in mud every time some doctor type would prescribe a new test or some goddamned prescription. Occasionally, I regarded the practitioners in the medical industry with distrust. Pills, tests, warnings, referrals, that's all they talked about.* I followed their advice anyway. I had to, or else Henry would pelt me with an endless series of his intelligent lectures. Going to the doctor was easier than listening to Henry.

I glanced at my watch and frowned, chastising myself for arriving at 7:32 AM -- two minutes late. The glass outer door of the salon was wide open, propped that way by a makeshift wooden wedge. No one was close enough to hear me exclaim: "Why the hell is the door open? This is April and we're in steamy South Florida!" Continuing my saunter through the open door to the reception desk in the front section of the salon, I remarked, "Either the air conditioning isn't working or somebody burned something."

A wisp of smoke made its way out of a waste basket behind one of the chairs. Most of the early morning regular customers knew each other -- usually not by name, but by hairstyle. I quickly identified a woman with more pink scalp showing than her geographically scattered silver curls. She always arrived in a wheelchair pushed by her maid. As I smiled at her, she whispered, "That old lady over there, see the one with the purple-framed eyeglasses? She dropped her cigarette in the basket. Everybody knows there's no smoking in here." I had to laugh at the customer's use of the term "old lady." Every patron in the shop at that hour fitted that description.

Gladys, the chic receptionist who never had a dyed blonde hair out of place, looked at me, having waited for my attention, and blasted out the bad news. "Monica isn't doing your hair today. She's not here."

"Why?"

"I'm very sorry, Mrs. Sternberg, Monica up and died."

"What?"

"We just found out. Her landlady called us."

I caught myself staring with my mouth open -- the shock of it all hit me right in the gut. "How, er, do you know what happened?"

"Apparently she was taking out the garbage, walking over to the big can in the back of her building, and, it seems she fell into it head first."

"Oh no, poor Monica. I hope she didn't suffer. I thought she was healthy as a horse. There must have been some problem."

"They're thinking an aneurysm, but nobody's certain."

"Is there a funeral or something I should go to? I don't think Monica had any family."

"She had nobody but a poor little cat. The landlady took in the animal and will probably send it to a shelter. Listen, you can still get your hair done. Salvatore is available, if it's OK with you."

I motioned for Gladys to lean toward me so I could whisper something. "I know who Salvatore is. He always wears a red vest and, well, I think he eats a lot of food with garlic."

"You're right, but we know about that. A couple of weeks ago all the girls gave him a large box of an assortment of Tic-Tacs."

"How did he take it?"

"Oh, he laughed and now instead of that garlic smell, he reeks of peppermint. But he is great at styling hair."

"And does Salvatore have my formula?"

"Monica had it written down and it was in the card file. You don't have to worry."

"I'll worry a lot -- Monica has been doing my hair since I moved down here from Milwaukee. She was like a sister to me. I can't just relax and not miss her -- the way she dug her long nails into my scalp and gave me a good rub -- it used to wake me up. I told her my funny stories and she told me hers. You don't just forget all those, oh, those, I'm going to cry, oh, while I'm recovering, tell Salvatore I'll be happy to give him my head. Just give me a minute."

I sat down on one of the reception area chairs and felt my pulse. It was throbbing -- the usual rhythm, I assumed. Apparently, I was going to be able to weather the loss of my expired hairdresser, but whew, what a kick in the old cranium! The gal didn't look a day over fifty-five or so. She didn't even have any relatives to get a sympathy card from me. Who could I feel sorry for? Monica was most certainly in heaven, or wherever a person of her faith went when her time was up. I stirred my reluctant frame by glaring at my reflection in the mirror. "Too many mirrors in this damned place!" Gladys masked a smile as she heard my whispered complaint. She'd heard it before.

"Why don't you sit in that chair over there, Mrs. Sternberg? Salvatore will be with you shortly."

I sat in that chair like an obedient student. Thinking time. *Sure, everybody takes care of me shortly. I'm barely five feet, so they look down on me and I'm "Mrs. I'll Be With You Shortly." I've spent my life waiting for tall people to treat me as an equal. It wasn't happening. Might as well look around and enjoy the taller types around here doing their taller things. Ooh, looky there, the Sunrise Salon has a new hairdresser. Boy, does she look young. I went through the change, probably, when she was still in diapers! Oh, now she's sweeping the gray hairs off her black floor mat -- the droppings from her last customer. Now what would a young woman be thinking, doing the hair of all these gray-haired ladies?* I'll just ask her. "Hi, there, I was watching you, Miss, gee, you sure are a hard worker. I was wondering what your thoughts are with all us, uh, mature folks?" The woman stared at me like I was a rude old biddy. Well, she was wrong -- I wasn't rude.

I rose from the chair and went to check out this Salvatore fellow, who had returned to his station. It was a bit of a crushing discovery. He didn't have long fingernails and he held his arms like they were wings. But the worst was that he talked constantly -- even more than I did. I walked right up to him in order to introduce myself and thought Gladys had her facts wrong. Salvatore smelled of cinnamon. He was a rather handsome chap and dressed as though he had adopted an Esquire look although he seemed to have ignored their advice about neckties. His smile saved the day, however, because on that unbearded closely shaved face I saw dimples. I was a sucker for a guy who had dimples. Soon I began to enjoy his style, as he greeted me with a gesture indicating I should proceed to his customer chair. He seemed very talented with his hands, waving them as he spoke with a muted flamboyance, but not quite at the level of an opera singer. Perhaps he could have auditioned for a movie role as Liberace, but his voice wasn't squeaky enough. "A baritone," I mused to myself, "just like my Robbie! I wonder if he sings."

"Mrs. Sternberg, it's good to see you. You came in for color and cut, right?"

"Yes I did."

"I'll go mix it now. You just make yourself comfy."

"Of course. I'll just make a quickie cellphone call. My son in Ohio hasn't been answering his phone for several days. Wonder what's going on."

"Be right back."

My new hairdresser disappeared into the back room while I once again went to Robbie's contact number in my phone list. The designers of the cellphone never had me and my kind of fingers in mind because every time I pressed a contact number I felt powerless. I never knew who to blame for my connectivity problems, so I chalked it up to a war on technologically delicate women. This time I heard the ringing sound for about ten seconds and then Robbie's not there recorded voice answered: "I'm always happy to speak to you, but right now I'm away from the phone, please leave your name and number." Robbie's answering message was just as jovial as he was. The younger generation seemed so cool and relaxed about technology. Whenever I needed to compose or revise my own recorded message, I had to wait for an especially confident feeling to arrive. Sometimes I had to wait almost a month.

People had suggested to me that I was an over-protective mother. It was true. I still regarded Robbie as my little boy, even though he was an adult now and, at age 42, had passed over the threshold they called "eligible" and entered the threshold considered "suspect." One of the customers who had been sitting across from Salvatore's station with her head stuck in a dryer, emerged and called out my name.

"Marlene, it's me -- it's Sondra!"

"Oh, Hi, Sondra, I guess I didn't see you. I was looking at my cellphone, you know, trying to call one of my kids, my son, actually."

"You look worried. Is anything wrong?"

"Well, not exactly, but something's up. I'll bet he's on vacation or busy with some project. But until last week, he always answered his phone because it's glued to his ear usually. Oh well, he's a big boy. He'll catch up soon."

I put my cellphone in my back pocket as Salvatore returned with my formula in Monica's cup. It shook me up a bit to realize how easily life could continue without that nice lady as though she was just passing through. Gee whiz, now the salon had her formula, her cup, and,

I noticed, Salvatore had even re-labeled her gratuity container with his name. *Ouch! What will they do with all my things when I check out? I would hate to end my life with my head in a trash can, but probably the poor dear barely knew it was all over. This Salvatore fellow has even benefited from his predecessor's demise, at least from my point of view, being that I'm such a good tipper.*

"Salvatore, this might be a silly question, but are you Jewish? You sound Jewish." The man didn't look Jewish at all, but I felt compelled to make conversation.

"I'm Eye-talian, Mrs. Sternberg. I'm from Brooklyn."

"Well, some of my Jewish friends come from Brooklyn and they talk like you. I just wondered. Do you know how Monica used to do my cut?"

"I do. I've watched you for a long time, Mrs. Sternberg. You have very nice hair. I know how old you are, and your hair is like that of a much younger woman. It used to be a dark brunette, right?"

"You mean it's not that way any longer?"

"Well, there are a few strands of your original color which I can see in your roots, but I suppose you realize that you're mostly grey. Monica's formula is perfect for you. I wouldn't change it in a heartbeat."

"Don't use the word 'heartbeat' just now, please? Monica and I were really like close friends." I refrained from telling Salvatore just how close we had become. She knew a lot about Robbie and his overtly feminine clues because I had spilled my guts out to her.

Monica could be trusted. We were able to talk privately while she did my hair because her booth was partitioned and somewhat isolated from the rest of the shop. She was the only person who ever suggested to me that Robbie's behavior was similar to another man she knew who was a transgender.

"Monica, dear, I've heard about a transgender before, but I've never known one. Tell me more."

"This guy believed he was really a woman, with a woman's hormones and instincts. He even wanted to go through a sex change operation, but he didn't have the money."

"I've heard that somebody did that, but it was years ago."

"It's more common now. Maybe your son is going to do it."

"My son? I don't think so. He has big muscles and he works out at a gym regularly. No, you must be wrong. Besides, he surely doesn't have the money."

"Well, then, he's stuck, I guess, but from what you've told me, I think he's like this other guy."

I said no more to Monica because it bothered me so much. Certainly, I never mentioned the conversation to Henry.

Salvatore looked apologetic for something he might have said. "Sorry, if I accidentally sounded casual about Monica's passing. I only knew her slightly, but from all indications she was a wonderful person and very understanding."

My heart did one of its thumps as he mentioned my beloved hairdresser. It was a signal for me to change the tone. "Oh, did we ever talk, talk, talk. I did love the way she did my hair. She was the one that suggested this deep auburn shade. Even my husband likes it."

"Who wouldn't? You're an attractive lady. And that brings up an important question."

"Yes?"

"Before I cut all that nice hair off, would you like to try a more glamorous look?"

"I don't know."

"Well, it would give you more height."

"Height? As in, uh, I'll look taller?"

"That's the general idea."

"Look, if it's too fussy, I won't be able to fix it myself between appointments."

"You will when I show you the solution!"

"OK, I'm tired of being a short lady with boring hair. Go ahead. Do it."

I'm not sure why I gave in to this unfamiliar man's sales pitch. He was patting my back, figuratively speaking, with two biggies: He used the word "glamorous" and then hit me again with the "height" thing. I must have been just ripe enough for being picked, because I walked into that hair salon feeling dowdy and insignificant, and now I was being brave like I had been electronically zapped. The bravery didn't last long, however. As soon as I agreed to the new style and let Salvatore ruff his hands through my unkempt mane, I was seized with new hairstyle buyer's remorse. I missed Monica's fingernails. What if I was about to look dreadful? How would I be able to sleep worrying about what I'd look like the next morning? Well, maybe I needed this kind of change.

Before I left the salon, I gave Salvatore his tip and thanked him. "I just know I'm going to get accustomed to this hairpiece, Salvatore. You seem to be good at knowing just what a woman needs to feel attractive. I'm glad you had it in stock and that I waited for you to dye it just right."

Salvatore smiled at me. The smile suggested he understood older women. I walked out the door with better posture. Monica was dead and I and my hair were still living.

Was I jealous because she was at peace and I still had to wrestle with my comb while coaxing my temperamental mane into good behavior? OK, I get that I won't be able to discuss yeast infections or other female afflictions with the new guy, and he is definitely a blabbermouth, but maybe this change in my style represents a change in my whole presentation. We'll see how it goes. Oh no! I just thought of something! Monica was going to talk to me about everything she knew about facelifts. She was going to bring surgeon information and other stuff. I shouldn't be angry with her because she died, but I know what my therapist would say. He'd say it was OK for me to be angry she died! And how did she know so much about a transgender? Could it be that she was knowledgeable about the LGBT lifestyle? Maybe she was gay herself? No, she would have indicated that to me. There's nobody I can ask about this. With her gone, and Robbie not calling me lately, I'll just have to manage. I still want a facelift, however. Life goes on.

7

I eyed my new hairpiece in the full-length mirror in Henry's closet. The added height was a plus, but I worried it made me look fatter. Well, I was overweight. Maybe thirty pounds or so. And the "so" part was the number I didn't want to see on the scale. I usually cringed when I weighed myself, and if I didn't like the number, I hung onto the towel bar, which subtracted about two pounds. I had spent serious money on Salvatore's solution -- a hairpiece that resembled a coiled snake. Henry wasn't to know about what I spent. Then I burst into tears, and for what? Crying wouldn't fix anything. Henry would still be rigid, Robbie still wouldn't call me more often and Linda still wouldn't hang on the phone with me until I experienced satisfaction. I wasn't so jaded as to think that a volume of tears would help me lose my ugly fat, but I took one more peek in the mirror anyway. I was taller, just as overweight and now my makeup was streaked. In a few minutes I had washed off all evidence that the wife and mother of the Sternberg family was feeling short-changed, but it was difficult to keep the hairpiece in place as I bent over the sink. I had caught myself being negative and knew without a doubt that it was time to turn positive. My system was to write down my thoughts on one of my notepads. "For the rest of today, I will refrain from my normal routine and rest, even though it's not the Sabbath, or even a national holiday. I will look for a better waterproof mascara. I will stand up to Henry. I will reflect on how I got to be this suffering person. I will once again quote Dickens and repeat, again and again, 'Tis a far far better thing I do today than I have ever done!'" I was done writing and ran to my office cubbyhole where my captive computer awaited my strongly worded assertions. Most of my philosophical concerns were listed and described in a folder I had entitled: "Philosophical concerns." Actually, the name of the folder had to be truncated by the operating system, so the caption read: "Philosophical cons." I opened the folder and typed: "Be more Courageous. Cry less. Act more. Talk is Cheap. The Hairpiece is on Trial." I closed the folder and cried for about one more minute.

The new hairpiece felt wobbly, so I didn't return to my bedroom with my klutzy walk. Salvatore had turned me into a fashion makeover, and fashion makeovers don't walk with their heads down or tally up the amount of lint on the rug. With uncharacteristic dignity, I removed the black A-line dress I always wore to the beauty salon the way I once taught Linda how to undress her Barbie dolls. I was alone in the house, and had a habit of speaking aloud, but I figured I was typing my thoughts in the air around me as though the molecules carried ink. Sometimes my speech was defiant, like it was right then: "If nobody appreciates me, then tough, I'll put up a new sign over my desk. "Appreciate Thyself." Was that from the Bible? No, it was Socrates. He said "Know Thyself." Well, shit, he didn't have me for a pupil! I got dressed in my "being lazy around the house" outfit, with more grace than usual. The ensemble was on my bedroom dresser because a "lazy around the house" outfit meant that it didn't belong on hangers. I slipped into my most elegant pair of designer blue jeans in the fat size before last year's diet and the loose-fitting man-sized green tee-shirt with the words, "I Yam What I Yam." It had an embroidered Popeye flexing his biceps. I flexed my own biceps and shuddered as I gazed at my upper arms. Did I ever look like a reptile! Why did females of my age have to degenerate into one of the lower animals? And why did I have to go to a psychologist to deal with my identity crises? I removed two pillows from the cedar chest which was usually too stuffed to stay closed, and then I was able to sit on it. Now I was in my favorite wondering location. My current wonder was whether I was really getting anywhere. "So much introspection, and I'm never finished doing it. I'll bet Henry never does it."

There was this high class shrink I went to irregularly who taught me to do positive declarations. I paid him out of my hidden cache of money, although it killed me when I had to make subtractions in my auxiliary checkbook, which was dedicated to my personal expenses. Our main checkbook was for important things that Henry approved of. His distrust of my financial skills was rough on my ego. The shrink's technique was supposed to teach me how to avoid negative feelings. We agreed that I should make an effort to write down good thoughts, but most of what I wrote sounded like what a desperate old female would write. Whenever I attempted to think positively, I took out my homework and reviewed my notes. I got bad vibes from most of those notes. One example from a typical session read as follows:

"The doc is really desperate to help me today. He fixes his gaze on my eyes, which he claims squint, even through the new bifocals, and I pull out my scratch pad to read my entry.

"I had a great day yesterday. The dishwasher conked out and Henry promised to help me do dishes by hand."

"What made that a great day?"

"I didn't burst into tears."

"And how did you manage that?"

"Oh, clenched fists and a dose of my favorite medical remedy."

"What medication did you take?"

"A cup of lobster bisque, which I keep frozen for emergencies, with Italian seasoned croutons. It works every time."

Then the good doctor taught me something I could try. He advised me that a positive declaration could also be done by speaking it aloud. I decided to try the shrink's suggestion and addressed the clothes hamper in the corner of our bedroom. He'd told me that any inanimate object would suffice. However, the clothes hamper wasn't my husband or a child of mine or even a sympathetic neighbor. That damned thing wasn't even up to handling my soiled laundry, much less serving as an object of enlightenment.

My family already had the solutions to my concerns. Henry and the kids accused me of being a procrastinator. They said that everybody had my number. Why me? Lots of people had gone on diets for thirty years and gained thirty pounds. I worried about making radical behavior changes, while the kids told me that changes which required decades weren't helpful. I told them that I didn't want to feel deprived, and that I needed comfort. They suggested I speed up that feeling of comfort. I had one answer: "I can't do that!" Whenever I protested, they seemed to tune me out, but I simply protested louder. **"Children, don't either of you understand that effective procrastination requires a methodical approach? Don't I have to be me?"**

Despite my earnest efforts, I couldn't convince my family to have just as high a regard for me in my plump state as my sister Julie Sue's children had for her -- Julie Sue who wore miniskirts. She bought her clothes in the junior size department. There was little doubt that the truth as to my age and gluttony was written all over my body -- my love handles, my arms, and most likely my butt and thighs also. But the worst was the part I presented to everybody -- my face. Those creases on my overtaxed complexion seemed to shout to the world that the skin covering my fat wasn't doing so well. I didn't even want to look at me because I wanted my image to be that of a young siren. Oh, I knew that wasn't possible, but couldn't I just trim a little here, there and everywhere? The most revealing clue was that I'd been smiling differently of late. I was afraid to stretch the old lips and cheek muscles too far for fear they might tip off the rest of my features.

Who in their right mind would think highly of an overweight woman like me? Maybe an overweight doctor? Medical types weren't perfect either. After all, the psychologist had a pretty big rump. And while I'm dwelling on this issue, it seems wise to refrain from any hasty action to deal with the problem, since there is no emergency.

I walked over to my clothes closet and opened the door. I could barely step into it to get to the slacks I knew were in there but had become invisible when I searched for them. The whole inside of that generously proportioned walk-in space was filled with outfits that no longer fit me. And Henry, ever the tightwad, had told me in no uncertain terms that I couldn't buy any new slacks until I got rid of the ones that I couldn't zip up without breaking a blood vessel. His terse comments about my wardrobe habits really stung.

"Get rid of things you don't wear -- you won't miss them. And that goes for your shirts and blouses, as well as your slacks!"

I had complained about not having enough drawer or closet space, which proved to be a huge flop of an argument. Henry's debating skills outweighed mine.

"OK, instead of thinking about more storage space, do simple long division -- half of everything you call your wardrobe goes to charity and the other half gets to be yours to keep. Then you'll have some breathing room in your depository of indulgence."

"Dear, that's a lot of work. I have to keep coordinates coordinated."

"If you take my advice you'll have enough clothes for three women instead of six."

For once, I had taken Henry seriously. The rods in my closet were sagging from the weight of my clothes. They were bunched up against each other like outfits on a clearance rack in a discount department store. Walking into that bedlam was beginning to pose a health hazard. I backed out of the closet with care so as not to disturb the shoe boxes stacked up against one wall. The stack was as tall as I was and swayed as though to warn me not to defy gravity. I shut the door to avoid further despair and walked back to the clothes hamper to pull yesterday's slacks out of the pile. "No problem," I thought, as I sniffed the crotch part. "Never do today what you can put off until tomorrow." Then the shrink's advice came drifting into my space, possibly through the air ducts. "When you think you're locked into a position, try to unlock it. Use an imaginary key if that helps."

"OK", I agreed to my better instincts reluctantly, "I'll get back on a sensible diet and then get my face lifted and then even my kids will have a little respect for me." Just then, the clothes hamper, which consisted of a fabric bag suspended on a wire frame, shuddered and collapsed. My first reaction was that I might have overstuffed it over the years, but at a very deep level, I knew the truth. It had become my alter ego.

8

Henry loved to joke about how a woman always worried about her hairdo while making love, but a day after I'd gotten the new hairstyle, we enjoyed one of the best lovemaking mornings in weeks. I remember it distinctly because Henry was acting especially nice to me.

"Honey, I love you. Not only do I love you, but I think your hairdo is very pretty. It's smart of you not to wear the hairpiece to bed. And you don't need to sleep with it. Your real hair is hardly mussed up at all. Did you train it?"

"Yes, I gave it an ultimatum. I warned it to stay put while I writhed and shrieked with pleasure. I threatened to cut it all off if it gave me a hard time."

"I speak to my hairs once in awhile too. All eighteen of them."

"You have more than eighteen hairs, Henry. But it's true that the biggest bunch of them is hugging your neck."

"Give an old guy a break, OK, woman?"

"I guess you didn't like my reference to your neck hairs."

"Marlene, did Robbie ever return your call?"

"I'm talking about your neck, dear, not about Robbie not calling back yet."

"He's never been good at getting back to either of us. He'll call you on your birthday, I'm sure of that. Probably at the last possible minute."

"That's helpful. Thanks for getting me to look on the bright side. Even if you're way ahead of me getting dressed. Where are you going now in such a hurry?"

"Where do you think I'm going? To the kitchen to eat breakfast. I've got to get some stuff for the garden and I want to get it done early. Aren't you going to join me?"

"I'm feeling a bit slow, but I'll be staggering in there soon."

I thought to myself that Henry was always more disciplined than I could ever hope to be. He kept his grooming and his attire and his schedule uncomplicated. Being nearly bald was easier and consumed less time than affixing fake hair to real hair. Having an uncluttered closet was more efficient than having a space where confusion reigned. Keeping one's weight steady throughout the years meant fewer hours of having to roam through shopping malls searching for wearable attire to replace outfits that were no longer wearable. Sometimes I wanted to put a curse on those of my ancestors who had been responsible for my genetic imperfections. At the same time I kept wondering who was to blame for Robbie's problems. Why had such a nice handsome fellow like our son remained single, causing us to wonder if he was secretly gay? He certainly hadn't been easy to read in those years when he was a teenager and still living with us. As for the time after he had moved out on his own? There were clues and rumors all over the place, but as for Henry and me, well, especially Henry, we hadn't taken the leap into that abyss yet.

9

I struggled out of bed and limped over to the mirror in the master bath to begin my AM routine. Henry had been right about Robbie's poor communication, of course, but not for the reasons we both assumed. How could either of us have guessed what was going on? And then, when the bomb went off? We were like two dying dogs on the way to a hospice for canines. My seventieth birthday had come and gone. Our family had changed. Henry had difficulty discussing anything. His periods of silence said it all. How does a wife describe the facial expression of a husband who is dumbfounded? If Monica were still alive I could have confided in her, so I spoke to her ghost:

"Henry changes the subject every time I have a certain look on my face. He pastes on a smile like he's fixing himself in Photoshop, but I can see through it. There's something in his eyes that reminds me of our next-door neighbor's cat. If you try to make nice to that cat, you can read the eyes and they're saying: "Don't you dare try to pet me, or I'll get my cousin, the Tiger, after you."

Monica would have said, "Give the poor guy time. He'll work it out." Even her ghost had more wisdom than I did.

I couldn't seem to get through to my husband the way that I once did during those years when our luck had gone south. We suffered as our friends suffered -- not enough time, not enough money, not enough peace and quiet. Still, we hung in there, solid as two bookends and aligned as two adjacent puzzle pieces. Had we lost that bond we always shared? Or were we simply out of touch with where social mores were headed?

When I married Henry, we had all the problems that all newlyweds have -- compatibility, household spending, how to bring up kids and when to have them, and how to have better marriages than our parents did. I figured all my parents' mistakes weren't going to be mine. My problems would be easy to fix. After all, I had been so thoroughly indoctrinated in what not to do. My mother was a spender and my father wasn't, but their money vanished anyway. Mother always seemed to have enough jewelry around her neck and dangling from her ears and weighting down her wrists and her fingers, so I just assumed it came from my father and that all mothers needed to have those embellishments. My folks were always redecorating the house and often when I came home from school it wasn't uncommon for me to have to search for some new chair to sit on and where to put my books.

Henry's parents had more modest means and didn't seem to spend on anything but canned food, bottled juice, Kitchen Klenzer and cleaning rags. If his family had an abundance of anything, it had to be the number of rags. I remembered them because Henry told me that everybody's underwear eventually got that way. When an item in their rag collection had more holes than fabric, they attached the newly cheesed cloth to others like that and made a mop out of the lot of them, using some old broom handle. It was an early version of recycling. Henry's mother's wardrobe was apparently confined to a couple of floral print house dresses. Their furniture was always falling apart. The first time I visited and was getting used to them being my in-laws, I sat on a low upholstered stool and my future mother-in-law cried out: "Not that one!" It was too late -- one of the four legs collapsed with me on it. A future daughter-in-law doesn't forget those incidents. One consolation was that Henry told me that his dad had a hidden cache of dollars somewhere for emergencies.

Neither of our sets of parents were much help in how Henry and I were to blend our different styles. He became the chief breadwinner of the family as an insurance salesman and I was nominated for the position of chief caretaker of the premises. We couldn't afford hired help, so I won the election unopposed. The breadwinner had the bigger say over our major purchases, like furniture, and the caretaker had the bigger say over which carpet sweeper swept better. Henry was good at a lot of things that I wasn't good at. We returned from our honeymoon in Door County, Wisconsin in our little green Studebaker, gloating over how nice a week in the rain we had experienced learning how to make love. Henry had read a very explicit book and told me he studied it so thoroughly it had fallen apart. After I was able to absorb what I hadn't read, it was time to settle into our real life. We made our way to the small apartment we had rented. I signed the lease with Henry, but he had made decisions he hadn't told me about. He considered love-making more worthy of discussion than furniture.

"I've decided that we have to start out very carefully. Instead of permanent furniture, I've got a better idea."

"Temporary furniture, like wooden crates?"

"We don't need a kitchen table, for example, we can eat on an ironing board and that could double as a place to dine as well as to press my shirts."

"You know that ironing board we got for my shower, dear? It's so narrow that you can't sit across from me -- you'll have to sit next to me. I'm not sure how those bridge chairs will work out, though."

"Yes, I've thought of that. And don't forget that my folks haven't given us our wedding present yet. Well, I told them what we wanted."

"I don't remember you asking me about it."

"I did, I asked you if you wanted to earn more money than you are making from writing articles."

"Oh yes, I do remember, that's when we discussed it."

"Anyway, Mother is sending us some modern plastic snack tables and very large cushions for lounging. If we stack up the cushions about three high, we'll be able to sit on them and use the snack tables when we have company."

"What about lamps and other illumination?"

"Listen, Marlene, if we really need more light after sunset than we get from the fixtures that came with the apartment, I'll pick up some pole lamps at a thrift store."

I thought Henry was kidding because the fixtures attached to the ceilings were really not fixtures. They were low voltage light bulbs which screwed into brass fittings. Henry was able to stand on the floor and reach the end of the beaded metal cord which turned each light on and off, but I could only reach the one in our small bedroom and then I had to stand on a chair or a bed. That one chair and our full-size bed were the big deal items we had picked out together. Then I told him that I thought the woman often made the furnishing choices.

"You're right, dear," he had agreed. "Tell you what -- as soon as you publish one of your wonderful stories and get some serious money for it, you can have your say."

"That's unfair, I think."

"It is unfair. Life is unfair. Paying bills while on a budget is unfair. Coming from a poor family is unfair. The way to get ahead is for the bigger earner to take care of the smaller earner."

"I guess I'll have to wait for my breakthrough, dear. Will you still love me if I turn into an Edna Ferber or a Lillian Hellman?"

"Only if you stay as sweet as you are."

"Well, that just ruins it, I guess. Famous women writers have strengths, but I don't think being sweet is one of them."

I gave in to Henry because I never wanted to give up my writing. In order to peddle enough of my literary efforts to pay for my shoes, handbags and some of my clothes, I had to work really hard. So we lived on the cheap. It wasn't so bad. I never had to leave the house wearing a floral print house dress. And Henry never left the house without kissing me goodbye and telling me to avoid impulsive actions. I needed to interpret his words so I could translate them into action I could take.

"So, honey, did that impulsive thing you told me to avoid -- was that meant to keep me away from department stores? And Henry, what about the fact that I married you impulsively?"

"Were you thinking of making a change?"

"Of course not. I'm just trying to figure out when our democratic relationship became more of a dictatorship."

"Don't worry, I'm doing pretty well with my commissions. Remember what your mother said?"

"I do. She thought you were practical because you had a good job, so I followed her advice. She said: 'He makes a living? Don't knock it.'"

Despite my failure to become a big-time author, I gradually increased my income with some free-lance editing and advisory services, so I felt I was making a contribution to the household budget. Eventually I began to make outstanding choices of furniture and other stuff. These choices were not always translated into actual purchases.

The second assault on my original programming came when I missed something. My fertility had never been tested, nor had my ability to keep track of the days of the month. It's common knowledge that self-employed writers who have their own work schedules often have a poor sense of what day of the week it is. In my case, I wasn't too skilled at remembering the month either. We lived in Milwaukee, so it was either cold with snow on the way or warm with a promise of bugs in the air. Henry never hesitated taking over as creator of the shopping list during my apprenticeship as a budgetress. He had a system of calculating which regularly purchased items should get purchased each week.

"Hey, honey? Don't you need a box of Kotex for your monthly curse?"

"Henry, I have almost a whole box left in the cabinet!"

"Well, didn't you use it up when you had your, you know?"

"Uh, when was my 'you know?'"

"You're asking me?"

"No, I'm asking the Kotex box."

"Where's your calendar?"

"I put it somewhere."

"Marlene, didn't you, oh, did you?"

"No, I know what you're getting at. I didn't. I'm late."

"How late?"

"Not sure, but I don't feel very well. I thought I was getting the flu because I puked this morning. Don't worry, it didn't get on anything of yours."

Well, so much for careful budgeting and family planning. Robbie probably heard the whole conversation from his emerging fetal sac in my tummy. But I'm not sure about the science of that and I never asked him. Was I naive about taking care of an infant? No, the term "naive" was too ambitious when it came to my expertise. Henry suspected that I was a know-it-all, a characteristic that overwhelmed what should have been some pre-birth learning on my part. My reasoning was: "How hard could it be to take care of a helpless little thing that weighs less than seven pounds?" Well, that attitude sufficed until the obstetrician who delivered Robbie remarked at the end of his final round at the hospital: "You're doing fine, Mrs. Sternberg, and call my office in a week so my assistant can connect with your pediatrician."

"What pediatrician?"

Somehow, Robbie's safety was not endangered, at least it wasn't until the last of the hospital maternity nurses handed me the tenderly swaddled bundle and ordered the obligatory wheelchair for the new mother to use as she made her exit. I told myself that being a parent was a cinch as I struggled to diaper my first kid without making the cloth so loose that the poop would fall out. It was an important skill -- don't stick the pin into the baby's skin -- practice, practice, practice, while the infant is shrieking and kicking and making you feel guilty for being such a klutz. And how many times did that itsy bitsy weenie of his squirt right into my eye? Did my troubles all start with the diapering thing? And Oh My God, what about Robbie's troubles? Was it possible I did something wrong when I pinned him up after cleaning out his whoosis? I had to learn stuff just like my pushy mother did. Except that she only had to diaper us three girls and never had to worry about gently lifting up an infant's scrotum! I decided not to be so pushy. *Was that my great error? Did my more gentle approach rub off on my new son in his formative years? And why am I beating myself up so much like I still do? I didn't do anything really wrong when I raised my own two kids. Society had something to do with it. Did I know what the future was going to spring on a well-meaning mother who failed to predict the transformation of peoples' attitudes about sex or miraculous medical breakthroughs? Not a chance. Well, maybe I could have predicted that Robbie wasn't going to grow up to be a drill sergeant, but any clues there during his little kid years must have gone right by me.*

Now that I know the truth, it pains me how patiently I waited for Robbie's call to wish me a belated Happy Birthday. Well, not so patiently. And all that time he was convalescing from the sex doctor's reconfiguration. How the hell did he pee while the new plumbing was healing? I would have been sympathetic. No mother wants her kid to endure pain. But I was in the dark, so I got angry. I kept crossing off the days after my birthday passed without his good wishes on a spare calendar I had. I used different colored markers. Two days late got an exclamation point in soft purple. Five days late got five exclamation points in red. Ten days late and I tore up the damned calendar.

10

My children and their lives took a back seat to our lives because they lived in different cities and there weren't any grandchildren to have fun with. Henry played with guns and fishing gear and I played with words on my computer and thought about getting into swimming as a refreshing form of exercise. Our community had a pool. I knew it was there, but whether I felt anxious to use it depended upon my zeal about getting into a bathing suit. I tried surfing the Internet to discover where brain cells governing embarrassment were lodged, but got nowhere. Henry tried to encourage me to engage in friendly exercise, like at a gym where I could meet women who didn't mind panting and sweating while they watched TV. He told me I was more stubborn than a mule, because at least a mule would respond to a kick in the butt.

"Henry, why would you compare me to one of the lower animals? A mule wouldn't call the cops or a lawyer."

"Marlene, I've talked myself blue trying to encourage you to swim or do something. I'm giving up."

"At least you're faithful. You are, aren't you?"

"Maybe you shouldn't press your luck."

"OK, OK, so I need to do something. Don't turn blue."

Henry wanted me to feel better about me. His system was to stay fit with exercise and disciplined eating habits. He never alluded to the fact that his metabolism and height might have had something to do with his leanness. The man loved manly activities. He enjoyed skeet shooting, which required certain arm movement, but he claimed that it was his fishing that kept him lean. I remember him telling me about all the muscles involved in successful fishing. He never explained to me why there were so many overweight fishermen, but maybe those fellows didn't work as hard as Henry did in the acquisition of fish. Henry developed very impressive biceps and triceps reeling in inedible varieties which he had to throw back. One day he hooked an old sunken rowboat in shallow water and used up hundreds of calories until a chunk of algae-covered wood showed up at the end of his line. He came home exhausted, too tired to eat dinner.

My system was to think about staying fit. In addition to my slowly walking over to my computer, I occasionally drove over to our clubhouse to look for ideas posted on their bulletin boards. That's where I saw the ads for numerous volunteer opportunities. At first I didn't think they were for me because they seemed geared for older middle class types. It finally hit me that I was in that category. That's how I got into volunteering at a library.

One day my neighbor who lived in our cul-de-sac approached me about her imminent retirement.

"What should I do with myself when I quit work? I don't play golf and I'm pretty bad at tennis."

"Well, I have to be frank with you. Do you consider yourself middle class?"

"Listen, if I were upper class, I wouldn't be here asking you about this subject. I'd be hostessing political teas or having my face in the Palm Beach News for some charity benefit."

"Then we understand each other. I'm a writer and you've been a mid-level banking executive. OK, here's what I've learned: Middle class mature women in our South Florida neighborhood who no longer work for pay either volunteer their services or participate in athletic activity or fester. Do you agree?"

"I couldn't agree more."

"I'm going to be helping at library events. My husband had to kick me in the butt a little, but it really isn't bad at all."

"That's an idea. You're a word person and I'm a money person. I think I'll lend my financial knowhow to one of those adult education classes. I don't even care if I get paid."

"I make a little money writing articles. We couldn't live on it. I couldn't even live on it. To tell the truth, even a puppy dog couldn't live on it. Not with today's dog food prices and the fees veterinarians charge."

"Thanks for your input. I'll let you know how it goes."

After reeling from Henry's likening my stubbornness to that of a mule, I began to unbend a little and managed to blow past my resistance to change.

"Henry, I just have to get out of the house. I can't sit here all day pecking away at a keyboard like a chimpanzee, hoping that my selection of keys turns into the Great American Bathroom Reading Joke Book."

"Why don't you do something useful where you can get out of the house where there are books, like a library?"

"That's not such a terrible idea -- too bad it's your idea."

"And you know a lot about nature. You could go give talks to people who can't distinguish a newly planted palm tree from a wooden telephone pole."

"So you think I should do some volunteer work at a library or a nature center?"

"Do something that's fun."

"Most of my fun is when I get paid and then spend the money."

"I'm thinking that the library environment would be good for you. Listen, you like people and you like books. Last time I checked, libraries had both."

I never want to agree with my uppity husband right off the bat because it only increases his smugness. After we have a chat that he controls with his moderator voice, I wander off to the front yard to smell the hibiscus, which has no discernible odor, and then I sneak back into the house and find something which needs help, like the top of the dust-laden curtains in the kitchen. I have to stand on a chair or find that long-handled broom attachment to our outdated vacuum cleaner. Neither activity proved to be a satisfying addiction, but I had to do something to avoid serious concentration on my issues. Since I wasn't succeeding with my anemic forms of anger management, I finally told Henry that the local library nearest our house could use some unpaid help. I actually pleaded with him to let me off duty at home for a few days a week. My strategy worked perfectly.

On Tuesdays and Thursdays I volunteer at the perfect place for me -- the newest branch of our county public library. I should have thought of it a long time ago because as soon as I became immersed in the routine, I acquired an excuse for buying a few new outfits. I kept track of my weekly clothing selections in a card file. Henry even coughed up the tab because he was only too happy to get me to stop bitching about my ennui. A week before I was scheduled to show up for my first stint at the library he came home with a large box from Neiman Marcus.

"Henry, are you spending our savings on something extravagant? You've never bought a new suit, or at least not since we got married."

"Well, you'll just have to guess what's in this box."

"I don't think Neiman Marcus sells camouflage clothing for hunting or fishing trips, or do they?"

"Guess again."

"I give up."

"Open the box."

I grabbed the box and tore it open so fast I gave myself a paper cut. Inside the tissue paper was a beautiful new lounging robe and a peignoir set. It was for me. I was so unaccustomed to having Henry purchasing anything luxurious or for me that I had this spontaneous outburst: "I think the store people gave you the wrong box! This stuff is for some rich woman!"

"You're not poor, dear."

"I don't believe this. Henry, you've cut off the price tags. What did you spend on these duds?"

"None of your business. Just make sure the stuff fits. Open the card."

I opened the envelope and then a card popped out which wasn't even a birthday card. It was a general purpose card with space for a message. Henry had written on it: "Just to show you I'm not so much of a penny pincher, try these on for size. These gifts are my way of congratulating you for getting out of your shell and into an activity I think you'll enjoy." There was a check made out to me inside the card. It was for $1,500.00.

"Henry, I can't believe it!"

"Don't get mushy on me. Buy yourself a few new things so you'll stop being a kvetch."

"I don't like that descriptive Yiddish word 'kvetch.' Can't you say, oh, 'conscientious objector,' or something? Am I really that kvetchy?"

"That's your word -- you got it from your mother. But you do complain a bit."

"I definitely got that from my mother. Anyway, thank you, honey. I love you and I love the presents."

Henry smiled a sly smile and left the room to leave me alone with my joy. My cynicism couldn't leave me just like that, however. I was convinced that the gifts were part of Henry's secret plan to get me to stop depending on a therapist. No matter how long we were married, there were always surprises.

The library volunteer work was fun and took me away from my worries, at least for the time being. I enjoyed my time with the books and even talked to the county employees, who seemed to appreciate my interruptions of their humdrum duties. But there came a day that was destined to live in my overweight infamy. I needed such a jolt because it gave me pause and opportunity for more reflection. I was, and still am, very talented at reflection.

The day in play happened to be a special event in the upstairs reading hall, so they had moved all the chairs and tables to one side to make room for the big crowd of literate men and women. I usually spied on the women more than the men because their outfits were more conspicuous. Men don't need conspicuous outfits because they are already the center of attention, especially at libraries, or at least in our library, where women outnumber men about 2 to 1. One of these overdressed women, Nancy Westerville, a woman of about forty, looked different from the last time I had seen her almost a year before. I wondered why she hadn't been around, but now, here she was. She appeared to have lost at least eighty pounds, but it could have been ninety. How could one tell at that level? There was a big change in every aspect of her appearance, especially in the way her hair hung across her shoulders. Where was the ponytail? I had been accustomed to admiring Nancy's rosy cheeks stretched to the limit across her plump and merry face. In my opinion, she would have made a terrific female Santa Clause. She definitely had a jolly personality. But now? This was some alternate person clacking along the floor with amazingly high heels. I couldn't help thinking: "She didn't wear high heels before, like ever." I glanced down at my own smudged sneakers, practical to the point of fashion rebellion. They were so worn out, with two different shades of shoelaces and one loose rubber sole flopping about, it was embarrassing. I had taken so much time and effort to dress myself nicely from the ankles up that my energy gave out when it came to footwear.

I didn't know the woman very well. Nor did she recognize me as we passed by each other in that congested meeting room. We were but two of about fifty humans milling about near the rectangular banquet tables which had been covered with plates of cookies and assorted beverages. I watched her for several minutes and she never went near the cookies. She didn't give any sign of a hello as I started my "Hi, there," approach, but instead pecked on the shoulder of one of the tall fellows chatting with a group of inner circle types. Had I been prone to affronts, I would have digested that omission as a social forward pass to a likelier receiver than me. But then, she probably didn't even know my name. This wasn't the time to give her my cute business card, so I just secretly snapped her picture with my IPhone. It was a back view.

11

Despite our fear about how our extended family would react to Robbie's sex change, we still had to deal with this big family wedding coming up. I was brooding about it openly and Henry was a closet brooder.

"Henry, did I get any messages, like from, uh, our older child?"

"Your incoming call light is flashing. I didn't hear the message."

"Thanks for hearing the ding-a-ling at least. I thought he, uh, she, was going to talk to me about Cissy's wedding. You do know that it's in September, don't you?"

"I know about it because I remember that Robbie, when he was Robbie, had agreed to stand up in the groom's party. I don't understand how that happened, but it happened. They're having a traditional Jewish wedding, aren't they? I'm assuming it's not like that simplistic style affair we attended a few years back where we sat in chairs in the woods and swatted mosquitoes while they had that do-it-yourself prayer fest."

"Of course it's traditional. They'll have a rabbi and an unbearably long procession on the way to the usual canopy thing, you know, the chupah, and the breaking of the glass, the whole shmear."

"I figured that. Well, it's going to look awfully silly when eight guys are lined up at the chupah and one of them is wearing a dress."

"That's why I'm anxious for the call, dear. We all have to decide what to do about that problem, and our elder child needs our input."

"Here's my input. The transgendered person, or should I say 'trans-sexual?' Well, it should stay home."

"He's, I mean, she's Cissy's favorite cousin. Cissy will be heartbroken. You know she's always been so fond of him. There has to be a better plan."

"Look, if Robbie comes as a woman, which **Robbie** spent money to become, wouldn't that horrific surprise detract from the bride and groom and their lavish celebration? I don't like it at all."

"Well, maybe she could still go as a man because none of the family or our friends know about the operation yet."

"Yeah, Robbie the fake could use the stall in the men's room, but I'm not having any part of that idea. You and Linda and the kid can go figure it out."

Nothing had been resolved about whether our son-into-daughter should attend Cissy's wedding, and if so, as which sex. The problem made me dizzy, because I figured my child would go along with the plan either way. I'd learned that she had already felt pressure to hide her new gender at the auto plant, at least until the medical bills were satisfied. The following morning I woke up before Henry's alarm clock went off and glanced at him to see if he was awake. His eyes were shut and I could hear his short and rhythmic wheezy breaths. Good. That meant I could continue to lie under the covers and worry to my heart's content. I was now a whole bunch of days into that Seventy Years Old category. That meant it was a perfect quiet moment to think about eternity. My thoughts ran as usual: "Will I be plump or thin as a dead old lady in a coffin?" I sensed that my calorie-laden days of getting away with murder were behind me, and I did mean that literally. Then Henry woke up and grabbed me with his morning clutch. I was right in the midst of a mind-meld -- trying to recall where I had put my dog-eared calorie counter. This husband of mine had little sense of timing, but a great sense of his needs. I felt impelled to alter the dynamic, even if only slightly.

"Honey, the alarm is about to go off!"

"No it's not -- I shut it off earlier."

"Do you know what time it is?"

"Of course -- it's before the alarm goes off and it's Tuesday."

"It's Tuesday? Oh dear me -- I think I missed a doctor's appointment yesterday. Oh, no, I'm wrong, that's for next Tuesday."

"Marlene, you talk too much."

Good old Henry -- so predictably warm and fuzzy in the AM, while I was engaged in deep philosophical debates with myself. Do men ever realize what women have to go through first thing in the morning to unwind their built-up anxieties, releasing certain vivid messages emanating from dreams which are left dangling in shreds, and at the same time, or in a protracted minute, let themselves hang loose? I desperately needed an answer to that question.

Henry was taking the whole boy-into-girl thing badly. I'd heard or read in books that every father wants his son to be an extension of himself. Baseball players wonder if their sons can throw fast balls or curves. Hunters and fishermen can't wait until they can take the male tyke out in the woods or on a boat and expose him to bugs and temperature extremes. Some fathers feel grateful and even relieved when the son resembles his dad. I could certainly empathize with that one. And Robbie? He looked a lot like Henry. When our son officially grew to measure an inch taller than Henry's six foot one, Henry gave him a tall guy present. It was a five hundred dollar open-ended agreement to pay for the boy's whole new wardrobe at one of those men's stores specializing in guys who were over six feet. That store had a custom-made entry door so their customers didn't have to duck.

Robbie had Henry's nose and his high cheekbones. He had muscles in the same places and went to Henry's barber, who had a tendency to cut

Robbie's hair to look like he was Henry. That's when Robbie's rebellion began to show up. He wouldn't go there any longer and began to use alternative hair stylists. The set-in-his-ways barber lost some business because that's about when Henry began to lose his hair and got one of his buddies to give him a monthly trim. We hated to admit it, but Robbie was rapidly moving in a different direction. He was destined to be more handsome than his daddy and he definitely had more determined hair.

One of my neighbors who knew all the local gossip told me that Robbie was considered the catch of the neighborhood. How did she put it? Let's see, "Marlene, that son of yours is the most sought-after young man I've ever seen. Why doesn't he ask any of the girls out?" I think I defended Robbie by telling her that he didn't have time for girls because he was too interested in scholarship and carving miniature male figures out of stale but unchewed bubble gum. That usually caused the neighbor to withdraw. Despite my intervention, I worried a lot about Robbie's failure to launch. I tended to blame Henry, because he tried to push our son around after he came home from college, where he studied art more than anything else. My sense was he pushed Robbie too hard, causing our troubled young man to get a job as an assistant to a glass blower in a very small factory in Ohio. He moved out and became a specialist in bud vases. Maybe it was a good thing that he learned about his internal sexuality in time and never ruined some girl's life.

Henry was more of a pessimist about Robbie's future, as well as everything else, and I was more of an optimist. We had a pretty good blend, similar to sweet and sour meatballs. Our mixture threatened to come apart after Robbie became a physical woman. After surviving a near nervous breakdown, I relaxed somewhat. Henry, on the other hand, maintained his rigid opposition. I kept trying to punch holes in Henry's logic, hoping that he'd be unable to plug the holes fast enough. One of my attempts revealed a shred of promise. Although Henry refused to believe there was such a thing as a transgender the way it was explained to him, he did do some research into the medical facts. I wasn't supposed to know about it. When I disposed of the trash one day, I saw three wrinkled sheets in Henry's waste basket that proved my suspicions. OK, so they were twenty-five pieces of three torn up wrinkled sheets, but I smoothed out one of the pieces to read what I could. It only took me forty minutes to paste the three sheets back together.

On the morning of my Seventieth birthday, I had a wonderful moment when Henry gave me an unusually large check as a present. The birthday card itself was a bit of a poke in the ego, however. It featured a photo of a very ugly old wrinkled woman and one of those old age jokes. Was I supposed to look like that? Fuck it. And since I had cried my eyes out the day before because I had taken a furtive peek in the mirror and noticed how much my face had aged with the saggy fleshy folds under my chin, the card bothered me all the more. I was ready to explode with anger and self-recrimination until Henry's big injection of money caused me to lose my bad temper. Truly, it was a great picker-upper. I actually had enough now to make a down payment on a facelift, that is, if I had the guts to do it. Except for my angst about having no calls from the kids, it was a pretty nice day.

12

It was five minutes to ten in the evening of my birthday and I was ready to go to bed thinking that both my children had forgotten they had a mother who was now a year older. Their neglect was something I could store in my mental repository of peeves as I searched for a fetching set of pajamas and slippers. The peignoir set Henry had bought for me was still in the box, waiting for me to deserve it. Suddenly I heard the phone in my cubbyhole jangle, causing my heartbeat to rev up a few notches. "They remembered, those rascals!" I put my hand to my chest and definitely experienced a tingle of excitement. It was similar to the way I always felt when I had a car that wouldn't start and then heard it suddenly it come to life. Linda was on the phone. She sang a few words of "Happy Birthday" and then told me that Robbie had asked her to be his proxy.

"What does that mean, Linda? What the hell is he doing that he can't call me on my birthday?"

"Please, Mom, Robbie had a big project and the day got by him and he didn't want to call you so late in the evening because you and Dad go to bed early and you're on Eastern time."

"Wait a minute, Robbie's in Ohio -- you're in Ohio, right? Aren't you both on Eastern time?."

"Yes, but our Eastern time is much later than your retired peoples' Eastern time."

"I'm not retired -- your father is retired!"

"Well, I think of you as retired, Mother, because when you do your writing you're sitting on your, oh never mind. OK, you're not retired. Robbie will be calling you in the next few days. Can't you just give him a break?"

"Oh, of course, I don't stand on ceremony, as the saying goes. Anyway, I hate that expression. You talk more to him than I do and that's a good thing. So tell him I appreciate his unspoken wonderful wishes and that I love him. And don't tell him how hurt I am that he didn't make the call himself."

"There's something in the mail for your special day, but I'll bet you didn't get it yet. It's from both of us."

"I didn't, but what am I going to say?"

"You're going to give me that bullshit that we didn't have to."

"Wrong, I'm through with that old crappy phrase. Actually, you did have to. I almost cut you out of my Will!"

"How could you cut me out, Mother dear, when my net worth is probably fifteen or twenty times your net worth? At least you don't have to worry about my future!"

"It was just a joke, OK, it wasn't funny. Anyway, at least you called, honey, to make me feel better, and I appreciate that. Actually, today was a pretty successful day for me. I'm making some big decisions."

"What?"

"Well, I'm thinking of having a bit of plastic surgery, like starting with my neck."

"That's so not you, Mother. I think you ought to straighten out your closet first."

"Do you think my clothes are more important than my wrinkles?"

"Last time I visited, all your outfits were wrinkled from being crammed in that closet so tightly, but I don't think you need any facelift yet. You could probably wait until you're Seventy-Five. Also, if you're going on another diet, you should get that handled first."

"I was thinking that if I fixed my neck I would lose a few ounces right there."

"What does Dad think?"

"You know what he thinks. He still tries to think of me as his twenty-one-year-old bride. He had our wedding photo enlarged and bought an expensive frame for it and hung it up on his wall, but when it comes to picking out a birthday card, he seems to get his reality back.

"Did he get you one of those old lady cards?"

"You know about those?"

"I almost, uh, nothing."

"You almost bought one for me too?"

"Our gift should be coming any day, Mom. Oh, I've got to prepare for tomorrow! Bye!" And with that, my adored Linda, speedy, dismissive Linda, cut-the-mother-off-at-the-pass Linda, hung up. Whew, it's a good thing I don't go crazy, just because my kids are weird. I knew all the time that I'd get at least one phone call before I got in bed with my resentment simmering.

I hesitated before applying my night cream at the end of the day of my birthday. It had occurred to me that Linda's call just in the last hour was one of the longer phone calls I'd had with her recently. I always gave excuses for Linda, even if she didn't require them. I was the one who needed my head examined for putting up with her quickie bye-byes.

Henry was already asleep, so I used my getting-ready-for-bed time to ruminate about my 37-year-old daughter's strange life. *Let's see, when was our last conversation before this one, and how long was it? At first we didn't even talk about that soldier she'd been allegedly "going with" for the last, what, nine years? I'd lost count. Most single women talk about their love lives with their mothers, don't they? But Linda's just different, so I brought up the subject. I think she said that I should stop calling him a soldier -- that he was retired from the military and was currently working as some kind of a researcher, with a specialty in the mating habits of birds. Yeah, that was it. "But Linda, you're so mysterious! Can't a mother even ask her daughter if she's shacked up with a fellow?"*

"I'm not 'shacked up,' as you refer to it, Mother dear."

I didn't like the way she said 'Mother dear.' Then Linda went on to describe the living arrangements with the birdman of nowhere. If he had a home of his own, I knew nothing about it. I didn't understand her explanation and she hung up before I could learn how often they played at being married. Now what does "once in awhile mean?" God Forbid, if I should even dare to ask if she ever had plans to start a family. The conversation ended when Linda needed to end it.

"Sorry, Mom, I have to rush -- I have a meeting of my Twelve-Step Program's Executive Board -- talk to you later." Click!

I knew about the Twelve-Step crutch programs because I had spoken to her on a previous two-minute phone call about which one she was active in, but I've lost track of her response because there have been several such groups. I know one of them had to do with too much excessive throwing up, but I think she graduated from that and moved on to Overspending on Travel Anonymous.

Did Henry just turn over on his side? I thought I saw movement.

"Marlene, will you please switch off the light?"

"I was just going to, Henry." I leaned over to my nightstand and groped for the light switch on the lamp. As I did, I accidentally knocked off a couple of books from the pile next to the sole source of light for my sleep-inducing reading pleasure. Served me right for stacking up my reading material about eleven books high.

13

My daughter Linda was one of those women who would never be overweight. She currently wore a size 2 coat and was eight or nine inches taller than me. When she was small, I used to compare her legs with those of a wading bird, even though she ate more like a vulture. Everything that went into that child's mouth had to have been absorbed into growth tissue, because I was constantly buying her bigger shoes, longer leggings and older girls' jumpers. She began to tower over me about the time she entered high school. After she reached seventeen, her height became fixed and her figure changed from thin to thinner. Her body could be described as on the bony side, but possibly a tad leaner than the average self-respecting skeleton. I feared she had become anorexic, but how could she be described as such when I knew she devoured in two days what would be a week's worth of produce for Henry and me. When I picked out a dress for her as she was getting ready for college, I had to go to the girls' department. She never inherited any of my cheeky genes and nobody ever described me as lanky. Somewhere I had read that recessive genetic characteristics are submerged until somebody from the next younger generation winds up with those fat cell markers. That was great news because the kids that Linda probably wasn't going to create would mean there would be fewer chunky people in the world.

My obsession about my approximately thirty pounds of overweight had accelerated as a result of staring at the photo of Nancy Westerville's backside. I went crazy with envy. The idea that some obese lady could shed all those pounds really got to me. I remember going home from the library late that afternoon and recording my reflections. I added them in bold font to my "philosophical cons" folder. "**Is it possible for a fat woman to take off lots of weight and suddenly be surrounded with hunks, dudes and other admirers? I'll bet Ms. Westerville is entertaining dates like mad -- probably acquired from one of those rabidly advertised meat market websites. Conclusion: I'm not only jealous -- I'm motivated beyond belief, but right now I'm mostly jealous.**"

My envy knew no bounds when I thought about how tenaciously that woman must have taken hold of her self-destructive ways, restricted her diet and done whatever it took to eliminate so much of her excess weight. It only took one aloof female to put me in a such a blue funk, but that one was meaningful. Oh how I begrudged the joy she must have experienced as she assembled a whole new babe wardrobe. After agitating for a couple of hours, I took a moment to retrieve my cellphone and the stored images. I quickly scrolled down to Nancy's rear end. Yes, she had most certainly dropped a big bunch of flesh. "It must have been surgery, it was too fast." Steeling myself to stop dwelling on an unproductive obsession, I exited from the "cons" folder. *Oh yeah, I was going to look up more data on plastic surgeons if I had time. Well, I'm not in the mood just now.* While I was bestilled in a type of suspended animation, Henry entered the room and handed me an envelope.

"Sorry, honey, this invitation was in my pile of stuff, but it's for you."

"Thanks, what is it?"

"Weight Watchers propaganda."

"Throw it out, I'm going in a different direction."

"I know, you're going to do something creative, like coming up with a different recipe for Key Lime Pie."

Henry left the room. I watched his slim hips vanishing as he shut the door to his private office sanctuary. There were no piles of paper in there and I harbored a deep resentment of his extra-long built in desk. It only held essentials -- a computer, printer, phone fax and a plastic pencil cup filled with sharpened number 3 pencils. What kind of athletic type preferred number 3 pencils? The rest of his fake granite desk surface was bare. He could dust his desk surface, while I didn't need to dust mine because it was completely covered with everything required for a messy desk occupant. If I wished to consult my "Things to Do" list, I knew precisely where it was buried.

Suddenly, the sanctuary door opened and Mr. Slim Hips emerged. "I forgot to ask you -- did you put your niece's wedding date on our social calendar?"

"Of course I did. September 16th, a Sunday. Actually, we'll have to block out a whole week around that date. I've even considered buying a dress for the occasion. They say it's 'black tie,' and I don't want to shock anyone by wearing only a black tie."

"You'd like to stick it to your rich sister, wouldn't you?"

"People who aren't celebrities or undertakers at a convention who make everybody spend unnecessary money on their egomaniac weddings have a lot of nerve. What are you wearing?"

"My blue suit."

"Blue isn't black."

"I know -- do you think I should have the dry cleaner apply something? Like you have your hairdresser give you a rinse? It eventually comes off."

"You shouldn't embarrass my family with your skinflinty apparel, even if I hate their uppity ways as much as you do."

"I'll wear what I wish and they can think what they wish."

"Will you at least promise me that you'll wear a white shirt and tie and try to blend in?

"I'm not making any promises this far in advance."

"Well, whatever you do, don't go overboard with trying to look stodgy. Be nice for our kids' sake. I guess they'll each be in the wedding party. Well, I know Robbie will. Linda's probably declined already, if they even asked her."

"I thought you knew everything."

"Henry, I don't know exactly who will be in the wedding party. Since our son is Cissy's only male cousin, he'll probably have to buy a tux or rent one."

"That'll be the day. That kid doesn't spend shit on clothes -- that is, except for those black leather jackets with those logos on the back of them."

"I really liked the one with the drawing of that rock group 'Kiss.' And dear, you should stop worrying about Robbie's tastes. It's out of our control."

"He's 42, isn't he? Say, don't 42-year-olds usually stop playing with games and toy furniture and chia pets?"

"He loves that room design software he bought and plays only on the computer now."

"You know him better than I do."

"He's more like me, Henry, he distrusts guns and loves beautiful things."

"Maybe he'll grow up in ten years."

"Why should he? Life should be fun."

"It's fun to shoot and fish and fun to be like me. Look at my exhilarating day ahead -- I'm going fishing with Mike and we're chartering a fishing boat from a guy named Greasy Gus Grabbit."

"That's the guy's real name?"

"No, his real name is Marion Gustopholis, or something like that."

"I guess the Greasy adjective describes his, oh, never mind. So you're going to have fun."

"What's Robbie do for fun?"

"It's Thursday, Henry. He has a job."

"First of all, it's Friday, not Thursday. Secondly, he hates his job. He spends all his take-home money. When I was his age I saved all my money."

"Henry, if everybody was like you, the U.S. economy would come crashing down with a thud."

"I never played with games of any sort."

"You were never young. When I married you, remember how I asked you if your boyhood things would require room in our closet?"

"No."

"Well, I did, and you didn't have any boyhood things. All you had were three business suits and a few shirts and ties. Not a single game or hobby or even a deck of cards. Just a camera and a few pictures."

"Games are for children."

"Our son likes games -- also decorator software. He also models things out of clay. You should appreciate how artistic he is."

"Maybe he came from Jupiter or Saturn, where fortyish artistic single men are hatched."

"It's supposed to be Mars, but not our son. He could be from Venus."

"OK, I'm not going there. But I wanted to show you a photograph taken last week of our nature center volunteer group. Actually, that's why I walked in here."

"I totally forgot there was a picture."

"Here it is. Take it."

Henry handed me the color photograph. I made the mistake of examining it and whatever hopes I had to enjoy the rest of my day ended in a crescendo of agony. My mind flitted to the last scene in the movie, "The Picture of Dorian Gray." The central character's real looks caused a shock and the audience gasped. I looked more intensely at the photograph and wanted to kill something. Just then a well-adapted Florida mosquito flew by. Even one of the most enduring life forms of all time can be in the wrong place at the wrong time.

14

In my generation, becoming a mother meant always having to say you were sorry. Before the arrival of children, you only had to be apologetic to one person, the husband. When I think about how unprepared I was during my years as a young mother, my consolation was that they didn't put me on a stool wearing a dunce cap in order to humiliate me into learning how to master the ABC's of juggling nap periods with cooking, shopping and the cleaning up of spills. Times were changing quickly as American families prospered. The new generation of kids were given all the fringe benefits denied to me. My children learned executive skills before kindergarten, and they soon became adept at bossing me around. They got their Pre-K education from watching older folks make mistakes. Eventually, it began to dawn on me that the only way to catch up with these smartass seventies babies was to survive to a very advanced age. I'm working on my Honorary Master's Degree in Sexual Preference Psychology right now.

The obstetrician had warned me that the baby that was to be Robbie might come early, at least from his observation of my cervix or my pelvis or whatever those doctors were so fond of observing. After Linda's birth, I remember that he laughed at me for worrying about how painful labor would be. Why he actually told me that each of them sprang from my womb like a lubricated puppy dog right into the arms of the nurse on duty. According to him, I could have borne them in some corn field or even a gravel pit the way it happened. Robbie was born sixteen days before my due date. I was in the grocery store buying canned goods and foodstuffs for a shopping averse fellow like my husband when I slipped on a puddle of gooey water. It had come from my body. A kindly customer who was in the aisle next to me helped me to my feet and arranged for the store manager to summon Henry from his place of business and get me to the hospital. The customer gathered up my purchases, paid for them with money I stuffed into her hand and had the store deliver them that evening, together with my wheeled shopping cart. The last thing I remember about that event is that when Henry arrived with his car, I asked the kind-hearted customer if she could grab another three cans of the chunk style tuna fish and add them to the order.

The embryo that was destined to be our Linda was, by my reckoning, created during a snowstorm in Milwaukee. Nobody in our neighborhood could get the outside doors of their houses open because of the three feet of heavy snow piled up during the night. Henry managed to crawl out of a window and lay his hands on a shovel. Everybody's vehicle was stuck somewhere, either in a driveway or blocking somebody's access on our narrow side street. We were all marooned for a week without electricity and the neighbors all got to know each other better. You've heard the tales about how couples with a power outage had nothing to do when night came, so they fooled around. We did likewise. Unfortunately, we were out of rubbers. They were on the shopping list and I would have gone to the drugstore the day after the snowstorm hit. I wasn't very good at planning for the future, but I made up for it by being creative after the fact.

Our marriage thrived after that second baby drop and eventually birth control came to town. Henry and I conferred about the size of our family. He said one of each was fine with him and I said I really wanted one more girl after we had both Robbie and Linda. I explained that the reason I wanted another daughter was because I thought Linda should have a confidante, but since there was still no way to guarantee a sister for our baby girl, we stayed away from each other whenever I felt especially fertile. Henry put away money for the kids' college and I taught them how to be self-sufficient. Robbie showed an aptitude for art and design, while Linda seemed inclined to take things apart and put them back together. Like our portable radio and her first two-wheeled bike. One day I caught Linda, then aged nine, with Henry's set of tools, playing with the loose wheel and the frame of her 24-inch Schwinn. There were screws and wing nuts all over the cement surface of the carport. I got crazy and shouted at her: "What have you done?"

She replied calmly, "I'm changing the alignment -- the wheel was rubbing against that metal thing. It's OK now."

"Where on earth did you learn how to do that?"

"From Mr. Jennings -- the man down the street. He owns a bike shop."

"Oh, from Mr. Jennings, I see. Did he explain to you what an alignment was?"

"Not exactly, I just showed him the problem and I heard him using that word."

"Linda, be a good girl, put your bike back together so those parts don't get lost."

"Sure, Mom, but Robbie's bike doesn't ride so good either."

I had been thinking of sending Linda to a college for girls only, but Henry and I conferred and his practical side ruled. We sent Linda to the state college at Madison, where she graduated with a business degree in three years instead of four and then worked her way through classes in automotive repair. Somewhere along the way she began to fool around with the motors and other equipment on school buses and built a reputation as a skilled transportation vehicle grease monkey. Henry was quite proud of her as she formed her own bus company and hired employees. He now had the resourceful children he always wanted -- a girl with masculine abilities plus a business mind, and a son who could design original shapes for ceramic containers and sell them for less than his costs. I told Henry that Robbie needed a trade if he wasn't going to make a serious living selling overpriced jugs and cupid figures or do statues like Henry Moore, the famous sculptor, so Henry gave Robbie some advice. Of course, Robbie never took it, and that's when he moved to Ohio and got into glass manufacturing. After a few years of low pay, he had an extended long distance conversation with Henry. I wasn't there and it didn't end well. Then Robbie consulted Linda, who was on her way to success. She was practical to the core. She told him to leave his job as an assistant glass blower and get a union job with a better future, so he went to work for General Motors. Robbie then moved from Cambridge, Ohio to Lordstown, Ohio, and settled in. One day he called me and told me about his illustrious interview.

"Mom, I just sent you a note that I got a good job here, but guess how I got it!"

"Tell me, I'm falling off my chair from the suspense."

"Well, you always told me that I was good at artistic pursuits and I was good with my hands, so you remember how I did all those models of cars and then started to construct my own versions?"

"How could I forget -- you used to have all those parts of models all over the floor and your father tripped on one of them and broke his toe, and-----"

"Well, instead of reminding me of that unfortunate accident now, just listen up!"

"I'm listening -- one of my ears is glued to the phone and the free ear is a backup."

"I went to the interview and showed this fellow my best two self-constructed models and he started to laugh."

"OK, I know the joke is coming -- keep going!"

"I looked at the two models and one was of a Ford Mustang and the other was a Lincoln Continental!"

"So, what am I missing?"

"The job was for General Motors and I had their two big competitors in my demonstration!"

"So you were embarrassed?"

"Was I ever, but I still got the job. The interviewer excused himself and left the room and when he came back he told me I showed a lot of initiative. So now I'm in this union and I was put on the wheel assembly team and I'll be making enough to live on. Aren't you proud?"

"What about your art? What we sent you to college to learn?"

"It's a sideline -- I'm tired of always being in debt."

"I can't believe I'm hearing this from you. Didn't I always tell you that when you grew up you'd get the value of money? Oh, I'm sorry I'm sounding bitchy -- I've had a downer of a day, and --"

"Mom, I don't have time to hear your apology. I have to leave now. I have a union meeting."

Was this my son, the artist with his gentle ways, commingling his daily activities with the bums who talk like they've all been trained in the empty lots of Brooklyn? The Jimmy Hoffa gorilla types? What will Henry think? Well, he'll think about the money first and then let me do the rest of the worrying. I had to say goodbye to Robbie with a motherly tone: "Watch out for those brutes -- I hear they have a lot of tough guys who think they run the world."

"You know I've learned how to keep my mouth shut. I will never forget that day I got beat up in an alley for voicing my opinion to a couple of thugs."

"Sure, you learned your lesson about talking at the wrong time to the wrong people and now, maybe, maybe, you'll also keep some money in your wallet, maybe."

"Don't you trust me?"

"I trust you like you like you were my own flesh and blood. Unfortunately, I don't always trust me. The trouble is, you've got my creative genes and none of your father's miserly instincts. Does this new job mean you'll finally be able to visit us without our sending you the plane ticket?"

"Got to go, Mom, we'll talk about this later." Sure, later, I thought, like later after I'm in my oversized coffin from worrying about him. Well, at least my middle-aged boy has turned the corner. Now he has a job with benefits, and boy, does he ever need them!

15

Cissy's wedding was going to be a lavish affair befitting her father's station in life. I think his station was in Bridgehampton, although he never took the bus. I shouldn't have been surprised that Howard Rosen now earned so much money. He had become a real hotshot entrepreneur who required the services of several brokerage houses, multiple lawyers and an accounting firm where several employees assigned to his businesses worked nights and weekends during tax seasons. Even when he was courting Beth, years before his big-time business success, our mother referred to him as "Howard, the financier." When Beth was in the process of ensnaring him, Mother would tell the neighbors what "Howard, the financier" was wearing when they had dates, or what "Howard, the financier" brought as gifts. It grated on me why she couldn't just call him by his name without the description of his line of work. I had to ignore all those not so subtle inferences as I got to know him. Actually, Howard wasn't a bad sort, being friendly to me and Henry, but it was hard to keep track of a guy who was always in meetings in Rhode Island or some other foreign location. If I asked Beth, Howard and Cissy over to dinner, only Beth and Cissy would come. Her reason was, "Howard's gone to Montreal, or maybe Philadelphia, or occasionally Berlin, and it always had to do with some business deal. Eventually, we forgot what he looked like, so Beth had learned to drag out a magazine or some company annual report which she brought with her. There, on a bookmarked page, would be Howard's picture, often standing and smiling along with other big business types. On one of these visits, while Beth's attention was directed to Henry, I took one of these annual reports and flipped to a page where Howard's salary was listed. I had to excuse myself to deal with my bladder, my moment of heart stoppage, and the repair of my makeup.

I must have enjoyed questioning my sister, even though her answers made me feel foolish that I'd even asked. Her lifestyle reminded me of a TV show.

"Beth, with a husband out of town so much, how do you manage, like, socially?"

"Oh, I get involved in organizations that give money away."

"Of course, so silly of me to ask. I've always thought that giving money away might be amusing." I wondered what a woman like my sister would do if she didn't have all those organizations. If it were me, I would have picked a different husband. Actually, Henry and I agreed that Howard was probably quite happy with his life. Our whole family felt rather sorry for him because he was married to Beth.

I got along just fine with Cissy, but now I had a big worry. With her wedding date scheduled, and the planning already happening, how was the family going to handle Robbie's sex-change? Linda and I had been talking to Robbie and the three of us had tentatively agreed that the name "Robin" might be a good choice. Henry hadn't been consulted yet, but Robbie wanted the name decision to be unanimous. In the meantime, we managed with "Rob." If Cissy called me before we'd had a chance to plot our approach, what would I say to her? Sure enough, before we could fabricate a plausible scenario, the phone rang and I was certain it was Cissy. The timing of the call was the tipoff because Cissy always had a habit of calling me when it was cocktail hour in the Hamptons.

"Hello, Cissy!" I answered, even before she spoke.

"You told me you didn't have caller ID. How did you know it was me?"

"I was looking at my calendar and figuring out when you would be calling about your upcoming nuptials. Unfortunately, I was just going out. Can I call you back?"

"Sure, Aunt Mar, I'll be here for awhile. You have the number?"

"I guess you're home now. But which home?" I had to ask because by that time there were more than two.

"I'm on the island. Our Suffolk County place."

"I have it in my book. I repeated the number to her."

"Right, Auntie, I'll wait for your call."

I wasn't just about to leave the house. The truth was that I had to collect myself. Robbie's presence would certainly be a subject of the conversation. So would the details of my niece's wedding, because it was going to be a "destination wedding." Destination weddings meant that guests would be contributing to the health of the destination's economy. Henry had heard me on the phone and walked over to my cubbyhole to hear the latest gossip.

"Why was your phone call so short?"

"I know she wants her cousin Robbie in the wedding procession and nobody's supposed to know about he's a she. But you knew that this was an issue and you didn't want to talk about it. Well she is willing to come as a man, just to keep the spotlight away from her, but I still need to stall for time."

"I guess Robbie is willing to play at being a guy once again. I wish she'd make up his mind which sex she enjoys being. I still think he should stay home and make some kind of excuse. She shouldn't try to look cool wearing a man's tux. Also, she'll have to flatten the new boobs, won't he?"

"Watch your pronouns, Henry. You still don't understand. Robbie has been a woman inside his head, inside his body, and only has had to play at being a man to avoid stuff, what kind, I'm not sure, probably the embarrassment or the notoriety, you know, everything. She's OK with not going as herself, as a woman, if it avoids making everybody else in the family uncomfortable. He's always been accommodating, and now, she's the same way. She even agreed that it would be tough to spring the news on the Rosen clan at this time. Listen, nobody in the family outside the four of us will know what's inside those trousers!"

"Well, I think you're influencing her to go as Robbie because you're still jealous of Beth. You're envious of her lifestyle and her natural slenderness."

"I am not. Besides, Beth's being skinny isn't natural. She's too old for that model's look and too young to be dried out from life. Everyone knows that rich people can afford to stay skinny and still enjoy their food. Eating cake and pie costs a few dollars and adds up to high calories, but eating lower calorie caviar and chateaubriand costs ten times more."

"You're always accusing me of being in denial. Well you're in denial about your diet and, oh, never mind. I'll get in trouble if I discuss your food issues with you."

"It's because of the way we grew up, and you know it!"

"What I know about it is what you've told me again and again. Your mother's still in the kitchen with you when you decide what to eat. You even have her picture on the wall by the table!"

"It's time I took that picture down. But what about the fact that our older daughter, Cissy's adored cousin, wants to come to the wedding?"

"Well, she can come. One less guy can stand up. The couple can still get married."

"She told me she's ready to stand up as a guy. Should I call her and tell her to come as herself?"

"I can't make that decision."

"OK, then it's final. Our older daughter will come as Robbie."

"Sure, you're the one who knows all about being natural."

Beth and I had our differences growing up. I was the kid who could hit a baseball like a boy. She stayed on the sidelines watching me bat -- always smoothing her skirt and making sure her sweater was tight enough. I did better in high school and sports and she did better in the last row of the movie theatre or when we both dressed up on the High Holidays. I tried to understand the Hebrew prayers, while she just wanted to understand the Hebrew boys. Then she met Howard. She thought he might be the one, so she decided to string him along. He took the bait and I do mean bait. Beth wouldn't tell me what she did, but every time Howard came to call he had a gleam in his eye. I wasn't good at whatever Beth was doing. My mother got tired of trying to train me to marry rich.

Beth turned out to be even more devious and cunning than my mother. She had been married to Howard for several years without any signal that the stork was on the way. Then she began to lay plans for something she learned from a fertility specialist and her method was successful. Somehow she managed to conceive Cissy without actually letting Howard in on her scheme. One day my phone rang with gusto while I was lecturing little Linda on the merits of clean fingernails for girls.

"Hello, whoever it is, hang on!" I didn't mind putting the unknown caller off for fear that my daughter was about to take something apart that needed to stay together. However, a loud and nearly hysterical voice from the speaker caught my attention.

"It's me, Marlene, it's Beth! I'm pregnant!"

"You're what? Linda, come here where I can see you!"

"Aren't you happy for me?"

"Wait a minute, Beth." I screamed for Linda to stop getting charcoal all over her overalls. She had been learning something destructive in her first grade class. "Beth, I'm sorry, how did you? When did you? Are you sure? And do you really want to go through with it?"

"Of course I'm sure and I want a baby so baaaad!"

"Beth, it hasn't been that easy for you! Did you make an appointment?"

"I sure did! How did you guess? Howard had back to back trips with a free day in between two months ago when the blessed impregnation happened!"

"Oh, I wasn't, I didn't mean that kind of appointment -- I meant with the obstetrician."

"Oh, him? Well, that part was a snap. All I did was call his nurse and tell her I was late and then they did all the tests."

"So, sister dear, that's great. I'm happy for you. How do you feel?"

"Like shit. Can't keep food down."

"Try sucking on a lemon for awhile."

"What does that do?"

"You forget how nauseated you are. Tell me, how does Howard feel about being a father?"

"He made sure I get the best treatment there is when the time comes. He arranged to buy a significant share of the private hospital I'll be using."

"Oh that's good, at least you won't have to plead for a bedpan or jelly for your toast like I did."

16

I woke up in a tizzy this morning, imagining that my niece, Cissy Rosen, was sitting on the edge of my bed, criticizing me because I hadn't let her play catch with Robbie. That's the funny thing about dreams -- they take reality and twist it out of shape so that the distortions haunt one's inner life. Cissy's phantom in the dream was her present age of 31, but Robbie was this little kid of 11. Why did our 42-year-old transgendered daughter show up in my dream as a little boy who could be a playmate of his girl cousin? They were never playmates. When Robbie had his eleventh birthday, Cissy hadn't been born yet! Wow, here was solid proof that my therapist's reliance on dream theory was misplaced.

"Dreams can't even get the math right!"

"Are you talking to me, Marlene?"

"No, Henry, I'm dictating a sentence to the invisible secretary in the room -- the one whose name you mentioned in your sleep last night."

"I did no such thing."

"Henry, when you're snoring regularly and I'm awake, I can hear you say things out loud!"

"I don't believe you."

"OK, then who's Laura?"

"I don't have a -- I don't know a Laura."

"The woman who called the other day and left a message. Her first name was Laura."

"Oh, there is a Laura who works with my dentist."

"Does she get anywhere near your mouth?"

"Of course she does. She squirts the blood off."

"Then you do have a Laura."

"Oh, go make breakfast. You drive me nuts."

"I will, as soon as I change your pillowcase. You got lipstick on it."

"I don't get -- what?"

"Don't worry, dear, it's my shade. Just testing."

Henry left the room while I went back in my head about the Robbie and Cissy dream. Was it possible that my submerged memory knew something I didn't? Did Cissy ever have a crush on Robbie? Whew, I think she did, and I had forgotten all about it! What was that dream really all about? I wasn't ready to trust the shrink about that one. Aha, maybe that Robbie and Cissy dream sequence had something to do with her upcoming wedding. It was approaching so quickly I pretended I was caught up in a time warp. I learned about time warps from watching numerous Star Trek re-runs. They were useful tools because they helped me gloss over my ongoing grief and quickly get to the good parts. Every time I had a moment to think about how luxurious Cissy's wedding would be, I was able to consider the source: The parents, my sister, Beth and her husband, Howard. Beth was eight years younger than me, but that meant she was eight years smarter about the newest avenues of spending money. Who were they if not rich, richer and richest, compared to Henry and me, middle, middler and middlest? One particular day stands out for me when it hit me how my sister and I lived in different worlds. I had been visiting her at their lavish townhouse in Pound Ridge, New York. They had just finished furnishing the place. . . .

"Beth, your home is so beautiful. May you and Howard spend many happy years in this delightful area. Great schools, lots of trees --"

"Marlene, guess what? This townhouse has just been sold."

"You're moving already? I just sent you two toss pillows that match your mauve walls. You said you loved them!"

"I do love them, but Howard can be rather impulsive. Yesterday he brought me a real estate sale contract for my signature. What could I do? He put a down payment on a place in Long Island. Even better schools and more trees!"

"You want me to return the toss pillows? I still have the receipt."

"Of course not. Cissy loves them. She won't let them go, even though most of these new furnishings have been included in the house sale. Howard said the buyer was in a terrific hurry and he wanted the deal done before she realized she was overpaying."

"Well, you know what I always say, 'whither the man goest, thou goest too,' or something like that."

"When I married him I knew he was ambitious. But I didn't get the whole gist of it until after our honeymoon."

"What happened then?"

"I had a choice: accept life as a wealthy wife and put up with a few inconveniences, or complain about everything and have luxury forced upon me."

"So you chose ---"

"The inconveniences. I had to buy my outfits in more exclusive stores or Howard would be unhappy."

"Oh, I would so hate it if I couldn't shop at Penney's. They have these terrific sales that make you think you're investing instead of splurging! Really, Beth, I give you all the credit in the world."

"It's better to have a happy husband. I was naive to think we would live in one place for a long time. Now I keep the phone number of the moving company handy. You never know."

"Are you going to have to buy furniture all over again?"

"That's another compromise I made. Howard hired this interior designer lady, and she practically forced me to go post-modernist."

"Oh, sure, post-modernist. No wall-to-wall carpeting, but that's good. Less lint to vacuum."

"You should see this designer lady! She has green hair and wears it down to her tush."

"Is she Irish or something?"

"No, she's Jewish. Does a lot of the multi-millionaire families in New York."

"She's Jewish, all right."

"Cissy is holding out on the modern, however. She's doing her room in Federal style."

"Federal, as in, uh, oh, when you said 'Federal,' all I could think about was the Washington Monument. So what's Federal style that goes in a bedroom?"

"You'll have to ask Cissy. I think you're right about Washington, though. It's probably the style furniture when he was President."

"I'll make a note of that."

"Can you stay here a few days? I'd like to take you with me when I pick out some new accessories."

"Can't, Beth. My plane reservation is for tomorrow."

I was reluctant to tell Beth that I had to get home to do the weekly laundry and shop for groceries. Big wealth made me nervous and realizing that my own sister was living with it made me even more nervous. Had I known about Beth's rising circumstances, I wouldn't have selected the pillows I did. They had a luxurious look, but I would have died if she knew they had been on clearance. I changed the subject.

"Beth, tell me, do you have much time to do any reading?"

"Sometimes after tea and before dinner."

"You drink tea?"

"That's what my neighbor friends with British tastes do in Long Island, so I guess I'll be doing it. They refer to it as "taking tea."

"Great. You'll be taking tea and I'll still be taking aspirin whenever Henry gives me a headache. I suppose Howard never gives you a headache?"

"I have more tsouras than you know, but I won't go into it."

"I have that too -- Linda takes bi-polar medication."

"Robbie's always been healthier, hasn't he?"

I wondered at the time what Beth was thinking when she made that remark. I never liked to discuss personal stuff about Robbie, except for his accomplishments. "Say, Beth, did you know that Robbie won a sculpture contest?"

"No! But I'll bet Cissy knew about it. She and Robbie gab all the time on the phone."

So now I understood why Beth's husband purchased a mansion on Long Island. Beth didn't seem to complain much at all, once she got over the fact that the new interior designer slept with most of her male clients. In fact my good sport sister got right into the swing of being a resident of the Hamptons because she felt it was a perfect place to bring up a girl for whom she had big ambitions. I had begun to like my sister, even though I once hated her when we were kids. I never asked Beth if she still had the scar on her knee where I once threw one of my mom's china figurines at her. Things were different now that we were grown up matrons. Beth had maids to clean her homes and run errands and was known to time her tanning sessions to the second, while I had dishwater hands and avoided the sun and the pool in our community because I hated having to put on a bathing suit.

As soon as I returned home, I managed to adapt to a residence with a husband who was home every night and sat in a worn out chair to read the newspaper. Beth had lots of chairs that were brand new or restored antique, but most of the time she had to look at her freshly perfumed twelve pound Chihuahua because Howard was somewhere else. What was there to be jealous about?

It was a Sunday -- the day when Henry scheduled his once-weekly inspection tour of our house. His military training had never left. He had a chart. We had his and hers chores. He was tall and I was short, so he got the high up cleaning tasks and I got the low ones. I was too short to check him out, but he could do all the checking he wanted. First he would check the volume of the dust under the beds and then he would check the tops of the pictures that were hung at my eye level. I kept visualizing Beth being out somewhere taking tea while her maids did the dusting of their place. She was being entertained while I was being scored.

Henry was an active participant in our housecleaning. He didn't sit like a lump and say, "Marlene, it's time to use the dust mop." No, he gave me a passionate kiss with one hand on my chest and waited for me to take a breath. Then he would hand me the dust mop, which he had been holding behind his back with his other hand. He enjoyed watching me mop the floor and clean low-lying objects, but he actually had the more demanding job. He had to get on a stepstool and clean everything up high -- the fixtures, the higher up pictures, the skeet shooting trophies, the ceiling fans, and the tops of the cornices and vertical blinds. The best thing he did was to deal with the spiders. They kept showing up again and again to rebuild. He even had names for them. One was "Eight-legged Charlie," another was "Seven-Legged Henpecked Willie," and a third was "Wanda, the Destroyer." I had a name for the dust mop. I called it "Marlene's Third Leg." Henry and I were a team, and so what if he was the captain and I was the whole crew? Maybe I was being entertained after all. And on a brighter note, maybe, just maybe, Beth didn't enjoy her tea as much as I thought.

Most of the time when I thought about my sister's lifestyle was when I went shopping. I simply figured I needed a purse or a pair of slacks and usually ran straight to Dillard's in the mall. Beth had told me she shopped at a luxury boutique on "the Island" that was so exclusive it had no name that was publicized, no catalog, no website and no listing in the yellow pages. Its customers were sent invitations to their periodic showings. Once I asked Beth if she bought purses or slacks there. She told me they were afterthoughts. "Beth, what do you mean by that, uh, 'afterthought' term?"

"Oh, after I bought a few new dresses and coats and shoes, I had thoughts that I might need some new purses and slacks, so I drove over to Park Avenue in Manhattan."

"Beth, you drove all the way there yourself?"

"Well, Larry had the steering wheel."

I knew that Beth didn't like to flaunt her privileges in my face. Larry was the chauffeur. He supported his family on what Howard paid him. Larry's family didn't have it too bad. His wife had a maid too. So not only did I envy my sister's lifestyle, I envied her chauffeur's wife's lifestyle also.

Most of the time I had few regrets about my situation. I had two nice kids and Beth had only the one equally nice daughter. I was twice as fertile as Beth, which meant she was half as fertile as I was. My kids were industrious and Beth's daughter was illustrious. My kids worked for a living and Beth's daughter dated men who had grandfathers who started out working for a living.

17

I was at my cubbyhole trying to finish a story about a woman who found out she was going to have quadruplets. Just as I got to the part where the poor husband got fired from one of his three jobs, I decided to take a stay-at-home writer's coffee break. Normally, I would be deep in thought over which delicacy to have with the coffee, but then I did something that was beyond the boundaries of my playing field. Instead of going for a nosh, I lapsed into a visualization of how Beth would take her breaks. She wasn't a writer, but she must have used her down time to do something. I remembered that she played tennis regularly and that she wasn't very good at it, but she kept trying to improve. The part that stuck with me was how she had emphasized how she usually dropped about two pounds after a match. I didn't care if it was sweat -- it was two pounds! What did I drop after my coffee break? One-tenth of a calorie from searching for a snack bar and then, negating that one-tenth calorie, the addition of the one hundred eighty calories listed on the wrapper. I took out a calculator and discovered that I would be up five percent of a pound while Beth would be down two pounds. I didn't like the spread. That was the end of the way I did my coffee breaks.

I tried to stop focusing on my sister Beth and her family, but it was difficult. Their doings were so deliciously evocative of the flood of

Americans moving on up. Like the way Beth's world changed so dramatically after her labor pains gave way to the joys of motherhood. When Cissy was just a little kid, not even two years old, Beth began bestowing, no, make that lavishing, her total attention and careful instruction in luxury on the child.

We knew Cissy was extra smart. As soon as she reached school age, she developed into quite a prodigy, that is, a prodigy of a certain sort. When the girls at her private school went on a field trip to a natural history museum, Cissy made a careful study of the gem collection. As a sophomore in high school she learned how to distinguish sable from mink and vicuna from wool blend. Her education at home focused on the importance of clues to a boy's background. She was coached to eliminate all the poor guys with few prospects. I recall that when Cissy began to date Sherwin, and was still interviewing a few other contestants, Beth gave her a list of which questions to ask the unsuspecting fellow on their first date. One of the questions was, "What was your favorite subject in high school and what was your major at college?" If her date indicated any path less practical than pre-med, pre-law or finance, and maybe engineering if the guy was a genius, then the second question was, "What's your favorite pastime?" If the fellow answered that he liked fishing, bowling or going to neighborhood movies, then there probably wouldn't be a third question, unless it was to inquire what time they would get home.

I liked Cissy. I liked her sense of humor, the way she adapted to being spoiled rotten and how she treated her possessions. She was becoming accomplished in many upper class skills and had learned to ride horseback English saddle. For a time they rented a horse for her, and she gave the horse commands with a British accent. Then they bought her a horse of her own which she kept stalled in Duchess County, New York, but it was inconvenient for the family to keep driving all the way out there, so Howard picked up a mansion nearby for a cool million or three. Beth had phoned me when this happened and actually exclaimed, "Marlene, we've just bought a lovely home to go with Cissy's horse hobby." Talk about putting the horse before the house. And that wasn't all -- Beth and Howard weren't finished with their guidance. They gave her a sailboat for her twenty-fifth birthday. She kept it moored somewhere in a marina on the Hudson. Cissy didn't know much about operating a sailboat, so I guess that's when Sherwin, who had always been in the picture, began to take on a whole new aura. He taught Cissy the difference between a jib and a mizzen mast and a few other things. She had already studied his family's Dun & Bradstreet report. The real turning point came when she found out his father had just purchased a hundred and twenty-five foot yacht. Soon she fell deeply in love.

A male screech broke into my cloud of concentrated envy and jarred me like an unexpected clap of thunder. It was Henry calling me from his sanctuary.

"Marlene, what are you doing?"

"If I tell you I'm daydreaming instead of finishing my story, will you give me a hard time?" I realized that Henry put daydreams in the same category as night dreaming and that he considered dreams as unconscious manifestations caused by childish reverie combined with indigestion.

"No, not this time. I need help with something on my computer."

Whew, Henry needed help. What a lift to my spirits! Now I could forget about the fact that I had entered into matrimony without sufficient training to land a yacht owner for a father-in-law! The only downside was that now I had to postpone scribbling out an outline for a short story I was thinking of writing. It was about a rich girl marrying one guy while being in love with her cousin. I walked into Henry's sanctuary.

"Say, Henry, what if Cissy isn't really in love with her fiancé?"

"What I want to know is, has she missed a period?"

"You dirty old man."

"I'm like that tee-shirt you have -- I Yam What I Yam. Can you show me in Excel how to put gridlines on this house-cleaning chart?"

Before I could actually make the important return call to my niece, I had to consciously refrain from revealing Rob's new identity. Except for occasional slips, I wasn't calling our sex-changed daughter by the boy's nickname any longer. Getting the pronouns correct had also been a struggle. Henry kept asking the three of us, "what's with the 'R?' The name decision was a very big deal and our four-person family presided as a committee. Henry was adamant that he not be on the committee, but he had finally come around. I had to give him an ultimatum: either he would agree not to abstain from voting, or he wouldn't be invited to any more family events. Henry had never in my memory caved in to any of my ultimatums, so I was treading on thin ice.

"Are you in or out, Henry?"

"So I won't attend family events, I don't care."

"Henry, you won't be invited to your own surprise birthday parties and possibly not to your own funeral. That's how serious I am."

"That's goofy, I don't have a choice about my own funeral!"

"That's right. But you won't be welcome at mine, not at Linda's, and not the one for our transgendered daughter either."

"I'll probably be the first to die anyway."

"OK, then you can abstain from the naming committee, and the three of us will remember this for as long as you live."

"I heard that the three of you like the name 'Robin.' All right, I will agree to that name, and that's my final vote."

"This is a democracy. I'm okay with that name, but I'll have to tally up the kids' secret ballots."

"They sent you written ballots?"

"Not exactly."

"What then?"

"Never mind."

"I just know I've become a victim of a conspiracy."

"Well, I can't deny that. Linda thought "Reba" sounded contrived, and both Robbie and I thought "Roberta" was too old-fashioned. We really hoped that you'd go along with the gender-neutral name "Robin."

Robbie now prepared to change his paperwork, actually, her paperwork. She reminded us of two important things she needed and wanted from her father: The first thing was Twenty Thousand Dollars to help with the hospital and surgeon's bills, which were quite hefty. Linda's big loan was a game changer, but he had also taken out a loan from his retirement plan at work. The second thing was Henry's promise to love his son's new female self and understand that he had always been a woman in a man's body and wanted to go all the way and have the operation to complete the process. Henry wanted to separate his concept of fatherly love from his acceptance of the operation. He still didn't understand why the surgery was so critical, so Robin got on a plane and came to our home to make the case. I marveled at how our new daughter sat his father and me down on our sofa and gave us an elegant prepared lecture. Dressed in a two-piece slacks outfit which was quite convincing, although the hairdo still seemed masculine, Robin did her best to be reassuring. The voice was still Robbie, I thought, but there was something different in the way she spoke. I watched closely to see if any of Robin's explanations were sinking in with Henry. I had my doubts.

After Robin's visit, I asked Henry about his feelings toward his child.

"Marlene, I can't accept what he did -- maybe I'll never accept it. So just let me be, please?"

"All right, Henry, I do understand. Let's just let it cook."

I was angry with Henry, while at the same time I empathized with his attitude. It wasn't anybody's fault that our son was born with a different set of sexual transmitters, or whatever went on inside those mysterious cells. Also, both Linda and Robin had finally convinced me that during the year leading up to the actual operation, Robbie's need to keep it secret from us was imperative for his self-confidence.

I was completely blown away by how our child had managed the transition. If ever a transgender person should have gotten a prize for a well-reasoned presentation, it was Robin. I kept thinking that she had another talent even beyond her art. She could have been either an actor or an actress. He and she (he and her?) (???) (whoever). Anyway, Robin might have been the first to win Academy Awards for both.

I thought the presentation had been awesome. He/she had explained that femaleness resided in every fibre of his being and that medical science had finally perfected those hormonal and surgical techniques that made such a drastic switch feasible. In addition to Robin's two conditions which were so important -- one involving mere money and the other involving emotional considerations -- Robin, had a simple request. She insisted that Henry please not refer to her as a son any longer. I was impressed with how she pleaded for her father's blessing on the sex change thing. We all suspected that it wasn't going to be much of a blessing. Two days after Robin left, Henry sent her a check for the money. He wouldn't show me the card enclosing the check, but I peeked when he left it on his desk. The card said, "Don't thank me for this -- just get your damned bills paid and then leave me alone about why you did what you did. Love, Father."

18

Cissy's wedding had me worried about something other than Robin's decision to attend as Robbie wearing a tux. My lingering problem was me and my vanity. I was intent on buying a new dress or two, especially one that was suitable for the evening of the ceremony and reception. But spend precious money to drape my thirty-pound overweight self? Unthinkable. I had been granted three whole months to prepare. How much could I lose in three months? Starvation calories were out. Eating sensibly made sense -- that's why they called it eating sensibly. I knew I could lose two pounds a month without too much fuss, but six pounds down wasn't going to hack it. I couldn't even see a difference in my cheeks after a whole month of sensible dieting because that two pound loss seemed to come from my boobs. When I considered all my body parts, the section I least wanted shrunk were my boobs. The tush was first, right ahead of my thighs. A single visit to the shrink had given me some much needed impetus, but mental strengthening had seldom been known to slim down one's excess fatty tissue. The shrink asked me if I could relate the incident which got me into my "shrink Marlene Sternberg" mode. I had it down cold, and it wasn't exactly Nancy Westerville's drop dead dieting fame -- it was when Henry showed me that horrible photo of our volunteer group and the sudden shock of my seeing what the camera saw . . . .

There it was in my trembling hand. When I first saw that print, I had wanted to rip it to shreds, but instead, after seething appropriately, filed it with the "D's" under a "general" category, which meant any old designation beginning with the letter "D." It could later be re-labeled as either "Diet" or "Destroy." The photographer had made multiple prints on glossy paper of our corps of smiling unpaid nature center workers. The shorties were displayed sitting on the ground in the front row with their legs crossed, the mediums were standing in each of two rows behind them with arms hidden behind their pals, and the taller individuals stood in the rear with chins jutting out bearing expressions of body superiority. I should have been in the shorties row, but I couldn't sit with my legs crossed. They must have put me in the second row of mediums, on one end, so that the shorter mediums wouldn't destroy the symmetry. I couldn't find me at first, but there was a woman in that row sporting my hairdo and my weird affected smile. It was the fake kind that always showed up when they said, "Cheese." Sometimes the person who snapped the photo, being a nature lover, would call out: "Trees!"

That just couldn't be the way I looked to the outside world. It was a certainty that the creature in the photo was beyond redemption. Who was the imposter with my face? She was definitely wearing my new outfit from L.L. Bean. Yes, it all figured. It was me. I had worn those serviceable sporty nylon slacks with pockets planted all over, down the sides of the legs, under the zipper that provided easy convertibility from long pants to shorts, and even with another secret pocket inside the waistband. I had put junk in the pockets because what were pockets for? I called out for Henry.

"Hey, honey, you know that nature center group photo? Was that the only picture they took of us?"

"It's all I had. Please don't ask again. I'm trying to concentrate."

"Sure, you're trying to concentrate. Sorry I asked."

Now why did I allow the photographer to take a picture of me with full frontal exposure of the bulges in my side pockets? I had even put my smart phone in a dumb place. It was in one of the side pockets where I couldn't sit on it. That phone stood out like a peculiar bulge in my already ample hips. If I had foreseen how I looked, I would have stood on several stacks of their nature guide books in the back row and jutted out my chin with the biggies. "Except for one problem, and that is, would my saggy neck skin have showed?"

Henry must have completed his concentration because he soon asked me if I had examined the group photo.

"Why are you asking me that question?"

"Because I was just wondering if you liked it."

"OK, so you looked it over. So what?"

"That's all, I just asked."

"**You saw my fat hips, why don't you say it**!"

"Please don't shout. I'm right here."

I lowered my voice a few tones. "Those weren't all my hips -- there were things I had put in my side pockets."

"Of course."

"OK, I'll admit, the part that seems to be my thighs also seems to out-thigh everyone else."

Henry shifted his legs around and looked down at the floor. "There's no way I'm getting drawn into this subject."

"You have to get drawn into it -- you told me about the photo and gave it to me and planned to use it as an introduction to your new idea of how I could lose weight."

"No, you're twisting the whole thing."

"Oh yeah? You want me to stop having desserts and write down the calories of everything I eat for the next thirty pounds of my suffering another weight loss attempt!"

"I want you to be happy."

I guess that those issues which begin as little things have a way of getting bigger. An untreated sore gets bigger and worse and so does a leak in the roof. A few extra pounds on a short lady like me doesn't go away as easily as one-two-three. It's not like simply tossing a bucket of water on a waste basket fire. It takes a whole rescue squad effort and months of planning. But once in awhile I get a kick in the conscience. This time all it took was a jealous fit over a single woman who had shed a third of herself, and then the knockout punch -- a single photograph haphazardly handed to me, and look what I'm doing now! I'm embarking on a purge of our pantry. There, I'm ridding it of all the stores of goodies that Mr. Perfect wouldn't touch with a ten-foot pole unless we became poverty-stricken. No, strike that, even then he would never open a plastic container of tapioca pudding that contained nutrients. Plain, yucky tuna fish yes, but never anything creamy. He would once again remind me that the only hungry people in the world lived in Somalia.

19

When I finally got up the courage to call Cissy back, I had to leave the gulp out of my conversation. I was caught up in a situation I hated -- having to weave a web of deceit for which I had little talent. Even Henry knew I was a terrible liar, with the possible exception of when I told Henry what I had eaten for lunch with the girls. Now I had to falsify the facts about Robin's situation when the truth was, we needed more time to adjust to the facts ourselves -- like a few years. Oh how I wished that everything could be simple and above board. Why couldn't Robbie just come out as Robin and be done with it? We could have issued a straightforward announcement of his arrival and status: "Girl born to Henry and Marlene Sternberg -- Age 42, six feet two inches, 165 pounds and six ounces. Mother and daughter doing well." Etc. Well, that would be if we had a perfect world.

I picked up the phone to dial my niece's number and my fingers froze. "I can't do this." There was the clock on the wall, ticking away my last few moments of honesty. My thoughts raced on. *Why can't Robin make this call? She's the one who did the deed. Oh, I guess that's silly. Cissy would tell her favorite cousin to go as the woman she was, at least I think she would. I just don't really know. On the other hand, Linda's got a knack for fast talk -- maybe she could get me off the hook. What about Henry? No, scratch that -- he's the one who thought Robin ought to avoid the wedding altogether.* Well, here goes, I'll just have to do it myself. I'm the materfamilia here, or whatever I'm called. If I do this quickly, maybe I can fake my way through it with diversionary tactics and Cissy will believe that everything about our family is normal."

I crossed my legs and made the call. "Cissy, it's me, I'm able to talk now."

"Oh, Hi, Aunt Mar. I wanted to fill you in on some things."

"Oh good. I had some questions. Like, is it true the wedding ceremony will be held in Chicago? There are almost as many bad jokes about Chicago as there are about Cleveland."

"My fiancé Sherwin's from Chicago."

"I feel better already. I love Chicago, actually. It's beautiful there in September. Skyscrapers everywhere, breezes pouring in from the lake, high heels pounding the pavements on the Magnificent Mile, the favorite location for car chase movies. I could go on and on."

"Sherwin's father is a personal friend of the mayor. We hired a wedding planner who did work for Hollywood celebrities. He recommended the Drake Hotel."

"Oh, I know that place. When you drive South on Lake Shore Drive, it's right there in front of you and I heard that the original owners forced the Outer Drive to curve to avoid it."

"I'm pretty sure that's one of those bad Chicago jokes, Aunt Mar. By the way, how are you?"

"Oh, I'm fine, so-so, you know. Our whole family is fine. How are you getting along with the other lovebird?"

"We're doing well, Auntie, but it's been so hard to pin everything down for the ceremony and reception. Listen, I don't have much time to chat. I've been trying to reach Robbie. I must have left at least four messages for him."

"You mean sh--- he hasn't called you back? I just spoke to him a couple days ago."

"Is anything wrong?"

"Well, he was in the hospital, but he's out now and rehabbing, I don't know, somewhere near his apartment in Ohio."

"I didn't know! Why was he in the hospital?"

"Well, he was having difficulty molting."

"I don't follow."

"I don't know how to describe the procedure. He had a skin problem caused by, uh, lack of some kind of vitamin -- whatchacallit? Anyway, it caused some of his skin to peel off, but they did a graft, or something. It has to take, I guess."

"Oh, you mean the doctors have to make sure his system doesn't reject the graft?"

"You got it, Cissy. He's not getting his messages right now. I can look for the rehab place phone number, but can I give him a heads up on what you're calling about?"

"Can you find out if Robbie can be in the groom's wedding party? A few months ago, he seemed amenable, but now I need confirmation. He'd have to have a tux, of course."

"No problem -- I'll let him know. It's just a good thing he has time for his skin procedure to heal. At least we've got 'til September!"

"But he has to have a matching tux -- all the groom's attendants are being sent to this special wedding outfitter, but Robbie can do it online. There's no need for him to come to Chicago. He only has to make sure he has the right tux and the right fit. All this takes lead time and you'd be surprised how little time there is!"

"Cissy, I promise I'll have Robbie call you. But I have one important thing to say and you can't forget it."

"What's that, Auntie?"

"You know how sensitive Robbie is about his appearance. Maybe it's better you don't mention the skin graft. He's not happy yet about how his face is, uh, maybe it isn't healed yet, but he has enough time. It should be fine by the wedding."

"Auntie, he's a good-looking man -- probably the handsomest guy I've ever laid eyes on. What's his problem?"

"Too many years at that union job. I think the environment at that plant has gotten to him. Those auto parts give off toxic waste, you know. It can even cause some hormonal imbalance. I'll have him call you."

"You know that Linda has asked not to be in the wedding party, but she's been terrific. She's coming to Chicago to go to the bridal shop with us, just to be sociable --I'm so looking forward to our getting together."

"Linda's always helpful and chummy. She's mad about Chicago -- I've never figured out why, but she's even tried to establish a Bus Hall of Fame there. Something to do with a Chicago Motor Coach Company starting a new industry."

"Yes, Aunt Mar, I heard about that."

"Leave it to Linda. So how many people are you having?"

"We're trying to trim it down to 300."

"It's going to be a wonderful party. The Drake is really high class. Also, it's got a reputation for being affordable, that is, for those folks who don't have to reconcile their checkbooks every month."

"Oh, it costs a bundle. But Sherwin's parents are contributing. They're in the lumber business, you know."

"I didn't know. And it's bad manners to inquire about their financial situation. Are they very wealthy?"

"They must be. They're buying us a house in Lake Bluff. Overlooking the water. Contemporary, I'm afraid. I had to give in on that one. It will be our summer residence, if we ever get a chance to enjoy time away from New York."

"I don't doubt it. Can I ask, is Linda's fellow on your guest list?"

"You mean Captain Jimmy Japetto, that wild-eyed Italian chap who co-authored all those books about the mating habits of animals?"

"That's the one."

"I can't leave him off -- Linda would kill me. I don't think he's coming, however, didn't you know? He's in the South Georgia Island group, studying the sex rituals of penguins. And as long as you mentioned him, is she ever going to, uh, you know, make it legal?"

"You know Linda. She's very independent. Linda's a different breed of person. She's a single female industry, sort of."

"You mean because she runs a bus business?"

"I think she's getting bought out by Allied something, but she's going to keep fixing the buses. Who'd a thought I'd raise a female mechanical hotshot and a male artist who makes ends meet supervising lugs, lug nuts and engine blocks?"

"Your kids are both highly intelligent and extremely enterprising -- even daring."

"You don't know the half of it."

"How's Uncle Henry?"

"Oh, he's fine, as usual. Nothing to worry about. I could go on and on, but we'll have more time to talk when you're not preparing for your first marriage. It's better you should keep the stars in your eyes as long as possible."

"I appreciate your concern. Say, what are you wearing to the ceremony and reception?"

"I'm having a designer dress redesigned especially for me so you'll think I just waltzed out of a Vogue magazine model tryout. Well, what I really mean is, you'd think of the Ladies Home Journal fashion section that deals with older women with a middle syndrome."

"Middle syndrome?"

"Sure, middle class, too much around the middle, waking up in the middle of the night, the middle list goes on and on."

"You're a blast, Auntie!"

"Say, I'll also be wearing the new four-inch high heels to your affair and they're so stylish and upscale, words fail me. I've been practicing walking in them and my toes are recovering nicely. Oh, and I'm forcing Henry to get into a black tux or I'm leaving him. You know what he said?"

"I can guess."

"He said, "Lock the door on your way out."

"He didn't mean it."

"No, because then he'd have to get a paid full-time maid. The tux is cheaper than getting rid of me."

"Uncle Henry would never get rid of you. What would he do for companionship? He doesn't brag enough to make out as a single again."

"Right. That's cute. Cissy, dear, I have to go now. Don't mention Robbie's skin problems. He's so sensitive, he might say the wrong thing."

"I promise."

After I hung up, I had a lot of lingering misgivings. *That was one tough conversation. I made it up out of cheesecloth. Robin was probably not answering Cissy's calls to avoid the whole issue. She knows he's going to have a problem wearing a normal tux accompanied by a pleated dress shirt with her new chest. And she'll have to manage using the men's washroom and the stag party and everything. I'd better call her right now because of the lies I just finished spinning. I'll also have to concentrate on the selection of pronouns -- it's so hard to adjust one's verbal habits. But I have a plan. And this time I'd better get Henry on board too. Cissy deserves to marry the man of her financially secure dreams without letting Sherwin's parents find out what a weird family their pride and joy son is marrying into.*

20

Having and raising kids has always been a crapshoot. A mother doesn't know if the offspring will turn out to justify those moments of passion or accelerate the date of her death. Henry and I never figured out why Linda was such a financial genius with a growing investment portfolio, even with her lavish spending habits, while Robbie never had more than a few bucks in his pocket. Our fears didn't subside even after he'd been on the job at the auto plant for a year. We learned he'd spent half his take-home pay on therapy and a significant portion of the rest on a small apartment which he decorated in black with touches of red for his accent pieces. When we wanted him to visit us in Florida, he needed us to pay for the plane ticket. When we wanted to visit him and see how he lived, naturally he didn't reciprocate. We were good sports and flew or drove to his place on a few occasions, but on the most recent visit, there were some unnerving changes. It's easy to remember them. Upon arriving at his apartment, we were startled to see a strange man staring at us from his entrance hall with his finger pointed menacingly in our direction. I screamed until I realized that it was the cast figure of a life-sized body builder. "Robbie, where the hell did you get this, this gigantic statue?"

"Oh, Mom, I made it -- well, I had a little help. I took a class in large scale sculpture and a bunch of us students worked on these as projects. Isn't he cute? I call him 'Goliath.'"

"Is it worth something? Like art you can market?"

"It's just a sideline, which I'm hoping will become a money maker. When I get home from the plant I need an outlet. I hate my job most of the time."

"What's wrong with it?"

"My co-workers. They're all a bunch of red-necked bums. Some of them are alcoholics and they all swear like gangsters."

"Your father swears when he's angry."

"Well, Dad grew up rough, but at least he doesn't talk like a hired gun."

"I guess you can say that. Why is it so dim in here?"

"I put in low wattage bulbs. Even the track lighting is muted."

"You must be saving on electricity. Maybe you're more like your father than I thought. Dad wants me to spend less on clothes because my closet is so crowded."

"Mom, I know about your walk-in closet that you can't walk into. You have so many outfits you don't even know what you have in there."

"Dad says I could open a boutique. Well, I've had weight fluctuations, so I need three sizes of everything."

"I know -- you like cream pies and then you go on crash diets."

"I'm glad you got the slenderness genes from your father's side of the family."

"Let's not discuss my genes, please. Dad's been snooping around my place. Let's see if he came upon my French Doll yet. This doll has human hair on her head and black eyelashes. She's dressed in real silk and sits on the bed. Say, what's that noise? Where did Dad go?"

"Walk toward the noise -- he's probably looking for the bathroom."

"No he's not -- he's knocking on the door of my, oh, an extra bedroom I keep locked."

"Why is it locked?

"Well, I'm doing a new kind of art work and I don't want anybody messing around in there."

"What kind?"

"Just some experimental work. Let's resume our tour while I go explain to Dad where we keep the toilet and the guest towels."

"Who's the 'we?'"

"I have a guy who's helping me with the art work. It's pretty involved and he's good at helping sculptors and has some great tools for big projects. He's here a lot. Also, he helped me with the decor."

"It's amazing how you've turned into such an expert at staging. Now it's with a doll with someone else's eyelashes and it sits on a bed? She's a fixture there, I suppose. How could your dad ever discover this plaything if he even fell on it? Everything's black in there."

"Eyes get accustomed to dark surroundings."

"If you showed movies in your bedroom, you wouldn't need to dim any lights."

"How did you know I showed movies in there?"

"Just a hunch. Why else have a darkened room? Who do you show them to?"

"My friends from my club."

"And do you have any women over?"

"Sure, the girls from the revue love my movies."

"What kind of a revue?"

"You really want to know about my adults only club?"

"No, let's change the subject."

So Henry and I got a taste of where our son was headed. We had sent him to art school and what did we get for our money? He became a designer of depraved statues and room furnishings for a house of ill repute. Thank God he had a trade and a job with benefits.

21

Henry and I had engaged in our share of heated arguments, just like lots of married couples who hung on for the long ride. I learned that there were more jokes about marriage than jokes about lawyers or sex. I chalked up our disagreements to the way we were raised. My family was as different in its background and lifestyle from Henry's family as the Vanderbilts were from the Joads of John Steinbeck's tale of poverty. Perhaps that statement is slightly exaggerated, but it helps me to think that way, and I still need all the help I can get. I got the full story of my parents' marriage just by being as observant as possible right after I learned to see shapes. As soon as my father began bringing home greater sums of money, my mother began to collect things. Her favorite collection was to acquire every genuine Majolica platter ever manufactured, but we didn't eat from them. They were housed in a walnut breakfront with glass panels to remind us children that we were supposed to pine after lovely things until we came of age and developed taste. We three daughters were the hope of the future. First came me, the one with the gift for reading and writing. My dad wanted to send me to an Ivy League school for the class of girls who were called debutantes, but he spent all his money on my mother's acquisitions before he got his act together to accumulate a stash. I was sent to the state college where the tuition was affordable.

There was always a sense in our household that all our money was going to disappear one day. Actually a lot of it did disappear. My mother hid dollars in cookie jars, vases and unused broken Thermos bottles which she kept on the top shelf of a pantry. If we had company over, she asked my dad for a generous amount of money for refreshments for the guests, but I was aware of her hidden gift for thrift. She spent half of the money for the company and secreted the rest. As soon as she had enough dollars she would buy genuine jewelry plus a set of baubles that looked like the real thing. When Mom went out shopping or called on friends in the daytime, Dad would ask, "Where did you get that necklace with the purple stones?" Mom would answer, "Oh, these are real amethysts. I bought them on sale at the bargain jewelry store on Wisconsin Street." What a liar she was. The stones were glass which she got at a junk shop. The real gem necklace went on her neck when they went stepping out in the evening when it was dark out. Dad didn't know the difference. She convinced him that she was careful at saving money on her wardrobe. The truth was, all the money was saved because she was a wizard about how to scrimp on food for our immediate family.

Henry was smarter than my father about money. I had given up long ago trying to outwit him in that department. My edge was always going to be in understanding modern social trends. My mother didn't have a computer and she never felt she needed help from a psychologist. She got most of her wisdom from talking to her female friends and neighbors. A lot of this talk happened in back yards and in local butcher shops and fish markets. Neither she nor my father had a college education, like we did. Henry read books about investments and the rise and fall of civilizations. He was the intellectual of our partnership. That left me to be the psychological expert. The gulf between us was one I had to bridge every day. Maybe I was more like my mother than I gave myself credit for, but I had to manage my marriage using my verbal skills instead of hiding dollars in cookie jars and other containers. I wasn't very good at being brief, so I went to extremes. I tried thinking my way into better communication with Henry, but he had no aptitude at all for mental telepathy. In desperation, I roamed library shelves for books about how spouses could talk to each other effectively using a minimum of words. The closest I could get was a book about telekinesis, which dealt with harnessing the power of one's mind. I'm still working on that one.

22

Henry was swearing under his breath. I always wondered how that expression came about. I could hear most of the nasty words, so maybe he was swearing above his breath.

"Did you come to any conclusions, dear?"

"Yeah, our son needed his head examined, and then a funny thing happened to him on the way to the doctor's office."

"Dear, this sex-change operation isn't, or shouldn't be a surprise to you." We've always had our share of clues as to our child's misgivings about his manhood."

"Marlene, there was once a young soldier who decided to become a blonde woman and made headlines. She never had a normal life."

"The first person who comes out with a new idea often suffers. Think of Jesus Christ."

"I'd rather think of Robbie as meeting a nice woman and having a good life with some kids in the picture."

"That's because you did exactly that, Henry."

"You have a point there."

"You can't say we didn't have a number of clues while Robbie was growing up."

"I thought those clues were normal feelings young boys had about having to become men."

"Robin has always showed signs of certain female behavior. Remember the first drawings he made when he went to kindergarten?"

"You're more likely to remember them."

"Robbie drew pictures of himself wearing a strange outfit -- it wasn't pants."

"Was it a dress?"

"I don't know, but it was some sort of design with frills and bows and now I remember, we let his curly hair grow long and it looked like a girl's ringlets--"

"You're right. I remember asking you why we were letting his hair grow long like that when it made him look like a girl."

"Remember that fellow who saw him and commented that our daughter looked just like Shirley Temple? We didn't have a daughter. Linda wasn't born yet."

"I'm not sure, but in some of those old period movies, like 'Little Lord Fauntleroy,' having long curls was common for those young boys."

"Most of those curly-headed kids were English, I believe."

"Read your history. They copied the English look here in the USA."

"We're arguing about what we don't even remember. Let's agree on one thing -- this younger generation has developed new thinking about gay marriage and gay rights and all that."

"All foolish thinking. What's right about marching in parades about sex? If a man is gay, let him be gay in his bedroom. Robin could have remained Robbie and let it go at that."

"Henry, Robbie was never gay. Do you understand that what Robin has gone through is traumatic?"

"Yes, I do, but I can't reconcile myself to, oh, what am I trying to say? Look, have these operations helped the lives of these people who have them?"

"I can't speak for all of them. I'm rooting for our Robin."

"I know. I think I'll just keep my mouth shut."

"Oh, that's really helpful. Look, you love to read. You never read Robin's medical report. All I can say is, what's done is done and the parent who thinks he can control a child's lifestyle is a parent who can't live his own."

"OK, already, let's change the subject."

"That works for me. Let's talk about whether pigs have wings."

Henry didn't comment. I let my mind sift through our conversation and gave Henry some brownie points for beginning to thaw. We lived in Florida. Hopefully he would thaw rapidly.

I was recalling the time that Robbie became immersed in science fiction books. He was about twelve. There was this can of paint, yes, some of it wound up decorating two of his shirts and the bedspread. He told me he had recreated the Starship Enterprise. I was the one who had bought him those Trekkie toys. The shirts disintegrated and the mattress under the spread was permanently disfigured, but his rendering of the legendary space vehicle was quite realistic. Robbie was also fascinated with the character of Wonder Woman, the Amazon with the magic bracelets, but he also liked Superman and wanted to be some kind of a superhero. He jumped off the roof and broke his ankle. Landed on my geranium bed and fortunately it was a soft landing. The roots were OK, though, so I didn't have to replace the plants. Good thing we had a ranch house at the time and not a two-story Georgian.

After I decided to stop prodding Henry to open up about Robbie, he noticed.

"I notice you're not on my back about Robbie, uh, Robin, Marlene."

"That's accurate."

"Are you trying to get me to soften up by wielding your silence like a club?"

"Manipulation takes many forms. No matter what I do or say, we're married too many years. We can come pretty close to reading each other's minds and we get just as angry with each other about the things we don't say as the words we do say. We broadcast our ideas without a microphone. You're usually off the air anyway."

"I just was thinking about how conscious Robbie was about his muscle development and how strong he was. I thought he would become a body builder."

"Well, you got your wish."

"Now he has this job at an assembly line building cars, but I figured that was a male-oriented line of work."

"Not the way he did it. He secretly believed he was the only man on the assembly line who wore lace underwear."

"He told you that?"

"He told me lots of things recently. Like one day a co-worker accidentally saw a peep of white lace showing where Robbie's belt met his waist. It was in the locker room where the guys changed out of their work clothes.

"Go on, this is tough for me, but go on."

"The guy wanted to know if he was a queer and Robbie told him off. He told him he wasn't queer. He just liked the feel of silky underpants because his tush was sensitive."

"And?"

"The fellow told him that he wished he could wear women's underwear too, but that he was going to a shrink to deal with his own issues."

"So the co-worker was a queer?"

"Nobody with any sensitivity uses the word 'queer' any longer. If you think the man had a sexual orientation to men, use the word 'gay,' please!"

"You know who invented the term, 'gay'?"

"No, and neither do you!"

"It was invented by the wusses who were afraid to admit they were queer."

"Listen, husband, I've heard people call you a redneck and an old-timer and all sorts of names."

"I don't go all soft on what other people think about me."

"Anyway, Robbie and the guy he met in the men's room, his name is Fred something, became better friends and that guy quit the plant and became an art gallery owner. He and Robin are now working on some business deal. And I'm pretty certain that man is gay."

"What do you think about Robin's art ambitions? Did you hear any details?"

"Yes, Robin thinks she can make a living doing a new kind of sculpture."

"It would have to be new. The old kind that became valuable was done by guys who died in a previous century."

"Our sculptor child seems to have attracted the attention of people who have money. They're apparently seeking out emerging artists."

"Did our son have to trim his organs to emerge?"

"I think I know more about art than you do."

"I like that guy Chagall -- he's a real intellectual -- and can he ever wield a paintbrush! His work is in all the museums."

"His work isn't as valuable as the work of Picasso."

"I know all about Picasso. He kept replacing his women when he got tired of them and he was a big scribbler. He couldn't draw, so he put boobs where butts should be."

"What if Robin/Robbie were to do well? Would you change your attitude?"

"What attitude?"

I kept trying to use a version of my silent treatment to get Henry to appreciate me and my opinions. It was impossible for me to be completely silent, so I called the technique my brevity system. One evening at dinner I was innocently ladling my flavorful chicken vegetable soup into his bowl, when he couldn't contain himself. Beginnings of sentences began to sputter out of him and then erupt, like one of those early propeller airplanes revving up. First you heard the tentative spinning and then came the ear-splitting noise.

"Will you, oh, will you, geesus, will you STOP THAT!!!!!"

"You don't want the soup?"

"No, dammit, I'm used to your gabbing all the time. And I know exactly what you're not talking about!"

"You do? Fill me in."

"Look, I wasn't brought up to think it was OK for a man to act like a girl. I sure wasn't brought up to think it was OK for a man to turn into a girl!"

"So get over your upbringing. Isn't that what you tell me?"

"Look, I do lots of things to help you out. I dust, vacuum, help with the dishes and do all the grilling of meat and chicken. My father never did that stuff!"

"You're wonderful. Now project your adaptation into the future and add new technology. They can clone a sheep and they can change a person's sex. Didn't you read "Brave New World?"

"That was science fiction. Yeah, I read it."

"I know you love Robin. Eat your soup."

"Your arguments are getting a little too slick for me, Marlene. Can you ladle me a second helping ?"

23

The wedding of Cissy and Sherwin screamed out from my calendar as though it had lungs. "I am coming, and you, Marlene, aren't ready!" Why wasn't Henry that nervous, especially when he kept rolling out his usual reminders of what I should be doing every minute of the day. Like this morning, when I heard him shouting from the kitchen:

"Marlene, did you shop for the kind of potatoes I specified? The ones shaped like ovals and not the ones with growths that look like tumors?"

"It's on the list, dear, really, honey, can't you be a little patient? I've got lots on my mind." What an understatement! The three "R's" had taken on a whole new meaning for me. Robbie, Rob and Robin. Linda had phoned and assured me that her sister was on track with the family's plan. I wasn't so sure about that.

"Do you think she's comfortable about it?"

"I think so."

"Are you comfortable with the idea?"

"I think so."

"That makes two of you who feel comfortable."

"Well, Dad is Dad. But what about you?"

"I'm a worrier. I wouldn't be me if I didn't worry. What about how Robin is going to dress?"

"She's renting a tux and has a breast-flattening upper body corset."

"And?"

"Please, Mother!! she's not going to have one of those things!"

"Say it, a strap-on dildo."

"I didn't even bring that up. I told you Robin is comfortable."

"Well, I'm not comfortable. I bought a girdle."

"Spanx?"

"Whatever they call it. That's worse than a dildo. At least a dildo has a small chance to make you feel better."

"Mother! How you talk! And as long as you brought it up----"

"Don't do plays on words, Linda. What are you doing for jewelry?"

"Fastening it and packing it carefully so the different pieces don't turn into a tangle of spaghetti. Mom, I have to go now."

"That dildo reference got to you, huh?" I didn't get an answer. Linda had hung up.

I stared at the tangled telephone cord, perturbed by my daughter's reference to carelessly packed jewelry. I certainly didn't want my packing system to turn into ten minutes of wrestling with knotted up twisted chains which required a roadmap to untie. Scientific types who understood chaos theory would nod in agreement. Why couldn't I just learn to relax, like Buddhists who had attained a state of nirvana? Always feeling perturbed was a characteristic of people with guilt complexes. *I had nothing to be guilty about. It was acceptable to fake an orgasm once in awhile. And how many of the Seven Deadly Sins had I committed? Let's see, wrath, avarice, sloth, pride, lust, envy and gluttony. Well, maybe I wasn't slothful.*

I tried to relax after my conversation with Linda, but something didn't ring true for me. How could Robin be comfortable? She was a physical woman preparing to masquerade as a man for the sake of the bridal party, the wedding photographers and our collective family egos. Linda and I were the real perpetrators. Henry would have voted to have Robin call in sick. It was too late to reverse the decision of our four-person committee now, there being no simple path to predict how the gamble would turn out. The dice were being tossed and all I could envision were snake eyes. I picked up the phone and called Robin and felt my adrenalin level drop when she answered immediately.

"Robin, Linda says you're comfortable going as a man. Is that correct?"

"Mom, it's all set. I rented the male formal wear already. I know how to fake it. Did you forget I had to work at the plant while my hormone treatment was going on? It's still going on. I can do it. Tell your guilt complex voice-over to hit the road already."

"OK, I'll pretend that we all made the right decision. Maybe I'll get each character starring in my multiple personality cast to go along. I had to call you because they were all arguing and driving me nuts."

"Well, as I've heard Dad rib you again and again, it's a short drive."

"You're a lot like Henry, you know that? You've got his confident foot-in-the-door style, his sarcasm and his flat stomach and compact tush. I'm beginning to believe that my big contribution to your life was to teach you how to dress for all occasions and all circumstances."

"I can't talk now, Mom, I'm working on a sketch for one of my new sculptures, and I don't want to lose my idea, which is still in my head."

"I know a genius when I hear one trying to be polite. I'll redirect my energies to your father. I think he's cussing about something sinister anyway. This morning the air conditioner was moaning. This afternoon there was a short in our kitchen ground fault circuit interrupter, or whatever you call it."

"They call it the GFCI."

"Go finish your sketch. This conversation helped me out. I can be an elderly princess again, protected by an assortment of smartasses. Call me before long when you get a chance."

I hung up the phone feeling over-matched. Linda was right after all. Robin was comfortable. Henry was fixing the house. I was a work in progress, reviewing the plans which didn't need reviewing. At Cissy's wedding Robin would act as a guy and dance with the girls and even lead as though her transformation had never happened. She had adapted to her female body so well, I began to wonder if my motherly instincts were becoming superfluous. If I couldn't do something for my new daughter's well-being, even if it was just a small gesture, then what was my role? Was I to become an accessory? I needed to get out of the house or I would go mad. I got in my car and didn't have any personal shopping to do for myself, but since I needed a fix, I headed for the women's department at Macy's. Robin had mentioned that she had purchased a new snakeskin handbag, so I bought I a belt for her that promised to be a good match.

Linda called me one more time to work out the details of our meeting place at O'Hare Airport in Chicago. I had placed a note by my phone with an important reminder: DO NOT QUESTION LINDA ABOUT HER RELATIONSHIP WITH THE BIRDMAN. But then she introduced the subject herself. I asked her if she thought that Henry was beginning to accept Robin's new persona. She surprised me with her response:

"Mom, Dad's not the same person. Something's happened! He even asked me how my relationship was progressing. He hadn't broached that subject for years."

"What did you tell him?"

"I told him that Jimmy and I were still on second base -- uh -- tying-the-knot-wise."

"What would third base be?"

"Oh, I guess we'd be looking at housing developments in the suburbs."

"I guess buying Parenting Magazine is out, then?"

"I have to ask you a question, Mother?" *Oh, oh, she said 'Mother,' not Mom. That meant I was straying too close to my daughter's frequently invoked boundary lines.* "It's about the wedding. Here's my concern: If any one of us accidentally reveals Robin's real situation, do you have a plan?"

"I guess I do. The plan is, we all act normal."

"Pretend that Robin's operation was routine, like having his appendix out?"

"Well, so the thing that they call an appendix is smaller, so what? I think we should act like we understood why the operation was necessary."

"With a transgendered woman wearing a man's tux?"

"We can say that it was too late for Robin to get a dress fitted."

Linda wasn't buying that excuse. "Mom, I'm not buying that as an excuse."

"I'm out of ideas."

"Mother, this is serious. Don't give me your nonchalant avoidance chatter. I mean, let's say Robin herself spills the beans -- how would you respond?"

"Oh, I'd probably go to the ladies room to repair my make-up and ask Robin if she wanted to join me."

"Uh, huh. That would really be pushing the envelope. Could you do it?"

"I can do anything. I'm the pioneering mother of a New Age BoyIntoGirl!"

"Amazing. Did you come up with that expression?"

"Yes and No. I mentioned it to my other daughter in one of our recent phone conversations, and she said, "Way to Go, or something to that effect."

"I'll have to call Robin again -- we need to get our lines a bit rehearsed."

"Linda?"

"What, Mom?"

Whew, she was back to Mom. I must have pressed the right gizmo on her feminist dashboard.

"I guess we're aligned. Robin goes to the wedding as Robbie, you go as you, I go as me, and Dad goes as he always goes -- reluctantly."

"Bye, Mom. I really love you."

"Same here. Give my regards to your boyfriend, the birdman."

As I hung up I threw the note in the wastebasket. Linda and I were each so agreeable, an observer might believe we were behaving well. One or both of us was maturing. It hadn't always been smooth with us. We'd had such a big fight the day she told me she didn't want to be called "the baby" any more. I'm fairly sure that happened about the time she redid her room and got rid of all the pink hydrangea wallpaper and replaced it with racing car motifs on a wood-grained background. On one wall she had attached a larger than life-sized photo of Dale Earnhardt. She even considered having us change her name to Dale, but agreed to drop the idea if we let her smoke cigars once in awhile. We won that round, but our daughter's negotiating skills had improved from good to stratospheric as she grew up. I had regressed, of course, since the best I had ever come up with when I needed to negotiate with Henry was the brevity system.

24

"Henry, how do I look in this dress?"

"Marlene, I'll be there in a few secs."

I waited with the patience of a fashion model. Didn't they always have to wait while the photographer fiddled with the camera settings? Henry emerged from the bathroom with half his face shaved and the rest still soaped up. He was right-faced, a right to lefter.

"Oh, you want my opinion of how you look, honey? That's a very nice dress -- it looks beautiful on your new slimmer figure -- when did you buy it?"

Henry and I were engaging in a performance. Did most long-married couples go through this ritual for ritzy social occasions? He would try on his entire formal ensemble, including cuff links, fake flower in the jacket pocket of the tux, and even the rented shoes, in the same length of time it took me to struggle into a dress I might never wear again. The next lavish affair might be a wedding for one of Julie Sue's teen-aged daughters, and by that time I could be wearing a shroud. I donned Salvatore's expensive hairpiece for the Marlene and Henry show and carefully nudged my feet into a daringly high set of heels. Between the extra two inches atop my head and the additional three which raised my feet, I was now nearly five feet five. I wouldn't be able to engage in a spirited dance or run or stoop to pick up anything or kiss anybody without fear of hairpiece misalignment, but I could always make up for these handicaps by bringing a large purse capable of enclosing a pair of flats and a travel size curling iron.

"I bought this dress two weeks ago, dear. I'm happy you approve."

Henry didn't care a whit about fashion, since his favorite clothing item was a knit sport shirt which was long enough and roomy enough to hide his holster and utility knife. But Henry was always on the alert to refrain from being conspicuous at a social gathering. He'd even voiced some ideas regarding male grooming recently which could be categorized as emerging twentieth century.

"Marlene, should I buy an electric razor?"

"You buy an electric razor? What for?"

"Oh, not to use, just to display when I have to join the other guys in the john. In the movies, upper crust men always exchange financial success stories while they're shaving -- you've seen it in films -- the communal bathroom mirror over the urinals. In case I want to fit in, I might have to drag out a two hundred dollar gadget for the purpose of trimming a hair or two on my chin."

"You know nothing about electric razors, honey."

"You wanna bet? I'm as modern as you are. Last time I went to the mall, I actually walked into Brookstone's."

"Did you buy anything there?"

"No, but I sat on one of their vibrating chairs and got the ride of my life."

"Why was it the ride of your life?"

"A very attractive young girl tried to talk me into buying it. I thought she was going to demonstrate all the settings herself and I'd be able to watch her vibrate."

"Maybe you should stay with your old razor."

In the mad whirl of our getting ready for the bash, my facelift plans had been relegated to the back burner, even though my new dress would be draped on a slimmer woman. I had lost seventeen pounds in the last eight weeks. In a fit of desperation I managed to eliminate one meal per day of what I termed "real food" and substitute one of those all-in-one drinks. I counted calories with more care. Butter, cheese and cream were out. Broccoli crowns and spinach leaves were in. I filled up on a nutrition bar if I couldn't sleep. When the bathroom scale failed to record more significant reductions, I eliminated bread for sandwiches and substituted wheat crackers. I regarded these changes as medicine that I would have to take for the rest of my life. Or at least until after the wedding.

I made one afterthought purchase -- a new girdle in a rather small size because it totally flattened my stomach. When I wore the new dress there wasn't a hint of a bulge in my middle. So what if the high heels hurt and the girdle was uncomfortable? I'd only have to feel like I'd been mummified for a few hours during the ceremony and the reception. The item wasn't even called a girdle any longer. So many terms for things had been altered to fit the mood of the times. I looked up the word "girdle" in the dictionary. A "girdle" was described as "something that encircles or confines." Well, I needed to be confined. A girdle it would remain. What if I became trapped into dining on fancy meal after fancy meal during the festivities? The tight fit of the girdle might keep me so constricted that not even a demonstration dessert cart would tempt me. One girdle was so much less expensive than a session with a hypnotist.

Henry's packing took an hour, once he'd assembled his rental wear and followed his careful checklist. My packing took several days if I counted the hours I spent changing my mind about how many outfits to take and which jewelry should adorn the final selections. Jewelry choices were major issues. Cheap jewelry would mean that I didn't care. Jewelry that was too expensive meant that I was trying to care too much. Even good gemstone pieces that straddled the gap in social classes had to be selected with discretion. Henry wasn't the right person to consult. Unknown to him, I had splurged on a rather costly jade necklace using some cash I'd been saving for a year. The price of it bothered me so much that when he wasn't looking, I removed it from my suitcase and put it in my no longer used lace stocking drawer, right under the Victoria's Secret pair with the sequins. The necklace was returnable with the price tag still on it and I had already packed a very nice silver and turquoise pendant that Henry admired. I understood the psychological purpose behind my extravagance. An abundance of jewelry was a substitute for love. An abundance of food was a substitute for love. What was a girdle for? I knew the answer. It was a reminder that too much love in the form of fattening food was self-destructive. Just how much love did I really need? I put the jade necklace back into the suitcase.

25

Before we left town I had one more phone conversation with Robin. I made a serious effort to refrain from asking nosy questions which had been circulating in my mind. *How would she conduct herself as she shook hands with new people? What if someone knew a single woman at the affair and wanted to introduce the lady to Robbie? What if the woman made an overture and Robin had to invent an excuse why she couldn't meet for a lunch or go for a ride? Robbie had been an honest man. Would Robin have to tell the lady, "Sorry, but I don't date women and I'm not gay?" Only a lie on her part would avoid a real pickle. She could tell the person that she was about to take a traveling job in the U.S. which required that she live in a motor home. I knew of a guy that had that situation and nobody wanted to date him. Robin had plenty of time to rehearse her role, and certainly didn't need my help. But how could she not be nervous? I was nervous for both of us.*

I picked up a few vibes from the sound of her laugh when I told her about my jewelry and girdle issues. The laugh wasn't quite right. It should have been less like, "hee hee," and more like "ha ha." Couldn't Robin fake Robbie's former guffaw for the occasion? I offered my most tactful maternal advice:

"Robin, you'll be careful about your laugh, won't you? Your voice is the same as it used to be -- I understand that part -- but your new laugh is kind of weird."

"I'm working on it. I have a transgender coach who is also helping me get through this last stint as a guy."

"Oh yes, you mentioned that. What's the coach's name?"

"Aphrodite."

"I should have guessed. Well work on it as hard as you can."

"I'm working on a lot of things, Mother, at many levels. After the wedding, if we get a chance to be together without all the outsiders present, I'll show you how I do the Tango the way they do it in Barcelona."

"I'm not going to ask you what you wore for the dance lesson? What did you wear?"

"Oh, there's a big store in Cleveland where you get all those fancy duds. My skirt is very flouncy and I really kick up my heels."

"Robin?"

"Yes, Mom?"

"Maybe don't bury yourself in the new role, like until after the wedding."

"The operation's final, Mom."

"It's not that. I just don't want guys to think you're looking for a catch -- like you're after their money."

"I won't have to, Mom. You haven't listened to what's happened with the gallery show in Cleveland."

"I listened. You were working on a sketch. Did you complete that daring new marble sculpture you're exhibiting?"

"You're way behind, Mom. But it's not your fault. I purposely kept you and Dad in the dark because the inspiration for the first marble sculpture came way before I had the operation. Like two years before. That sketch was for a different version of the original design. Right now I'm in the process of photographing the work for the catalogue. The figures I'm showing are ready for exhibition. I've been working night and day with my assistants."

"Assistants? How are you paying those folks?"

"Guess."

"Linda?"

"Uh huh."

"Funny, she never mentioned it."

"I've had to keep this entire undertaking very secret."

"And you even used my suggested name for the sculptures, "BoyIntoGirl?"

"I did. That name, followed by the applicable Roman numeral, was actually in the publicity that got into the newspapers."

"So you mean people got to see the new sculpture, uh, in its raw state?"

"If they read that section, they did."

"Yikes."

"And Mom, it was reviewed. The comments have been astonishing."

"Astonishing good, or astonishing controversial?"

"Both, actually."

"I should have been more supportive of those cupids you once sculpted."

"I'm going to be previewed in the two top art magazines -- they say I'm innovative and that I'm on a creative path that is inspiring."

"That's great, but you said you'd be anonymous until after the wedding!"

"I still am. I took a fake name for the show."

"Can you tell me what it is?"

"Yes, it's just one first name. My art and pen name is, "Natasha."

"That's not a Jewish name."

"No, my Jewish name is, I told you already, "Rivka."

"My grandmother's Jewish name was Rivka. Maybe reincarnation is possible after all."

26

Henry and I were on high blood pressure alert as our pilot announced over the loudspeaker that we were about to land at O'Hare Airport in Chicago. I was a more relaxed airplane traveler than Henry. That didn't mean I was calm, since I always felt relieved when the personnel who held our lives in their hands gave full details. Yes, we were on the right plane and yes, the airport folks knew about it. As for the quality of the conversation between Henry and me, I was spewing inconsequential comments sporadically, and he was listening to me with his eyes half open and his mouth clamped shut. He blinked a few times, so I knew he was conscious.

"I guess you weren't able to sleep on the plane, dear, huh?"

"Yes."

"Yes, you dozed or yes, I was correct in my assumption?"

"Maybe."

I gave up trying to make reasonable conversation, and that my land-loving husband was entitled to clutch both armrests with an iron grip. As the plane landed with its typical bouncing series of thuds, I heard him mutter, "Safe once again -- I just counted all four landing gear hitting blacktop."

I muttered back, "Your seatbelt is mixed up with my seat belt."

"I really dread this part of the flight experience."

"Landing?"

"No, just reconnecting with the Earth in an upright position."

"Honey, everyone else is standing up, like they're actually fantasizing they'll be exiting in a couple of minutes. Can you please reach my carryon and give it to me?"

"Look out the window, Toots, it's pouring."

I hadn't noticed the rain, but Henry was right. Between the two of us, we had no umbrellas.

"I'm sorry I packed so light, wife -- I didn't think of bringing a rain parka or anything. How about you?"

"Maybe it will stop by the time we have to be outside, dear." Should I tell Henry that I had packed a pricey new raincoat which he knew nothing about? Probably not. If I needed the raincoat, he would marvel at my foresight. If I didn't, it was a moot point.

As I emerged from the crowded jetliner and tromped down the ramp in lockstep with the other trompers, I focused on Robin and how she would look dressed as a guy. Had she disposed of her man wardrobe? Did she still have the overcoat that fitted Robbie when he went off to his friend's wedding in Saskatchewan? I remembered being aggravated that two of his buddies were looking forward to getting married that year and he was looking forward to entering an ice sculpture contest. Henry was a few passengers behind me. He had given Robin a couple of suggestions: One, stick to conversations about foreign policy, and two, if she ran out of things to say, try sports talk. I guessed that's how Henry had always kept women from engulfing him in female chatter. Linda would be there for moral support. I had begun to think of her as the boxing coach who was also the one who wiped off the blood. That left me to do nothing but engage in harmless gossip. I had nothing to worry about except partial disaster or complete disaster.

Henry caught up with me and asked which way we should turn to find the nearest restroom. I wasn't sure if we should turn right or left. If it were up to me, I would have asked someone -- anyone. Henry would die before asking and preferred making his own decision. He cursed when he was wrong, which was about 75 percent of the time. Men cursed and women bitched. But Robbie never did either. He just solved problems quietly. Maybe Robin would have to learn how to bitch if she was planning to succeed in a relationship.

I sighed and then breathed in the welcome smells of a busy airport concourse. Human presence provided meaningful touches of imperfection to one of civilization's key enterprises, such as discarded half-eaten McDonalds sandwiches and water bottles that still contained water. I could smell the rain-soaked fabric overcoats on those who had just arrived. Travelers looked suspicious, but they could be excused because it was common knowledge that the last persons who were informed about the screwed up schedules were the passengers.

While I was gazing and philosophizing, Henry darted ahead with his usual vigor. He had no interest in looking out the big airport windows which seemed to stretch forever along the outer walls. Although the rain seemed to be letting up, this was one of those seasons when the few trees left standing on the fringes of the airport looked all bent over from wind gusts. Did these gusts come from Lake Michigan or the North Pole? I had never figured it out.

"Marlene, are you interested in retrieving our baggage, or are you preparing to compose a weather report?"

"I'm coming, dear." I caught up to Henry and noticed that he never looked to see if I was close behind. His legs moved as though he had never left the military. He was marching as in a training exercise, preparing for combat, while I was taking a sentimental journey. I disliked the strain of the long walk through the concourse, but distracted myself by employing my peripheral vision to gape at every window I passed, wondering about the sights and sounds outside the gates. Were all the suitcases now being carted to the baggage claim portal carefully locked and intact, or had they sat in a haphazard pile on those open trucks? I had often been seated at the window of a plane freshly landed, peering out as the airport personnel threw precious things onto large wheeled motorized carts. Those carts received the same respect from the cart-loading crew as dumpsters received from sanitation workers. What did it matter if passengers' gear, duffels, sealed boxes or outsized hard-cover fortresses of valuable equipment were bruised or soaked? And how many were about to slip through the cracks into unknowable caverns of mystery where lost luggage seemed to dwell?

It was still pouring rain outside, but I had my cellphone handy and was able to access the current weather for Chicago. Sunny with a ten percent chance of precipitation.

Robin and Linda were waiting for us at our baggage claim area, holding their luggage. I was greatly relieved to see my kids standing there together at our luggage carousel after hearing all the loudspeaker blasts about planes being late. Seeing their smiling faces gave me such a lift that nothing could shake my delight. After embracing my adult children, I watched while Henry permitted himself to be hugged and fawned over. I wished he could have been more demonstrative but at least he smiled and offered to take charge of the baggage.

"Let me take care of the luggage, kids."

"Thanks, Dad."

"I'll do it, Dad."

"No, Robbie, you stay right where you are -- I'll go get one of those wheeled cart jobs."

"Henry, I don't see our luggage yet."

"Maybe we'll be lucky. Stand guard."

This was the first time I was actually seeing Robbie as Robin, although dressed as Robbie, together with Linda as Linda. Did I have that straight? I was totally preoccupied with sizing up their appearances. *Robin was dashing and well-groomed, as he always was, except that now he was a she and should one call a woman dashing? Linda was even slimmer than I remembered. Would she notice my weight loss? Would she notice it even before I took my coat off? If I uttered the word "coat", would she look at my figure? Maybe she'd see that my cheeks were smaller.*

"I love that coat you're wearing, Linda, where did you get it?"

"Audrey Ames on the Magnificent Mile. Say, how much weight did you lose?"

"Seventeen pounds and five ounces."

"You look just great. You look younger."

"Really? I need outside assurance. Can you boost my morale at intervals -- perhaps on the hour?"

"You're the one who avoided junk food, or whatever you did, Mom."

"This series of parties will test my will power, you know."

"You might need a twelve-step group when you get back home. I'm certain they have one near you."

Turning to Robbie, Linda put her arms around her sister to comfort the person who had been pressured to attend the festivities still dressed as a brother. Being considerate of Robin's delicate condition, Linda lowered her voice to address her. "I think you're wonderful to stay in the closet for just a little while longer, Robin, and since I saw your new look, I have to say, I think you came out gor-jus!!!"

Robin's eyes flashed and she kept her voice low, but with an emphatic tone tinged with a hint of anger. It was the kind used by a baseball coach chastising a pitcher who had just walked three batters in a row. "I don't want that adjective! Nobody calls me gorgeous without risking a, a, punch in the nose!"

"You'd threaten me, just because I gave you a feminine compliment?"

"Yes! You're not complimenting me -- you're giving me the needle!"

"Who, me?"

"OK, my name is now Robin, we all agreed about that, you can call me good-looking, I'll even go so far as your calling me attractive! But not gorgeous! I hate that word."

Linda crossed her arms and looked first at Robin and then at me. I got nervous. Were my two daughters going to have an argument right there in the airport? Maybe it was time for me to step in.

"Kids, I want you two to play nice."

Linda ignored me and crossed her arms with a mean kid look. I could feel a vibration. As a young teenager she used to make our kitchen vibrate when she stamped her foot in defiance. It was scary, similar to when a jet plane took off. I hadn't gotten over those feelings because she was stronger than me, both then and now. At least this time her anger wasn't directed my way. I was cheering for Robin, although Linda seemed ahead on points.

"Damn you, Robin, I can say gorgeous if I think it fits!"

I couldn't control my knee-jerk tendency to intervene at this point, because what else is an overprotective mother of a freshly baked transgendered child supposed to do? "Shush, Linda, Robin doesn't want to be called 'gorgeous,' what's wrong with that?"

"Mother, she's still a HE in his head! It's driving me cuckoo! Robin, please explain to me what is wrong with the word 'gorgeous?'"

"Linda, it just doesn't feel right." Robin lowered the intensity of her hoarse whisper. Can't I have some time to adjust? I was brave enough to have the operation, knowing it was radical and controversial. Now, I just need a bit of respect. Lay off the overtly feminine adjectives right now, please, until I loosen up? I'm actually in a bit of pain from yesterday. I've got blisters on both ankles and the toes on my right foot."

"Oy vay, Robin, what happened to your feet?"

Had I ever heard my Linda, the least Yiddish of my clan, use that expression before?

"Maybe I shouldn't have tested out walking in stilettos until after the wedding."

"Why would you even want to walk in stilettos? You're almost six foot three!"

"It's expected of me in my circles, Linda. All the women in the upscale art world wear them. But now I have to get used to shuffling around in these guy shoes all over again. I went all out to play this game. Let's not dwell on it, all right?"

Linda turned to look at me. "What do you think, mother?"

I relaxed a bit. The old times never left and I was still the referee, so I made my call: "It's expected of Robin in her circles. Give her space."

"Space it is, but I'm entitled to voice my opinion. I'm just human."

Together, as if in a planned unison, Robin and I sang out softly: "You're not human!" Robin's next words were now barely audible. "Linda, you've always been incredible, and everybody knows that your emotions have been stifled since you were two years old."

"Well they're not stifled any longer! You really know how to hurt a person."

What had happened to Linda? She quickly grabbed a handkerchief from her purse and dabbed at her eyes. I had never seen her use a personal handkerchief before. The only wiping I remembered was when she would grab a rag to get the grease off when she was working with auto parts. I didn't want tension in the air. With four people having emotional conflict, one or two of us was likely to leak our secret involuntarily.

All the luggage had been retrieved except mine. Henry had been diddling around with the knot in his tie during our whole heated exchange. I needed to give him an assignment, so he could feel like part of a team. "Henry, mind the carousel, please? I see my luggage coming. Can you grab those two suitcases right next to that giant duffel? The large black ones with the yellow painted on leopard spots?"

I noted Henry's expression as he lifted the two overpacked suitcases and handed one to me and the other to Robin. The luggage cart was already full. He hadn't uttered a word, but I could read his face. It told me I packed too much stuff. We made our way to the outdoor exit. Henry walked the wrong way, but then Robbie put her arm on her father to guide him just like the good and affectionate son he had always been. "Daddy, put on your coat, this is Chicago."

"My suit is enough, son -- er, Robin, I packed my coat."

"Well, I have to say, you've never looked so distinguished and the last time I saw you in a real suit like that was for my bar mitzvah, I think."

"This is that same suit. I had it let out a bit."

"It's not the same suit, Dad, I know you're joking!"

"Just checking to see if you noticed."

My poor kid! How could he have a good time at his cousin's wedding if he had to talk like a man and dress like a man while he had all the problems of a woman, the worst being sore feet? Linda and I were barely getting accustomed to Robin's female self, while Henry could barely talk to Robin or about Robin without stumbling around with nomenclature.

As we passed through an exit to stand outside and face the nasty weather, Henry jostled me.

"Hey Marlene, you've been to this airport at O'Hare more often than me. Where do the taxis pick us up?"

"Henry, see that line of people over there to your right?"

"Oh that line? There's got to be a hundred folks there! Look at how desperate they look. I thought they were a bunch of refugees seeking asylum."

"Dear, refugees don't wear mink coats or have their suitcases handled by airport attendants."

"Well, I still think some of them are ready to pounce. Is that where we should be waiting?"

"Yes, Henry. Most of those folks got there before us."

"We're fine, Mom, we're used to this airport hassle."

Linda poked me and grinned, as she came to my rescue. "Are you cold, Mother, you look like you're shivering."

"Oh, don't worry about me. I'm not going to converse right now because I prefer to keep my mouth buried in my scarf to avoid getting a sore throat."

"Mom, your sense of humor is still alive. Don't let it die -- you need it to get along with Dad."

Henry had a slight smile on his face. Robin stood by Linda's side, trying to suppress a smile. The taxicabs were now arriving quickly enough to whittle down the number of waiting passengers. Just then an argument broke out between two women ahead of us in the pack. I heard the taller one yell at the shorter one, "I was here before you were!" Then the shorter one yelled back: "You were sneaking up in line -- I saw you!" Would these ladies come to blows? The crowd assembled around them in anticipation of a poorly matched bout between participants who weren't exactly dressed for a fight. The shorter one still had her hands in a muff. Ladies usually didn't trade punches. Instead they both did what women do so well, and that was to give each other the dirtiest looks possible. The taller one got in the next cab and I wondered if she would stick out her middle finger before the driver shut her door. I never found out because the man ahead of me obscured my view. As our taxi pulled up to where we were all waiting, the driver sprang out and opened the trunk. He and Henry worked as a team to pile all the luggage in while the three of us females stood demurely at the curb. I did catch the cabbie giving the once-over to tall and strong Robbie, but she held her ground at the curb innocently batting her eyelashes.

27

The wedding ceremony was scheduled to begin in fifteen minutes. I should have been ecstatic to see my favorite niece Cissy getting hitched to Sherwin Duberstein, a really nice rich guy. His family was so rich that Sherwin had no need to be that nice. Cissy would never have to suffer from any lack of jewels or designer clothing or a maid to help her fasten her necklaces or zip up her Armani dresses. Instead I was nearly in tears and they weren't related to resentment or its evil cousin, envy. Two major problems were ruining my day. The lesser one, my personal bulk around my middle, could be fixed with time and some effort, but the second was a social problem, a/k/a embarrassment. Robbie's sex-change operation might be hidden from public knowledge during the wedding, but what about afterwards? Everybody would soon find out and then I'd be forced to be straightforward. I was the conspiratorial mother of a male imposter.

I had seen Robin outside the ceremony ballroom, flanked by several real men who were most likely still real men. I might have been biased, but in my opinion Robbie was the most handsome, the most charming (could I still use the adjective "charming"?) and one of the tallest and most anatomically fit. The poor thing he was escorting would never suspect that the fellow beside her used depilatory, vaginal cream and pink plastic razors. It was the last chance I would get to see him dressed up like a boy.

My overweight issue had been diminished substantially. Henry had given me the nicest compliment:

"Marlene, I haven't seen you looking so trim in years. You look great, honey."

"Oh, Henry, I'm so miserable and upset. I want to thank you, but I want to cry."

"It's about Robbie, isn't it?"

"Well yes, but right now it's about my girdle."

"Let me get this straight, dear -- what's wrong with your girdle?"

"I made a mistake to wear it -- it's too tight."

"Did you buy the wrong size?"

"Oh, Henry, you just don't understand women, you don't understand me!"

What Henry didn't understand and never would understand was the difficulty of putting the girdle on and taking the girdle off. I gave up trying to explain it to him because we were on a tight schedule. We had to mingle socially and not look like we were rushed or harboring any devastating secrets. Then we had to find our seats for the ceremony all the way up front in the second row. As we said our hellos to all the right people, many of whom we had never met, the clock was ticking down to zero hour. All the close relatives were expected to be well organized, with programs in hand, and seated in gawking position. I wasn't quite ready, so I caught Henry on the shoulder. "Dear, you know my bladder isn't always up to snuff. I'm going to the ladies' room."

"Now? Well hurry up, and leave your cellphone on."

"Uh, I guess I should let you know that the battery on my cellphone is low."

"How low?"

"Like there's nothing on the screen but a black panel with an ominous-looking yellow warning, uh, like that."

"A yellow triangle with a red exclamation point?"

"Uh, yeah."

"Well, go take care of yourself and don't worry about the cellphone. I promise I won't call you when you're in there."

I didn't want to do a dance inside my girdle, which was now unwearable, so I scurried over to the line of squirming ladies waiting outside the door to the women's rest room. Once inside the stall I made the aggressive decision to abandon the girdle, so I removed my shoes, lowered my pantyhose, and managed to wiggle out of the thing without damaging my outer attire. As I hung it on the purse hook, I gazed at it for a few minutes with guilt as though I were leaving one of my babies on some doorstep. That girdle had cost $95 and there was no way I could stuff it inside my already overloaded purse. Henry would have busted a gut if he knew, so he wasn't going to know. I was counting on the fact that the lights in the ceremonial ballroom were so low he probably wouldn't notice that my flat stomach wasn't that flat.

Before I made my exit from the stall, I had to avoid the possibility that the next woman in line might immediately try to give my girdle back to me. The last thing I wanted to hear was, "Ma'am, did you forget your, uh, garment?" I told the lady about to enter that the bowl was clogged and she shouldn't use it. That was effective, and I made my getaway. It would probably end up being given to the rest room attendant. I wondered, how many girdles in the history of that high class hotel had already ended up in their lost and found? Probably fewer than the number of lace panties.

As I returned to the entrance to the hall where the ceremony was about to begin, I saw all the members of the wedding procession lined up. There was Robin being Robbie, chatting with one of the other tuxedo-clad men. I caught his friendly wave, but he didn't leave his place in line. Instead he gestured for me to talk to one of the young bridesmaids. She was several yards behind him and came over to speak to me.

"Oh, Ma'am, are you Mrs. Sternberg, Robbie's Mom?"

"Yes, I am. Sorry if I can't talk now -- I need to get to my seat in the front of the hall. But you are?"

"Carrie London. Robbie told me about you. He's my friend. He's just so, so, cool and handsome, and gifted! Oh, and most of the girls here are friends of Cissy, but, well, you know, we know some of the guys, and a few of us know most of the guys. Well, we, uh, most of us, like, came here together, like, you know, all the way from New York. I really wanted to meet you."

I listened to this attractive creature talk, like I should know what she was trying to communicate so precisely. My instinct was to be cordial, since I wasn't sure how to be cool.

"Carrie, is it? It's nice to meet a friend of my son. Look, catch me after the ceremony, we'll be at one of the front tables."

The young lady lowered her voice and said: "Robbie sort of asked me for a date."

"For a date?"

"Well, I think so."

"Excuse me, uh Carrie. I have to sneeze!"

I never thought I would need to fake a convincing ah choo before, but this was a good time to try it. Grabbing a personalized handkerchief from my purse, I gave out a real good blow, avoiding the monogram. This wasn't the moment for visible hysteria, even though what this girl was telling me was just too weird. Robin couldn't have asked her for a date. Unless, unless, oh no, could my daughter posing as my son have already become a, oh, I couldn't say it, oh, my, could she have already determined she was a lesbian? I felt like I had just been immersed in a "B" movie. There had to be some other explanation.

"See you later, Carrie, and don't worry, I don't have a cold. I'm just allergic to something in the air out here!" Then I let go another ah choo for effect. I was getting good at it.

My hands felt clammy and my pulse was racing. Before I made my way back into the ballroom, I spotted Robin again. I tried to catch her eye -- no, his eye - oh, never mind whose eye. There wasn't going to be any easy way to pry her aside for questioning, so I took the bull by the horns, no, the cow by the teats, oh, screw the wording! I had to go to the source without attracting Carrie's attention. I waited for the right moment and managed to grab his arm. "Robbie, can I have a word with you -- it's urgent!"

"Sure, Mom, what's the problem?"

"Over there, please.

She put her arm around me and we walked over to one of the sitting areas.

"What's up, Mom? The procession is about to begin!"

"This girl, Carrie from London?"

"Carrie London -- that's her name."

"I'm so distraught I can't think. OK, Carrie from New York, I guess that's what she said. Did you actually ask her for a date?"

"Oh, I know what that's about. It's not really a date. I asked her and some of the other girls to come to my gallery show in New York at the end of October. I told her we'd all get together after the show for drinks. I suspect, well, I think she has a crush on me."

"Are you leading that poor nubile beauty on?"

"Mom, I can't help it if girls come onto me. It's been happening for years!"

"You could help it. You could act a little obnoxious, for God's sake. You know how to be obnoxious. I brought you up, did you forget?"

"I can't act like you said. It's bad for my career and my image!"

"Oh, I see. So I guess it's better you break a few hearts then?"

"Well, don't worry about Carrie. She'll see my work and learn the truth. She's a very talented artist. Artists like her are carefree. If she does have a crush on me and I accidently hurt her feelings, why she'll do a great abstract painting of that experience with her emotion right in the brush strokes."

"Say, these girls that come onto you? Are most of them artists?"

"No, some are poets, and some are unemployed."

I didn't have time to get into a discussion of the New York creative scene, so I got to the point. "Well, Carrie seems like a nice girl. I hope you don't hurt her feelings and I hope she meets a nice guy."

"She will -- she lives in Soho." Robin then bent down to whisper in my ear: "There's lots of guys there who still have their you know what!"

I whispered back: "Well, does she know anything at all about the absence of your you know what?"

"Mom, some of these girls, maybe most of them, probably think I'm a gay man."

"Oh, thank God you're not! I feel so much better knowing you're a straight woman. Now I can relax during the wedding."

"I've got to get back in line, Mom."

"Me too, they're closing the door to the hall!" I ran over to the usher outside the door and he noticed the horrified expression on my face.

"Hurry, Ma'am," he warned me, "the woman inside will guide you to a seat, but you'll have to sit in the back!"

"But I'm the bride's aunt!"

"Oh, you are? Well then wait for the moment when you can join your family. But right now, you'll have to tiptoe in there. They're lowering the lights. Don't worry, you'll get a good up close view!"

28

I entered the hushed ballroom, where three hundred heads turned around to check the identity of the late-coming bumbler. The violinist at the front of the huge room did some minor key string plucking. In a movie, those sounds usually indicated that an ill wind was about to blow. A staff member with her finger to her lips guided me to the groom's side next to an exceedingly attractive young lady. That row could seat fifteen or so, but she was the only one there. I sat down and she graciously moved over so I could have the aisle seat.

I turned my attention to the procession about to begin and retrieved my purse to rummage in it for the program. Ah, there it was -- how could I miss it? It was the size of an extra-large greeting card, but most greeting cards don't have gold ballpoint pens attached. I opened it and a sentence beneath the names of the hosts and the betrothed read: "Seating will take place at 6:30 PM. There was a space below the script which I assumed was reserved for comments, since there were lines drawn. Did we have to hand it in and grade it? Like when it came to the kiss, were we to describe it anywhere from platonic up to sensual or even higher, X-rated? I slipped the program back into my purse.

The rest of the lights were lowered and the chattering of the crowd died down. The woman sitting next to me looked at her jewel-studded watch. It probably gave accurate time, but the real purpose of it was to make other woman envious. I wondered who she was, but it was too late to get friendly. I turned my attention to the procession and let my slightly protruding stomach relax. Aaahh, it felt so good to let it just go where it wanted to. There was something to be said about breathing naturally.

I had been a spectator at enough Jewish wedding ceremonies to know the routine. There are four mandatory rules, in my estimation, that have to be followed, or else the production will be a flop:

(1) The official selected to administer the part with the vows has to legalize the holy wedlock of the marrying couple, even though in modern times, it has become a formality. Their relationship has already been consummated, perhaps several times a week.

(2) The entire production must entertain the gathered guests and the most successful entertainment includes something those guests can talk about afterwards. Intrigue and intimate gossip usually trump visuals that mere money can buy.

(3) The ceremony itself must satisfy the religious requirements of the person or persons who write the check for the rabbi. If the ones holding the purse strings are Orthodox, there might be three hundred guests in attendance, but it is unlikely that the men and women will be garishly dressed and equally unlikely that the celebration will be a sumptuous affair at an upscale out-of-town hotel, especially if the guests cannot walk over to it. Conservative types can get away with most destination weddings and Reform types can get away with almost anything.

(4) The bride must look breathtakingly beautiful no matter what economic class she occupies. There are no unattractive brides -- only poorly designed veils.

My take on the wedding of Cissy Rosen and Sherwin Duberstein followed these four rules fairly well, but in my opinion, money was wasted. The room was too cold. There were too many ribbons, too many ceiling mounted balloons that served no visible purpose except to portray ostentatious intent, and way too many flowers. I heard a couple of people sneezing. The violinist was worth what they paid him, however. Even from the back of the room I could see his curly hair as he bobbed up and down like fiddlers do when they're passionate. When he began to play "Waltz of the Flowers" from Swan Lake, I was able to relax somewhat because the sweet strains of Tchaikovsky were pleasing and helped calm my nerves. At the conclusion of the music, my pulse began pounding again as I waited for Robin to appear. I had neglected to wear a wrap over my dress and the air conditioning was giving me goose bumps. My nose felt cold and clammy, like that of a dog I once tried to pet.

An orchestra hidden behind the curtains began to play music from a popular play, but by that time I was only in the mood for "Here Comes The Bride." If Cissy and Sherwin were going to go through with the whole shooting match, I wanted them to get on with it. I glanced at the woman seated next to me. She seemed anxious also. I would have been nervous as hell if my cleavage showed as much as hers did. Then the music stopped abruptly. How did the orchestra know when to stop? Did they have remote control signals? A wedding planner suspended from a catwalk directing the action? The room became silent except for people breathing. Three Hundred heads swiveled in unison one hundred eighty degrees around to the rear of the room as if choreographed. Ladies with brimmed or veiled hats adjusted them when prompted to do so. Men wearing yarmulkes merely had to shift their butts and necks. A few minutes passed and then all the heads swerved back up front as a man wearing a rabbi's skullcap and sporting a very long beard and a cheery smile entered from a door at the right front corner of the room. He was holding a thick hard-cover book with gold lettering indicating a sacred volume, so I figured he was ready to punch out a traditional ceremony with all the right messages, which Jewish people called brochas. As he reached the center of the room and stood in front of the chupah, he nodded to the crowd and gestured for them to return their gazes to the rear. Again all the heads went into reverse, waiting for the show they had come to see.

The orchestra played the traditional Lohengrin. Had I been directing, I would have shortened their intro by half. Finally, the strains of

"Here Comes The Bride" took over. Then seven characters darted out from nowhere holding cameras bearing lenses long enough for capturing gnats in the Himalayas. They began crouching in shooting position as the rear entrance door opened.

The first to emerge was a shih-tsu puppy, tethered to an elegant leash of pink leather, studded with purple gems, and was very well behaved. A teen-aged young lady following the pooch held the leash, and I recognized her as one of my nieces, Julie Sue's teen-aged daughter, Wendy, although I hadn't seen her recently without her nose, eyebrow or lip jewelry. The ring-bearer followed and then came the groom, Sherwin, who marched down the aisle with a wide grin and his thumbs up. After Sherwin's appearance, a buzz in the air was apparent as a series of beautiful girls dressed in pink satin accompanied by their escorts, handsome young men wearing black tuxes with ruffled lavender shirts, began their graceful walk forward, smiling all the way. More eyes focused on the revealed bosoms of the girls in their low-cut gowns than the fact that the guys wore purple cummerbunds. I looked for Robin and then I saw her, about three couples back. She looked exceptionally handsome! I had always wanted a good-looking adult child and now I was blessed with one who thrilled the hearts of very young and impressionable ladies. It was like a fairy tale, except that the story wasn't quite something you'd find in a children's book.

There was a bit of a pause and then out came four little flower girls, and finally, amid a myriad of excited whispering, the bride. Cissy was elegant in her white satin gown. As she made her graceful way forward, there was a pronounced rustle of fabric on fabric emanating from the extra long train of her gown. It was the size of three boxcars. Cissy looked as beautiful than any bride. I couldn't see her face, but I assumed there was only one imposter in the bridal party. Her form-fitting dress could have doubled as a nightgown, and maybe it would do so when the evening concluded.

The bride approached the chupah accompanied by her father. Howard bowed and retreated as Cissy took her place by Sherwin's side. The couple stood at attention flanked by two lines of attendants. Flashes from cameras went off. The sermon was next. I kept watching Robin as she stood as a guy stands, tall and confident in her male attire. Such a good actor, my daughter. It was impossible to see Henry and Linda from my back row seat, so I gave up trying. I strained to hear what was being said under the chupah, but I barely heard a word. *What was being spoken to join those two? "Do you, Sherwin, blah, blah, blah, take this woman, blah, blah, blah?" The word "consecrate" was in there somewhere.* I was able to hear Sherwin stomping on a glass followed by the applause of the crowd. Everyone in the audience rose to witness the kiss. I hated being so short because I missed the first part of the groom kissing the bride, and considered standing up on my seat, but I wasn't up to it for a number of reasons. It was a good decision, because as the crowd sat down again, the bride and groom were still locked in an embrace, with Sherwin holding onto Cissy like he would never stop. "OK, Sherwin," I wanted to screech out, "the audience gets the idea -- you're a real hottie!"

The couple were now officially husband and wife. I remembered the program, which seemed to require feedback, like a survey, so I retrieved it, signed my name and added the words, "Beautiful ceremony -- took my breath away." What a lie that was. Now that my girdle was off, I and my breath were doing just fine. Actually, I felt like crying. Not because I was the emotional aunt of the bride, but because I despaired that I might never be the mother of the bride.

29

The ceremony was over and irreversible. Any change of heart on the part of the newly married couple was now in the hands of rich lawyers, who could only get richer. I was intent on finding my family in the crowd. It was quite an ordeal, with me getting my toes stepped on as I barreled my way against the flow of people moving and jostling for position toward the rear of the room. Then I saw Henry, giving Linda's hand a squeeze, as they moved in different directions. Did Linda's nose need powdering or was she seeking a social opportunity? Henry seemed relieved to see me.

"Marlene, I missed you. What happened?"

"Oh, Henry, I got delayed talking to Robin outside the door while they were lining up for the procession. They made me sit in the back row."

"OK, what should we do now?"

"Well, we should follow the crowd to the receiving line. Why don't you go mingle while I look for the kids."

"I'm not a mingler."

"So then pretend you are. Our family is very big on pretense."

"You want me to go to the receiving line, don't you?"

"It's the socially correct thing to do."

"When was the last time I said to you, "Hey, Honey! Let's go do the socially correct thing!"

"Stop giving me one of your tests, Henry. Don't you want to congratulate Cissy and Sherwin and give Robbie a warm handshake for pulling off his -- uh, his --"

"His fakery."

"OK, but he's your daughter."

"I'm not going there and I'm not going to the receiving line either. And there's no quiet corners in this whole blasted hotel."

"Henry, you should be nicer to Robbie. I know you're avoiding the whole issue. This is a good way to deal with it."

"Marlene, where's your psychiatrist license? Tell you what -- if you see a couch somewhere in this room -- a place where you can analyze me until I dream the way you'd prefer it, I'll lie down."

My husband wasn't going to play ball. "Henry, look at me -- look at me very carefully. Do I seem any fatter than I did earlier, like before we got to the hotel?"

"Of course not, honey, you don't think I'm going to step into that one, do you?"

"Then stop walking away from me when I'm talking to you."

"I was just backing up to see your whole figure, dear."

"So now what?"

"I'm about to walk in the direction of the nearest bar."

"Well, there's Robbie -- right over there. At least say "hello."

"Hello, son."

Robbie came up to us and hugged me and Henry and beamed those expressive eyes at each of us. "What do you think, Mom, Dad, how does the tux look?"

Henry squinted up at the kid who was three inches taller than him because of the elevating heels on the formal wear shoes. "It looks good. I didn't know you got taller -- I know you got -- you look good. Are you going to be this height from now on?"

"Of course not. These shoes were rented for this ceremony. They're very special. The salesman told me they were from 'The Walking Tall

Bodyguard Line.' I picked them out because I thought they'd give me an edge."

"You need an edge, all right. What's going to happen if you dance with a normal-sized woman? She'll have her nose right in your chest."

I butted in before someone had a dad versus transgender daughter moment. "Robbie, I'll see you in the receiving line. Your father will see you at our table." *There, I did what the shrink advised, change the subject when the subject was like a killer whale ready to pounce.*

"That's fine, Mom. And Dad?"

"Hmm, what?"

"The cocktail lounge is through that door over there." Robbie was smiling as he walked toward the rest of the crowd.

Henry stared at the retreating form of his child. "He's walking differently, Marlene, do you notice?"

"You mean, like how his hips are --"

"You can say it -- he's swinging his hips a bit, like he's Marilyn Monroe, or somebody."

"He's practicing, I think."

"Keep your voice down, don't blow that kid's cover."

"Henry, I think she can pull it off."

Sure, maybe Robbie did have a new walk, but I hadn't focused on my child's posture since his first grade Red Riding Hood play at his school where he played the big bad wolf. What was in the cards for that person that I brought up to be attentive to women and a pal to his men friends? What about all those expectations I had for my firstborn as a new father? Could I make the mental shift to Robin's becoming a mother? I'd been too busy to see if guide books had been written for the transgender's parents.

"Henry, before you disappear, there was a hot-looking babe sitting in my row with jewelry up to her eyeballs, but no wedding or engagement ring. As a disinterested male observer, what sort of babe agenda might she have?"

"Who said I'm disinterested?"

"Come on."

"She's a slinker. She's looking for action."

"A slinker?"

"At a super-rich party like this? I'll bet they have a whole table of them."

We approached the receiving room line, which was a hundred folks long. Henry was still hanging on my arm, waiting for my "at ease" command, like I was his drill sergeant.

"OK, Henry, go to the cocktail lounge, if you must. So you'll miss congratulating Cissy and Sherwin. I can live with that -- chances are they'll still be in love during dinner. But honey, please don't get lost in there. Maybe have just one drink and then come back, OK?"

"Don't give me restrictions, Marlene. Are you worried that I can't hold my liquor?"

"You really want me to answer that? Remember George Marcus' party last year?"

"That was different. George forced me to try his special martinis -- I think he distilled the gin himself in his back yard."

"Henry, let's be honest. You're an occasional social drinker -- two glasses of beer, and maybe a shot of bourbon which you don't even finish. I've watched you."

"I'll be back in less than an hour -- did the battery on your watch fail also? If not, look for me in about forty-five minutes!"

30

I was alone to execute the required social amenities. I had no idea where Linda had gone. When my turn in the receiving line arrived, I performed the proper aunt-of-the-bride moves and embraced my Robin, then a few others, including Miss London, then the married couple and my sister, Beth, but not Howard, although I made eye contact with his cigar. My escape went smoothly. I looked for a table to sit at just outside the receiving line area and found one. It felt good to be off my feet. I saw waiters everywhere passing out drinks and watched hands reaching out to clutch them. I didn't have to look at my watch because I could count the times I said "No Thanks," to the waiters, about one every five minutes. Almost an hour had gone by and no Henry. I worried that it was now two bourbons past a couple of Heinekens. Just then I looked up and saw Henry swaying toward me. My fears about his will power weren't idle. He did not look like a person who had moderated his intake of liquor. I stood up and hastened toward him as he gestured for me to step away from the crowd so we could talk.

"Honey, I met shome guysh and shtarted a convershashun and losht track."

"Of what, the time or the booze?"

"Both. Lishen, I don't feel sho well."

"Dear, do you need to ---?"

"Yesh. But don't shay the wordszh. Jusht help me out. I think I might need a container."

My years of coddling my family members died hard. Henry was my teddy bear in bed, my meal ticket and my emotional prop, even if we bickered like two nut jobs over every aspect of life. My fool husband had just made me the rescue dog. Too bad I wasn't one of those St. Bernards because then I would have had a pail under my chin like in some movie I'd seen. I looked around. Close at hand was a small round server's table occupied by a sterling silver wine bucket. There was a bottle in it, getting chilled. I walked over to it quickly and noticed that the label on the bottle indicated it was Dom Perignon. What to do? This was an emergency. I took the bottle out of the bucket and placed it carefully in the center of the small table and brought the bucket back to Henry.

"Honey, here's a wine bucket, but it's got ice cubes in it!"

Henry managed to stagger over to the corner with me running after him in my high heels. We faced the wall and he didn't have three seconds left. Fortunately, the bucket did its job. We stood in our corner for about ten minutes until he felt better.

"Henry, I see a waiter approaching the table with the bottle on it not getting chilled. We've got to get out of here. Can you walk if I hold onto you?"

"Where are we going?

"Let's go to the dinner ballroom. I've still got the bucket under the sash of my dress if you need it again."

"I might need it again."

"Quickly, Henry, this bucket's heavy."

Henry whispered to me that it was important for me to hold onto him with a firm grip. Together, we race-walked toward the dinner ballroom like two pickpockets dodging capture. I had wrapped the full folds of my beautiful dress around the bucket, hoping the fumes wouldn't linger. We found our table and luckily, none of the guests had arrived at that ballroom yet.

"Marlene, honey, stick the bucket under that coat on that chair there!"

"That's somebody's coat, Henry! It looks expensive!"

"You're right. Look, I'm nearly recovered from my foolishness. Give me the bucket."

"This is crazy! Look, there's waiters arriving to finish setting up the tables -- there -- over there to your right -- see them? They're still working their way toward the far corner of the room."

Henry's glazed eyes followed my gesture and his expression suddenly lit up, indicating some plan to dispose of his iced vomit cocktail. He began walking over to the opposite corner from where I had been pointing and bumped into several chairs on the way. *Don't fall down, Henry, hold onto the chairs if you need to! Oh, goody, he's using the chairs advantageously. Somebody will have to rearrange them, but that can't be helped.* When Henry reached a table in the far corner of the room which had already been completely set up, he began unsetting it, moving the silverware, glassware and other paraphernalia to an adjoining table. There was only one small crash. I gaped as he stuffed the quickly snatched tablecloth inside his pants, suggesting a bit of a pot belly, and walked back to me. Somehow we were able to wrap the cloth around the bucket.

"Stay put, Marlene, I'll get rid of this thing."

I was amazed at how he managed to sail out of the room with his booty under one arm, but two waiters spotted him as he made his desperate exit. One of them scratched his bald head and approached me.

"Excuse me, uh, Ma'am, about that man who just walked out of here with that white bundle?"

"What white bundle?"

"Well, he had something under his arm -- we're just, uh, always looking for possible theft, you know, like the silverware?"

"I'll keep an eye out, but I have to go find my family."

The fellow thanked me and returned to his duties. I noticed a couple of staff members gazing at the now bare table. *Were they about to issue an all points bulletin for a missing linen?* I didn't wait to find out. On my way back to the receiving line, I prayed that Henry would be able to dispose of his frozen material without difficulty and would catch up to me. He was no thief, just a lousy drinker.

31

Henry looked sufficiently sober to avoid discovery as we seated ourselves before the rest of our party filled up our table. I stared at the centerpiece and searched for something to bite into. There were several condiment shakers, wine and water glasses and printed material that some bozo considered important, but not a crumb of anything acceptable for me to chew on with minimal consequences. I would have committed murder for a lousy breadstick or even a celery or carrot morsel, but no, my fate was to sit through the inevitable speeches and stare at chocolate bonbons.

Henry was making an attempt to appear friendly by smiling at everyone who passed by our table, even the waiters. I gave him a nudge to annoy him and serve as a reminder that our relatives expected his typical sarcasm, not the grin of a fool.

"I'm fine, Marlene, and you can stop poking me."

"You're not fine -- you look like a six-year-old who just got caught playing with matches."

"Would you rather have me grumpy and disagreeable?"

"No, I'm just nervous about Robin. It's affecting my mood. Actually, you're doing well, considering everything. Our relatives will be gathering very soon. I've seen all the place cards, and they did a good job."

"Yeah, they probably put the guests who could sit up straight next to the ones who couldn't."

"That's absurd."

"Just a little attempt at humor, honey. Can you find my napkin? I don't see it anywhere."

"It's on your lap."

"I need to watch my casual drinking."

"You could probably request Diet Coke."

"And look like a recovering drunk?"

"No, you'd look like an enlightened guy who was bored."

"Do you forgive me?"

"For having a weakness? Why should I? You've always told me you were perfect. I figured that perfection meant having at least one stupid habit."

"I've got more than one, but you're right. I am so much more perfect than you."

"Oh, Henry, you're so very Mars to my Venus!"

"Yeah, and there's another planetary test arriving. I see Robin coming to sit at our table."

Our relatives were about to sit down with us. Everyone seemed in a good mood. Julie Sue had greeted me warmly when we saw each other at the receiving line, and now I got to smile at her husband, Phil, and her two older daughters. Wendy, the youngest, was seated at one of two tables on the other side of the room. Its occupants were apparently groomsmen or bridesmaids. I had gotten a glimpse of that young group and it didn't take long to realize that they were all oversexed and underfed. It was just as well that they were confined to their own territory because nobody over the age of thirty could understand their language.

Robin seated herself as though nothing had ever changed about him. The kid would have made a good actor.

"Hi, Mom, Dad! I wanted to be at your table, and here I am."

I dug into Henry's ribs with my elbow so he'd let me do the talking, while he returned to his post-binge friendly smiling. "Robbie! It's you! I thought you had to sit with the bridal party."

"They're too young for me, mostly Tweetheads and Coke Snorters. I thought I'd be happier with you guys, so I overruled the place card placer."

"You look quite content, son. Your face is flushed. You must be having a good time."

"It's the wine, Mom, I had two glasses already. Did you know they had Dom Perignon and were offering it to just anyone?"

"I had an inkling about their choice of wine, yes. I hope they didn't offer it to the flower girls or the dog."

Whew, Robin was heavily immersing herself in the male role with the man's aptitude for drinking and decisiveness. How does someone go back and forth like that? First a guy, then a girl who doesn't want to be a guy, then a woman who knows her body has the Wrong Stuff, then she gets the Right Stuff, then has to deal with the family's urging her to do the man thing with the Wrong Stuff, which she agrees to do, and this Robin person can pull it off. She had to go from flaunting her pecs to being coy and unpredictable. Wait a minute, maybe Robbie never flaunted his pecs! I know he went to the gym to build his body, but he didn't do it to be attractive to women -- he did it to be a woman body builder! Thank God I've finally figured him out, no her out. Them out. Shit, I'll never get this straight!

I noticed the five o'clock shadow was now a barely perceptible fuzz.

"Robbie, here's a surprise for you. Dad bought an electric razor."

"Dad, is Mom joking? What did you do with your old Gillette? It's so old it's probably worth something now."

"When I die I'm leaving it to the shaving museum. I bought a Remington triple blade rotary. It's just for going to weddings and bar mitzvahs."

"That's so neat, Dad. I'd be lost without my electric razor."

"Marlene, as long as you brought it up, I need to excuse myself -- time to check out the stubble." Henry rose from his chair and disappeared into the throng of hungry guests.

"Mom? I can't believe it -- I thought we'd have to bury Dad with that razor and that old bristle brush, and, yeah, the shaving cup with the scum of a hundred old Lava soap shards."

"He's up to date now, Robbie, no more Lava. He's begun using Ivory lately for purity. I know he shies away from acquiring new habits, especially gadgets for his face with all those moving parts."

"Is he going to sit next to me?"

"I was thinking I should sit in between you two -- what do you think?"

"Oh, leave it that way. Maybe it's safer."

I greeted our arriving table mates as they sat down. "Hi, everyone, somebody's missing. I see you, Julie Sue, Paul, your kids, Mindy, and Sherry, Mindy's friend, what's your name? Davon? Hi, Davon, oh, we're waiting only for Henry and Linda."

Robbie leaned over to me to whisper that he'd been speaking to Davon. "Mom, I think you pronounce his name 'DAY-VONE,' to rhyme with the word 'intone.'"

"Oh, a French guy?"

"No, he's from Nigeria. Definitely not French."

"I'll be careful to pronounce it right. Thanks."

I've been an overprotective mother of a son too long. He's grown and leaving me far behind, and she's here now and socially adept. I shouldn't have to stretch my neck like I had a habit of doing to search the collar for a hint of dandruff. I wonder if the hormone treatments mean she doesn't have dandruff any more, or less dandruff. Shame on me. My son's no longer a son and I'm worried about whether the dandruff is under control?

Linda arrived and greeted the others. A moment later Henry returned from the men's room with only one discernible nick, but no active bleeding. I signaled him to make with some fatherly talk. He picked up the cue, knowing he was being monitored. Although he played around with his water glass, he managed to flash a smile at Robbie, while simultaneously focusing his eyes on a spot on the tablecloth.

"You still work out at that gym in Lordstown, son? What's its name? Muscle City or something?"

"The name you're thinking of is "Muscle's Last Stand," but now I go to one called "Peck's Peak Fitness."

"Hmm, clever, the owner must have the last name of Peck."

"She does."

"When I was your age I couldn't afford to go to a gym."

"Dad, you told me the story ten times. You kept up your strength by playing hockey with your older brothers. The family had no money for equipment so they swung you around for the stick."

"That's not quite what I said. It wasn't that bad, although we did use my mother's worn-out lace tablecloths for the net."

"I always laughed when you exaggerated like that, Dad, but I got the message. You had a habit of letting me know I was lucky to have more advantages than you did."

"Well, I know I didn't spoil you. You always worked hard. Marlene, did you say something?"

"Yes, Henry, I was thinking that young men today don't have it all that easy -- they have a harder time staying in relationships because young women are more independent."

"It's that feminist thing that's ruining ---- hey, stop poking me with your elbow, will you?"

"That was my gentle tap, dear, will you pass the water pitcher please?" Henry knew I wished he would shut up about his opinions. He always pretended he didn't have any social vulnerabilities, but his experience at the cocktail lounge had humbled him. I introduced Henry to DAYVONE, who was one big hunk of a black fellow. Mindy looked like a tiny doll next to him. Henry stood up and reached across the table to shake hands with Davon.

"Nice to meet you, Davon, and hope we get a chance to talk. Right now I can't hear much, with all the noise of the crowd. Davon smiled, rose and touched his yarmulke as a hello gesture. The yarmulke seemed lost among his dreadlocks. After the introductions were over, the table chatter seemed to fade. Henry wasn't about to break the ice, but somebody had to fill in. He leaned over to me to whisper a reminder that I had been anointed the designated conversationalist for the two of us. And that's maybe the first time in years I felt speechless. Several minutes passed and I couldn't think of a single safe thing to talk about.

32

I reminded myself that the wedding feast portion of a gala event of this nature had often been my undoing, so I grabbed my thighs as soon as I began to smell food. The tablecloth hid a lot of things I was glad to conceal, and my thighs were two of them. I glanced at my ultra lean Linda seated next to Henry. She was frowning.

"Mother, did you see the printed menu on the table? Did you read it?"

"Not really."

"Well, I did, and I'm asking the waiter if he can bring me a plain salad and some tomato slices. I'm not going to eat any of their bloody beef or the high carb potatoes. Do you know what poison they put on everything?"

"You could have requested fish, Linda. And if you're trying to influence my appetite, it won't work. I was born carnivorous and I'll die that way."

"You can suit yourself, but you know I don't eat fish -- have you any idea how fish are handled after they're mutilated?"

"With special fish gloves? Otherwise, you need hand sanitizer, right?"

"Oh, Mother, you'll never understand. But guess what they put on most food to cover up their culinary sins?"

"Sauce?"

"Never mind, Mother. Anyway, **you're** doing very well. I'm proud of you."

"Because of?"

"Everything. You're eating better, you look chic in your outfit, isn't she lovely, Dad?"

Henry nodded and grabbed a celery stalk.

"And Mother, even your voice is different. You sound like, I don't know, like every word is measured. It's just amazing!"

"Thanks, dear. I'm making every effort to maintain my new brevity system. Maybe I mentioned it to you."

"Your WHAT system? I can't hear you, oh, forget it, the speeches are coming. Let's wait till the toasts are over."

"It wasn't important. Isn't that Howard's brother at the mike?"

Linda and everyone else at our table were fingering their glasses, which had already been filled with champagne. I looked at the bubbly liquid and a scene at a Weight Watchers meeting appeared in my mind. Sparkling wines had nearly a hundred calories and water had zero. Henry's champagne glass was already half empty. Robin was raising her glass and staring at Henry, as though she had figured out what was going on with him. I forced myself not to care. If Henry got smashed again, Robin could deal with propping him up.

As soon as the speeches were over, Julie Sue offered her take on the expert management of the receiving line as a prelude to everything else she had to say. "Marlene, I thought the planners had a great idea for handling the pace of all the guests, didn't you?"

"Oh, yes they did. My only criticism is they should have had name tags."

My younger sister always liked to impress everyone with her modern views. She talked as much as I did, with an even worse habit of commenting on the details of every detail. She could never have handled a husband like Henry. I suppressed a giggle as she attempted to engage him.

"Say, where were **you**, Henry? I missed you in the receiving line."

"Oh, I had to help one of the waiters attend to some guy who couldn't hold his liquor. I just happened to be next to the fellow when he fell over."

"Really, who was it?"

"Never found out. The man was so shickered, he couldn't even tell me his name."

"You probably saved that man a lot of embarrassment."

"Not at all, Julie. I just happened to be on the spot when it happened."

It was time for my distraction move and I turned to Julie's husband. "Paul, did you try the wine?"

"What constitutes 'try?'"

"It's a step up from inhaling the vapor."

"I have never inhaled anything, Marlene. Not even Pall Malls when I was in high school."

"Julie, your husband is so straight and narrow -- a regular Boy Scout."

Julie Sue smiled slightly at my remark. Henry was digging his elbow into my waist to signal me to avoid a sensitive issue, like whether my brothers-in-law were straight and narrow or otherwise. So many secrets happening and so little time to think up the ingenious lies. I turned to check on Robin, and saw her winking at me. Actually, what I saw was the handsome son's wink, so memorable on that motion picture star face.

I used to watch Robbie with single girls at gatherings, fantasizing that he had the kind of wink and enticing expression that a girl would dream about afterwards. Would that girl take that wink with her the rest of the evening, wondering if it had been about asking her for a date, or at least a meeting in the moonlight? If Robbie wasn't attracted to girls, then why did he wink? Did I ever wink at my women friends? Oh my, maybe Robbie wasn't thinking about a potential screw session when he winked at a girl -- maybe he was just being friendly. Another clue misinterpreted. Our child was needy for friendship, possibly desperately. We never caught on. But I shouldn't berate myself for constantly suggesting that he ought to be dating. He'd just look at me and tell me he wasn't ready.

I spied Linda inspecting the bowl of vinaigrette for the salads. She could analyze the cholesterol and fat content of any food substance just by observation, although I had occasionally caught her dipping a finger into a splash of dressing on a buffet table and managing a surreptitious taste with incredible finesse.

The splendid meal to come was on my mind and I was no longer wearing the girdle.

The appetizers were wheeled in with fanfare. I could have kissed the server. Just as I was about to treat myself to bite-sized shrimp and scallop tidbits atop an herb garden of leafy stuff, plus an aperitif wine to wash it down with, the music began to blast away. It was so loud I couldn't hear myself think. How could I enjoy the remainder of the meal if I couldn't hear the sizzle of the meat? I was all set to dine with elegance and dignity, and now I wanted to strangle the bandleader, or whoever had hired them. I must have been cursing because Henry saw my lips moving and asked me what I was angry about.

"I don't like a blast of trumpets going off while I'm trying to keep track of calories."

"This is a feast. You shouldn't have to count calories now."

"You're right. But I do have to total up my points."

"Points?"

"Yes, Weight Watchers points. Don't worry, I've got it all handled.

And I did have it handled. To this day, I can't remember how I managed to restrain myself during that meal because I had put myself under a hypnotic spell.

"Mother?"

Linda was pinching my arm gently. I must have been in a daze. "Oh, yes, honey, I can hear you. What is it?"

"You ate sensibly, but it was strange to see you pushing your potatoes around the edge of the plate and making them into a decorative border."

"Did I do that? It must have been unconscious. But I've decided not to have dessert."

"What did you think of the speeches?"

"Well, if you really want my opinion, I've always believed that speakers should speed up their comments when honest hungry people are suffering. Dieters are like recovering alcoholics and they shouldn't be subject to prolonged food aromas unnecessarily."

"I'm going to the ladies room. Will you join me?"

"No, someone has to look after Henry."

Robin had left her seat. Henry seemed sober, but some others in the room weren't. I was still worried about caving in when the dessert arrived, so I pretended I was Spock from Star Trek, giving myself a mind meld. IT ISN'T LOGICAL TO RUIN YOUR DIET. I didn't think I was hungry any more, but the music was still so loud I couldn't hear my stomach. Photographers were like lemmings, scurrying around with their cameras and taking pictures of guests in various states of staring, laughing, noshing or whispering. They made the guests get closer to each other so they could get everybody into the frame. Henry looked bored. Before she excused herself, Robin had seemed very quiet and perhaps had to use a rest room. Julie Sue, Paul, Sherry and Mindy had left the table and were standing nearby arguing about something. DAYVONE had gone to watch the photographers prying some people apart and pushing others together. Was anyone having a good time? Henry put his arm around me for a moment and then took it away to take a sip of some after dinner wine which had just been poured into each guest's extra wine glass. Why did they do this now when most folks had left their tables? Maybe they had orders to empty all the crates no matter what.

"Henry, an awful memory is coming back to me. When you had to deal with your sick feeling back near the receiving room, it reminded me of a time years ago when I tried becoming bulimic."

"Really, you never told me about that."

"Well, after one experiment in gorging and purging, I concluded that it was more fun to be overweight. I had read books about gastric surgery and that route wasn't a church picnic either."

"You're really nuts, but I'm not exactly a model of sanity, so let's just try to enjoy ourselves."

"How can I? You've never had to go through withdrawal from freshly baked bread or au gratin potatoes."

"Everyone's left the table, including Robbie. Do you want to talk about his behavior?"

"You go first."

"It wasn't so bad as I feared, but I still think he could have given some excuses about being sick, or maybe even told the truth and given Cissy a chance to deal with it and let her make the choice."

"He wanted to come. He and Cissy have been very close. I saw them talking before. Oh, they're bringing the dessert now. I need help. Don't let me weaken!"

"Marlene, please, do your own withdrawal and leave me out of it. Here comes Linda."

Henry and Linda had been dancing while I sat alone, feeling left out. I spotted Julie Sue's handbag on the table and assumed she was making her rounds. She was a reliable gossip and could be trusted to return eventually to share it. The music seemed to go on forever. I looked at my watch and before I could decide whether to find someone to talk to or retreat to the ladies room, Henry came up behind me and squeezed my shoulders. I turned around, startled, and saw that his silly grin had reappeared.

"Marlene, I'm feeling a bit high, but I'm almost having fun. Why are you sitting there all alone?"

"It's my shoes. They don't want to go anywhere."

"Linda's too light on her feet and I'm too heavy on them to let me enjoy it. I guess I'm through drinking alcohol for tonight. I'll see if any of the waiters can get me some black coffee. Do you want coffee, dear?"

"Sure, why not. Oh, oh, I don't like the look on Rob-Robbie's face -- look over there -- he's having his photo taken with the other grooms-men."

"He looks constipated."

"Oh, Henry, how can you say that? He's fine."

"Constipated."

"Lay off."

"I'm going to the men's room. You can scrounge up the coffee. I hope Robin remembers how to use her---"

"Henry!!!!"

"I'll be right back. I owe you a dance."

"I'll be waiting here, staring at the bon-bons."

While I contemplated whether I could dance in my high heels. Beth appeared and asked me to join the family for some photos.

"Beth, I'd have to repair my makeup. I need a very big mirror and about twenty minutes of squinting."

"Don't be silly, you look fine, Marlene. Get up and follow me. Where's Henry?"

"He's roaming around somewhere. I guess I can redo my lipstick from memory, but I'm not sure I can walk another step in these shoes. That's probably why I was still sitting down."

"You could take your shoes off and then just slip them on again for the shoot."

"That's a good idea." *Should I tell Beth that I had brought flats and that they were in my purse? I'd been too self-conscious to change shoes out in the open, but this seemed like an opportunity. Would my stylish younger sister help me out? Say something helpful, Beth.*

"Listen, my feet hurt too."

Ah, that's all I needed.

"I understand you've got to greet everybody. I hope we get a chance to really talk some."

"Later. Right now everyone here is driving me crazy."

"Oh, here comes Henry. I guess I can walk. We'll follow you."

"Henry, Beth wants us to join the others to have our pictures taken. OK with you?"

Henry nodded and whispered in my ear: "Let's go do the right thing, dear."

I swiftly changed into the flats and we followed Beth over to a section of the room set aside for the photographers and their prey. The area was all dressed up with studio umbrellas, special backgrounds, drapery and lighting equipment. We were herded like pack animals into prearranged groups. The creation of the blood relatives with their mates portion of the album of the century took about forty minutes or so. Henry's best smile happened as soon as we heard the words "Thanks, folks, we're all done!" We scurried away like someone had opened the door to the cage. Henry described the session as similar to serving time in prison, but at least we didn't have to post bail to get out. After our release, he asked me if I wanted to dance.

"Just one dance, honey, and let's make it brief."

"You've been so quiet, I thought you were upset or maybe even sick."

"No, Henry, I'm not sick. Just a little worried about you know what. Why don't you find Robin and be nice?"

"Sure, sure, but you want to know the truth, Marlene, you're always telling me to be upfront with my inner thoughts, right?"

"Nobody's going to overhear you, dear, out with it!"

"I'm worried about Robbie, or Robin, and the damned sex change and his, oh, her new lifestyle. The whole thing is a huge mistake from which our son will never recover. Also, about this wedding fabrication?"

"Come on, let it all hang out."

"Oh shit, our totally screwed up kid! What the fuck has he done? Exchanged a perfectly good set of sex organs for some grafting specialist doctor's idea of satisfying the crazy notions of this generation? It stinks!"

"Henry, a wedding party is supposed to be fun, and just look at us! Suddenly, we're both in foul moods and we're not even enjoying the fact that somebody else is paying for all this luxury that neither of us appreciates! So they didn't pop for the plane fare, the taxis, the rentals, the dress I'll never wear again, or the hotel room. Big whoop! Let's just do the best we can, OK?"

"I'll brighten up, honey, I promise, but I can't stop worrying about Robbie. I just know that at any minute, like at this party, somebody's going to catch on that he's not who she is!"

33

"Marlene, how's my dancing?"

"You're doing well -- I've missed dancing with you, but I shouldn't have changed back into the high heels. You only stepped on my toe once"

"Did I hurt you?"

"Don't know, I haven't been able to feel any of my toes. Say, where the hell is Robbie?"

"Look to your right without being obvious. Our pretend son is dancing with Cissy."

I rotated my balky neck muscles until I saw the pair of them. "I see Cissy holding Robbie like he was her date, is that what you mean? My goodness gracious, what a dress on that figure of hers! I guess she had a committee of those nubile bridesmaids pin up the back of it so nobody would trip and fall. It's dangerous enough that it looks like a nightgown."

"Well, she doesn't have to worry about turning Robbie on."

We continued our moderately paced dance. As we twirled, each time I was able to catch sight of Cissy and Robbie, I gaped. Something was going on. I heard Henry utter one of his patented "oh, oh's."

"Oh, oh, what's the 'oh, oh' about?"

Henry stiffened up and turned us away so he could whisper in my ear. "Can you hear me?"

"Yes, your mouth is right in my hair!"

"Well, our daughter, ahem, 'Robin,' has challenges ahead. Very slowly, turn your head and see if you notice."

"You're right. Look at how Cissy is dancing so close to Robin's chest. She's saying something she doesn't want anyone else to hear! What the hell is Cissy doing?"

"She's being intimate with her female cousin -- that's what!"

"Oh, at last the music's over. Should I go ask Robin what was going on between her and Cissy."

"Do it. You're better at being nosy."

"Me, nosy? OK, I'll do it. Henry, the music's over. Finished. You can stop counting the beats."

There comes a time when a parent has to deal with the embarrassment of a child's behavior. It starts when the kid has its first poop in a public place and ends when the sun sets on your inhibitions, usually at the death of one of you. In my case, my capacity for humiliation was limitless, dwarfed only by my need to portray social correctness. I waited until Cissy left Robin's side to go off somewhere, probably to find her new husband. At the precise moment when Robin could be tactfully approached, I tapped her on the shoulder. She might have gotten her hormone pill dosage right, but they didn't much decrease the bulk of her biceps. Instinctively, I looked at her guy shoes to check for unsightly scuff marks.

"Oh, hi, Mom, are you having fun?"

"Lots of fun. Oh, Robbie, how are you doing, uh, son? You look nervous."

"I guess you saw Cissy getting close to me while we were dancing. Mom, she figured it out -- she knows."

"What happened?"

"It was really weird. She wanted to kiss me on the lips and give me a gigantic hug, like for old times sake?"

"Go on."

"I was worried that she'd had improper thoughts about me, like wanting to be too close. I figured she was tipsy, so I disregarded it. But then I felt her body against mine and soon I got the distinct impression that she was feeling me up."

"As in, uh, trying to check into what was under your shirt?"

"Well, not only that high up. She went further, you know what I mean?"

"Uh, you mean, she felt for something else?"

"That's right. I asked her what she was doing and she told me that she had noticed the change in my face. I wasn't sure anyone would see the difference, but she did. Also, I probably talk a little differently."

"Talk, maybe. Walk, definitely. Is she going to keep it a secret?"

"She promised me that she would, and I believed her. Well, I had seen tears, so I asked her what was wrong. She said that nothing was wrong, but that she wouldn't be able to explain her feelings. Anyway, it all spilled out of her, so I confessed and she swore she wouldn't tell anyone until I let her know it was OK."

"So, what's the problem?"

"Cissy couldn't stop crying and I escorted her over to Sherwin. She promised me again she would keep the secret. But a few minutes later, she found me and confessed that Sherwin had found out."

"Oh My God!"

"He thought she was unhappy with him, about something he said about the way she danced with me. Well, she couldn't let him think that, so she told him about me and asked him to promise to keep it secret. Mom, he's not the type we thought he was. Had to tell this one asshole guy in the groom's party, and I'm not sure who else."

"So what happened?"

"The asshole came up to me and made a remark I didn't like at all."

"Maybe I don't want to know what he said."

"He wanted to look at me in the men's room and see---"

"Stop, I can't handle this."

"I got really mad, but I didn't want to make a scene at the wedding. I never did like the idea of punching somebody out, even though I think I'm stronger than a lot of men, so I looked him right in the eye and told him I wasn't that kind of woman."

"That took guts."

"The guy was a bit tipsy, but an obnoxious boor is what I don't need right now. I don't know if I got through to him, but I told him to shove off or I'd have him thrown out. They actually have a bouncer here!"

"So now what?"

"Nothing. I'm going to have to deal with a lot of crap like that in my life. This isn't real life here, Mom, this is a shindig for rich people to show off their wealth. It isn't even Cissy. She's really just a nice person and I think she loves Sherwin. This whole party is what both sets of parents are about."

I didn't know whether to laugh or cry. Robbie, oh, blast it, Robin, was so very calm -- I was the one who was nervous. "Can I call you Robin now?"

"Not yet, maybe wait. There's a lot of people here who don't need to join in the side show."

"Robbie, then, Robbie, how can you be so nonchalant about it?"

"I'm not nonchalant. I got nervous. I'm still nervous. But I had a lot of coaching. I guess I was prepared. They actually have encounter groups and special counseling for people like me. I almost feel like a poster child, but here, I'd just like to act like a guest at the wedding of my cousin."

"I admire how cool you are. Say, that brings up a question which I was reluctant to ask you, but since you're being so frank, I'll ask."

"What's the question?"

"Robin, are you, uh, are you, a, uh, are you, oh never mind. It's not right to ask."

"Mom, do you want to know if I'm able to have sex like a woman? Nobody can hear us. Is that what's bothering you?"

"Yes, but this isn't the place to talk."

"I'll tell you this much. I'm technically a virgin. Did you read the whole medical report?"

"Honestly speaking, I read about half of it and then I got a killer of a headache and put the rest aside. Henry hasn't read any of it. I put it in a private file I have. The truth is, I felt out of touch with the technique where a medical specialist can change a person." I opened my purse and felt for the handkerchief. This was my grown child's privates we were discussing, and I didn't feel quite up to it.

"Mom, there's counseling available for parents and siblings of a transgendered person. They even have some in Florida. I checked."

"I love you, Robbie." Then I whispered "Robin dear." I had to blow my nose into the handkerchief. I looked around the room. "Where's Henry, I wonder?"

"Dad's gone over to get acquainted with Sherwin's folks, Mom. He's just fine."

"That's good, but is he still distant?"

"Maybe not as bad as before, but still in denial. And here, I can answer your question. You want to know my prospects, and how I'm dealing with it, just like you can't stop being curious about Linda's life? Well, I have a boyfriend, but we're not there, like, getting that friendly yet -- we've only had a couple of dates."

"So you wouldn't do it on the first or second date?"

"You're asking hard questions, Mom. I've still got a lot of remedial cosmetic work to do before I'm more, uh, normal. It's expensive, painful and time-consuming. Say, when I was a boy, you never asked me this personal stuff. And Dad pretended I was a eunuch. Now, it's like you've suddenly gotten wise. Well, if your friends and neighbors ask about me, just tell everybody I'm doing fine and they'll probably leave you alone."

"So at least we still are playing the part that you're a guy, like at these festivities, right?"

"Yes. I didn't go to the men's room. I used a small rest room on the floor above. After my transition is complete, I'll be able to fix my makeup where the women blab by the mirrors. I do know about those places."

"Oh, like specific gender activities?"

"I'm still getting the hang of it."

"Did you rehearse that line?"

"Sure, I rehearsed lots of lines."

"I'd better get back to Henry and reassure him. He worries, you know."

"Mom, I didn't mean to be hard on you. If you hadn't encouraged me with my art, I'd be in a bad way now. And don't worry so much about Dad. He's OK, he just asked me if my corset was comfortable."

What a strong person Robin is and how well she's adapted. She's actually a very attractive woman. I can see her in women's attire! Wow! There's that nice set of pearl and amethyst earrings that I don't wear any more. Linda doesn't have pierced ears. Maybe Robin's going to pierce hers? If she wasn't so tall, I'd have been able to see if her ears had puncture marks.

When it was time to part, Robin squeezed my hand as though to assure me that the two of us understood each other. I felt a great deal of compassion for her situation. Maybe it was my mothering instinct, or maybe I simply had empathy for the man, now woman, who had tried so hard to deal with sexual ambiguity. Wherever my concern for her originated, Robin was still my first-born, my baby, a person I had raised to be a caring soul, a good future mate and, with luck, a loving parent. It would be only a matter of time before I began to figure out if I knew anyone who had a son I could fix her up with.

34

Linda and Robin had departed for O'Hare Airport, while Henry and I were spending one more evening at our hotel. We had to kill time and Henry thought a good place to do it was in the bar on the ground floor. I kept an eye on him like I was a detective and he was a suspect.

"Henry, was there anything at all about the wedding that you enjoyed?"

"Yeah, when that crazy uncle of Sherwin split his pants while trying to do the kazotsky."

"I saw that too. That old fart was nuts to think he was still athletic."

"Did you have a favorite part?"

"Yes, when I found out that Beth and Howard learned about Robin and didn't go all nuts about it. Also, there's something really wild that Robin told me. You know that she's been creating those special trans-gendered sculptures under a false name."

"I sort of knew."

"I'll bet you didn't know that she had a team of assistants helping her."

"Were any of the assistants minus their balls too?"

"I think I'll ignore that comment."

"Gee, why didn't I have a crew helping me get established? These kids of ours don't have it so bad -- they should only know what I went through!"

"Henry, don't make me lose my train of thought. Oh, yeah, well, just listen to this one! Howard bought one of the sculptures and he didn't know it was done by his own niece! How's that for a crazy coincidence! He paid serious money for an artist's work not knowing Robin was using a fictitious name!"

"That is wild. I've known that Howard collected art, but that is something for the books."

"Henry, you have to take the good and the bad about a person. We both thought this whole destination wedding spectacle was the longest, most lavish, absolutely the most brazen display of ---"

"Crapola, use the term 'crapola,' because that's what it was."

"Well, it was brazen and lavish. But if Howard bought one of Robin's sculptures not knowing it was Robin's work, that's just so so small world and weird. It makes me think more highly of him."

"He's not a bad guy. He wasn't the only one orchestrating the affair. I heard that Sherwin's folks paid for half of it. The Dubersteins are as rich or richer than the Rosens. How do you like them apples?" Henry lifted his nearly full glass of beer halfway to his mouth, and stared at the glass. "It was almost worth getting drunk, actually. Too bad I sobered up so quickly."

"Well, at least you enjoyed something about this trip."

"I'm enjoying myself right now. We're leaving soon."

"Say, did you learn where the happy new couple is going on their honeymoon?"

"I was told that they're flying to Melbourne, Australia, and then on to New Zealand. I think the first leg of the trip is on some special non-stop jetliner. With Sherwin's glands running overtime, I'll bet they get a private space to monkey around right on the plane."

"They probably will. Women nurse their babies in public now, so why shouldn't Sherwin be able to pet his new doll baby 30,000 feet high like they do in the movies?"

"Linda told me the honeymoon would cost a cool hundred thou."

"A drop in Sherwin's bucket. I might be a bit jealous, but I can't help thinking that maybe it's not so good to have that much money to spend.

When I think about our low budget wedding, I still laugh. Say, do you remember your mother's phone call right after the ceremony?"

"No, but you do."

"Of course I do. She told you to make certain I'd never been familiar with a man before."

"My God, how times have changed. Even the advice that mothers give their kids. If Linda ever gets married, what will you advise her?"

"Good question. Well times have changed, but the advice is still the same. I'll have her make sure that her prospective husband has never been familiar with a man before."

Despite Henry's denials about being a gossip the way I am, because he insists that men don't do it, I didn't believe him. I was still wondering about the mystery woman who sat next to me during the ceremony..

"Henry, did you suspect anything about Howard and that woman sitting next to me?"

"I'm going to let you in on a little secret. You were right about her. Howard got sucked into inviting her or she was going to crash the scene anyway. It's not easy having a mistress who wishes she didn't have competition."

"I'm not going to ask you how you know about it not being easy. Say, I was going to bring this up last month. Did that woman, Judy something, the divorcee in our garden group, try to put the make on you? Your buddy Frank told me she gave him a sort of proposition."

"Yeah? How did you find that out?"

"Carol told me."

"You're such a busybody. No, Judy never approached me. You women are such gossips. How can a fella get away with anything nowadays?"

"It takes loads of money. Which brings me back to Howard and his cheating. He does it because he can."

"Maybe Beth is a cold potato."

"Hey, I never thought of that. So you're saying it's the wife's fault?"

"I'm not getting trapped here with your feminist mumbo jumbo!"

There he goes again. Squashing an innocent point I brought up. It was time for my brevity system. My first move was to make like a clam and avert any eye contact. It usually worked, but there was a time element. The key was to keep up the charade until Henry began to fidget because he really couldn't stand me being too quiet for too long.

"OK, wife, I get it. Suddenly you're quiet. Did I insult you?"

"Maybe."

"Say, what is your opinion of Sherwin? Do you think that, unlike his father, he'll be a saint?"

Ah, success, getting a man to be the one to shift from offense to defense! I had watched enough football to get that routine down!

"A saint, huh? Well, let's see, there's a Saint Joseph, a Saint Luke, everybody knows about Saint Patrick, but I don't think there's a Saint Sherwin. Besides, you actually believe that marital fidelity is really up to the wife. Did you know that Beth had Cissy consult a financial planner and a lawyer before the wedding, like right after the engagement?"

"But not a shrink? You consult those quacks."

"She doesn't have my issues. She doesn't need cosmetic surgery or weight loss aids or advice for how to mother unusual children. What she needs is to get wiser about financial stuff. I've even thought of sending her a gift subscription to Barron's."

"That's a laugh! You don't even know what Barron's is -- it's not a place where you look for ads for sales of handbags or jewelry!"

"I told you that I signed up for a course on basic domestic finance. After that, I'm going to start reading The Wall Street Journal every day. And I'm going to have you pay for it because you've kept me in the dark for so many years."

"Really? That's a big change for you!"

"I'm tired of leaving all our financial matters to the man of the house -- what if you check out before I do?"

"Let's change the subject before I have to start sending you flowers."

Wow, I really needed to apply that silent treatment more often. It definitely gave a push to my feminine power. I think it was something the male shrink suggested to me -- if I wanted my husband to fall at my feet, get him to be the one to want to buy the shoes.

The wedding was history and at least Robbie could comfortably slip back into her Robin skin. I got all the news from Linda on the phone that night. She was waiting for her flight and had a few minutes to kill.

"Mom, guess what? Robbie is gone and Robin is here to stay. Before she gave her best wishes to Cissy and Sherwin, she told Cissy that she was returning to her life in Ohio as a woman. She had brought a complete change of clothes to wear on the plane and gave Cissy the go-ahead to let everyone know."

"Good, no more secrets. What else did Robin tell you?"

"Robin told Cissy about her sculptures and Cissy practically had a seizure. One of them was on a pedestal in the front hall of their place in Duchess County. And Beth still doesn't know that Robin is the artist! Howard just buys expensive cutting edge works of art and never thinks to tell Beth half of it. But Cissy knew because she's very much into art. She immediately made the connection! The name was Natasha, remember, so the bill of sale never had Robin's real name!"

"Unbelievable! To call it a small world is an understatement. It's more like some higher power out there is orchestrating this whole thing! Listen, you get yourself back to Cleveland safely. Take it easy. We've all had our quota of stress. I think everything's going to work out for Robin."

"Sure, it will, that is, except for her relationship with Dad. He's in a lot of denial."

"Not about the operation, Linda, just about the wisdom of it. Oh, by the way, Henry has no idea about how you financed Robin's sculpture production."

"Don't tell him just yet."

"Good idea."

"Goodnight, Mom, I'm exhausted."

At last the whole family, including my sister, Beth, and her entire family and many of their friends, would now be privy to the facts about Robin. They could gossip about it to their heart's content. I hadn't realized that Beth learned of it before we wished them goodbye, so I was a bit dumbfounded with her parting comment:

"Marlene, you should count your lucky stars because you've been blessed with two gifted children.

"Beth, Linda's business success is common knowledge, but what gifts of Robbie are you referring to?"

"I know about the sex change with your son. Don't worry, I won't say anything now."

"Oh My God! So you know! But why do you call it a blessing?"

"What's Robbie's new name? Robin? She's very talented and very brave. Cissy told me all about the new sculpture series and how good it is -- she calls it 'cutting edge.'"

"I'm delighted at how open-minded you are, Beth. Thanks for the moral support."

"I wish I had your chutzpah, Marlene."

"What? With your successful station in life? Whatever do you mean?"

"I mean, oh, just be happy, dear sister. And appreciate your good fortune."

"You appreciate yours, don't you, Beth?"

"Oh, Marlene," she sputtered, "I just got so fed up with the wedding consultants we hired to plan everything. I'll never use them again!"

"You have another bride to give away?"

"No, what I mean is, I'd never recommend them."

"Oh, I'll make a note of that."

Beth was hiding her pain, just like she used to do when she was a teenager and wouldn't talk about what happened on her dates. I was beginning to figure her out as Henry and I walked into the lobby of our hotel. While we were in the elevator going up to our room, I took advantage of the fact that nobody else was in it. "Henry, Beth actually remarked to me that I had been blessed with two gifted children. Do you think she couldn't think of anything else to say because of the shock about our son?"

"I think she's a bit jealous of you and the fact that both our kids have been successful, whereas, her daughter needed to marry into money. And she's just a jealous person anyway."

"I wonder what she has to be jealous about."

"Who can ever figure out what a woman is thinking? Give it up."

As we got into bed, Henry gave me one smooch and then closed his eyes. For me, this was an opportunity to engage in deep thought about the family situation. Henry called my bedtime ruminations a waste of good sleep time while I called it constructive worrying. It still bothered me that my husband was so upset about the wedding and Robin and other matters. How could I ever help him adjust to our daughter's new self? *Let's see, we've been married 49 and a half years and the last time I influenced Henry's feelings was, oh, I remember! It was before we agreed to get engaged! I should make a mental note to tell my unmarried children the following: When considering a permanent and legal matchup, do all your negotiating before signing on the dotted line. After that, it's all high risk matrimonial maneuvering. If you don't get agreement on the basics before saying "I Do," then why even get married to that person? For an exciting adventure in risk-taking, you might as well do skydiving. It's a one shot at a time adventure, you don't need a lawyer to stop doing it, and after your jump at least you have a fighting chance to walk away with your freedom and not too many bruises.*

35

My resentment of my younger sister went back so many years, I had spent whole sessions with my psychologist trying to deal with it. It began the day she was born. She wasn't supposed to be a girl. My mother promised me that I wouldn't have to share my bedroom if the baby was a boy. They didn't have pictures of the inside of mommies then, so I had to wait until it was too late for me to adapt to a rival who was going to take away my privacy and half the space in my precious haven. I was told to get over it when I was nine and I still get told by Henry to get over it, and I'm now Seventy and counting. Much of my attitude had to do with Beth's natural slimness. Maybe it was the way she got treated and not anything she actually did. I remember all the details, even actual words, like they were stamped somewhere in my brain with indelible ink. My psychologist told me early memories were stored all over, but he said the hippocampus was the most important.

"Sure, that explains everything, doc. The prefix 'hippo' sealed my fate. Wouldn't you just know it!" I then described for him my version of how my mother spoke to me:

"Marlene, the reason you have such a big tuchus is because you eat heavy foods and everything sinks to your rear end. You should watch

Elizabeth Ann and take a lesson from her -- she never even eats cake or pancakes."

I told my doctor that I was only fifteen and Beth was only six and a half. Later we learned that she was allergic to wheat and some other foods, but why did that overly favored six and a half-year-old snot-nosed pipsqueak avoid bread products before anybody ever took her to an allergist? And why did my mother criticize my rump when I was still five pounds underweight and Beth was so skinny she looked like one of those stick figures the kids drew? One of my sharpest memories of her as a three-year-old is that my mother had to exchange some of the gifts of clothes from relatives because they were for three-year-olds. Poor Beth, as she reached puberty, she had to stuff socks and things in her bras because otherwise her side view made her look like a boy. Ha, I used to taunt her by telling her that if she walked the wrong way into a strong wind, she'd blow away.

My mother's unfair comparisons of my shape with Beth's were about as scientific as voodoo. She had the gall to blame our differences on her weird pregnancies.

"Marlene, honey, when you were in my tummy I ate everything! Pie, sugar, milkshakes, banana splits, and all those kugels that Granma kept shoveling at me."

"But Mother, Granma didn't stop with her recipes when Elizabeth Ann was born!"

"No, she didn't, sweetheart, but my doctor told me to watch my eating better, and he scared me. Remember cousin Shirley? She died young of diabetes and was a fat pig!"

"You always treated Beth better than me, Mother. You fed her every spoonful until she was ready for kindergarten!"

"I did not! She fed herself when she was less than four years old!"

It's interesting how I remember conversations with my mother like they were yesterday and can't remember promises I made to Henry last week. I've learned from some of my friends my age that they have the same problem! Even the shrink knew about this peculiarity of a person's memory. So I began to understand why I resented my sister and why she was attracted to Howard. She needed someone to feed her and coddle her, so that's why she married a wealthy man. And she married a guy who was never around much, so I guess she didn't bother to eat a lot most of the time. At least I understood part of my problem now. Henry stayed home too much.

I was deep into an idea I had retrieved from a dream. In the dream I was holding a fork and somebody was trying to help me keep food on it until I could get it up to my mouth. The food kept falling off and so I kept being hungry. When I awoke I couldn't quite put a face on the helper. I knew it was a woman. If that woman was supposed to be my mother, why did my unconscious wipe out her face? Then another old conversation with her emerged. It was one I must have carried around with me all these years. Aha! I knew it! My mother was obsessed with the eating habits of all three of her daughters, not just with Beth's! She used to hover behind my chair, waiting to see how daintily I could place food on my fork.

"Eat slowly, child, don't treat the fork as a shovel, treat it like a toothpick."

"Mom, get lost!" Then, when she got mad at me for being rebellious, I would soften it up: "Mommy, I'm starving. And what's this strange stuff in the salad?"

"Alfalfa, dandelion greens, shredded cabbage, and wheat germ mixed with a bit of vinegar and oil, you know, for dressing."

"Well, I hate it. I'm not eating this garbage. You're a rotten cook. I want my Granma!"

"You want to be a fat old lady?"

"Granma's skinny. And she bakes all the time!"

"Granma has had a hard life. I want you to have things easier!" After that speech, she would remove the salad dish with the uneaten stuff from the table and put it somewhere. One day I figured out what she did with it. I spied her mixing it into the dog's chunky moist food and putting it into its bowl. And eventually I figured out my mother's game plan. She was attempting to package each of us girls as a pretty woman with the appetite of a bird. In my growing up days, it was common knowledge that the prettiest girls with the smallest waistlines got the richest husbands! Her playbook wasn't so secret, however. Whenever she got phone calls from Mrs. Siegel, her lady friend who was married to a doctor dripping with wealth, I would furtively pick up the extension in the dining room, where I could hide behind the curtain. Mrs. Siegel was such a gossip, and a busybody. Why would a successful doctor marry such a dizzy dame? I had to know what they talked about because I had suspicions.

Mrs. Siegel always asked: "Ethel, how is Marlene doing in school? She's such a smart one!"

And my mother's answer was something like a dismissal of my scholarship and a putdown of my other qualities. "She's better at school than she is at home."

"Oh, how is that?"

"A's all the time, and such a vocabulary! I can't even understand some words she uses in her school compositions. The teacher is always putting notes on her papers and saying her stories are very creative."

"Oh, that's good, that's good. And is she helping you around the house, like a good future housewife?"

"Oh, a little. Her best quality is how careful she is with her hygiene. She's got such good straight teeth, and I see her brushing her hair over and over until you can hear the static. Her room could be a little straighter, but I think she's wising up. And how's your son, Larry?"

"He's learning how Manny works by going to his office. We're sending him for a fine pre-med program out East. But listen! He's always thinking about girls! I know he thinks Marlene is a peach."

"He does? Well, maybe, you know, maybe they should see if they like each other."

At that phase of the conversation I'd quietly hang up and cautiously extricate myself from the curtains so they wouldn't rustle. My mother's hearing was sharp. I'd learned that the hard way. And what a nerve! She actually thought she could pick my boyfriends! I was so mad, I resolved to show her a thing or two. If that greasy-headed Larry ever showed up here, I'd teach him what a real girl was like! I'd find a way to reduce him to mashed potatoes. I wasn't so dumb as my family made out. After all, my ambitions soared to heights my family never dreamed of. Each day that I got on the bus to go to high school, my attitude went with me.

As a senior in high school, I loved talking about my perceived failures of childhood to those of my friends who seemed like-minded. We analyzed and bad-mouthed like crazy. I was the ringleader and would ask one of my closer friends, like Barbara, "Hey, Barbara, remember the question your mom always asked you when you got home from school? 'Honey, what did you learn today?' And what was your casual non-answer answer?" Barbara was in my inner circle. We comprised a small group of victims entertaining early feminist ideology. She'd answer, "'Oh, we had a discussion about our bodies in health class, but I knew everything already" One of my weaknesses, at least the therapist called them weaknesses, was dwelling on the past. I kept defending myself. "I don't really dwell on the past, but my mother kept giving me advice that sounded so dumb. She would coach me on how strong I should be and then what did she do? She stopped talking and went back to her routine of cleaning up after the family, like it was the school's job to teach us only enough to end up just like her."

My mother wasn't dumb, just brainwashed. Little did she know about how I got my real education. Maybe she thought that high schools were repositories of higher learning, but she was clueless about the kind of learning that we students picked up outside the classrooms. My best teaching tool was the locker area in the corridors. If the nosy hall guards thought lockers were a place to store one's belongings, they were dumber than bologna sandwiches. Lockers were places where girls traded stories about how all the guys tried to feel them up when they got the chance. Ha, was I ever forewarned! If that Larry jerk ever did take me on a date and try to feel me up, I'd tell him off. Sure enough, my prediction came true. Larry asked me out and I had to go because I didn't want to make too many waves. Then that numbskull did try to put his hand on my left tit and I think I told him to go jerk off somewhere else. Maybe I didn't use those words. I've been too immersed in modern culture lately. But

I'm certain I told him to put his hands in his pockets and that I didn't feel like sharing my tits with anybody until I was ready. In my mind, I'd be ready when I found a guy I could control just a little. That Larry jerk must have been a pussycat because he left me alone after that one date, although he kept sending me photographs of himself half naked in one of those super-tight bathing trunks. He had a physique like Tarzan, but I figured I could squash him with a few words about his bad manners. I think I also told him he should stick his wiener in his mother's meatloaf. Upon reflection, did I really say that, or did I just wish I had said that? Funny thing, after that one memorable date I don't remember too many more conversations between my mother and Mrs. Siegel.

Maybe that's why I didn't seek out a rich husband. I was going to conquer the world and didn't need one. Big Whoop! And now, knowing what I know, well, I'll have to be even tougher! What did the shrink pound into me? "Stop living in the past!" What did I say to the shrink after paying him how many of my hard-earned bucks? "I'm not living in the damned past. It's just that my childhood was one pile of horseshit after another! And my damned sister pulled the longer straw!" Of course when I defended myself with the shrink, I got a look that could freeze helium. I guess that's why therapists earn their money. They have six senses, instead of five. The extra one is the sense of a patient's bullshit floating through the air. The best psychologists don't need lie detector apparatus. They seem to feel the vibrations emitted when a client's denial system cranks up and excuses are spewed out. Eventually, even I knew when I was being defensive after spilling my guts for forty minutes. Tears would come gushing out of me like a geyser. In one of my sessions the doc had to procure extra boxes of tissue from his upset patient closet. I kept asking him how and why he always got me to cry, but even with all the good money I paid him, I never got a really clear answer. My takeaway was that he was the one friend I could count on who never criticized me while I was wailing like a two-year-old. What a terrible fate I had been dealt! I had to pay somebody to be nice to me.

Even though Beth had treated me with kindness for years, I unconsciously blamed her for a few problems I had because she had the gall to get a facelift when she was so much younger than me. Now it's not unconscious any more. I'm angry that she did it and I've been squeamish about doing it and not squeamish about blaming Henry. I know in my heart that if I took a strong stand with him, he'd give in. My problem is due to my own doubts about the whole operation. I think about Beth's surgeries and the results. I still haven't figured out how she is able to empty her tear ducts with her skin so tight on her face. A loose wrinkle wouldn't dare expose itself on the mug of that fashion plate sister of mine. However, I'd heard rumors that Beth's husband was behind her cosmetic rejuvenation efforts. I learned the truth of this from Julie Sue two years before the wedding, when all the relatives got together at Julie's home to celebrate her daughter's high school graduation. Beth hadn't arrived yet, so she became the subject of the conversation. I was helping out with the appetizers in Julie's kitchen before the party started and we had a chance to talk privately.

"Marlene, I've got interesting news about Beth. Wait till you hear this and wait till you see her!"

"What now? Did they buy another house?"

"No, but Howard gave her a present for their anniversary -- a gift card for Fifty Thousand Dollars."

"Julie, there's no such thing."

"I'm exaggerating, of course, but Howard paid to have Beth get a full facelift, ears flattened, neck tightening, the whole works. She went to a New York surgeon who does these surgeries on celebrities."

"Did you see her?"

"I saw her and she looks like Beth, but ten years younger."

"Fifty Thousand for only ten years off?" That's 5G's a year. For them it's pocket change. How does she feel after going through all that?"

"Well, you'll get a chance to ask her. She should be here soon. And how would you feel?"

"I'd feel like buying out Nordstrom's designer department. Unfortunately, I'd have to wait until all the clothes were marked down ninety percent."

"Me too."

"Now why did Howard come up with that? Wasn't he happy with her looks before the renovation?"

"Well, I can't say, but I know how he does things. Howard trades in his car every year and I happen to know that he has a private chef on the payroll!"

"You're not suggesting he's had thoughts of trading in something besides a car?"

"You mean like a wife? How the hell do I know? Maybe he has something going on the side."

"Do you know something you're not telling me, like is he making sure the old lady's face gets fixed up so it doesn't cramp his style?"

"Marlene, you're kind of hard-assed about how Beth lives, aren't you?"

"Who me? No, she treats me very nicely. Every year we get an anniversary gift that makes Henry's head spin. Last month it was a painting with an engraved title on a gold leaf frame."

"You too? What was the subject of the painting?"

"It was a beautiful waterfall with trees and plants overhanging and mist rising from the lake below."

"Oh, we got a painting just like that for our anniversary. What was your engraved title?"

"It was called "Falls Over Lake Lucy."

"Well, ours was different -- it said "Falls Over Lake Horatio."

"Julie, I hate to mention this, but the two family dogs are named Lucy and Horatio."

"So did they name the dogs after the two lakes?"

"No, I think it was the other way around. They had those two dogs before they bought that big place with all the acres. They have several waterfalls on their property in Duchess County. I guess if someone owns a waterfall and a whole lake, they can name it whatever they want."

I heard Julie Sue sighing. Then she spoke slowly, her voice choking up a bit. "You know, that's quite an estate they have. Their own set of lakes and a golf green and an Olympic-sized pool and all. Howard not only knows how to make a buck -- he sure knows how to spend it!"

"I keep telling myself that happiness is just a guy named Joe, but my husband's name is Henry. I better get back to my little world. There's dirty laundry and dust piling up, just waiting for my attention."

I couldn't help wondering if I would be insulted if my husband gave me money and told me to get a facelift. It would suggest that he didn't fancy the way I was showing up for him as I aged. At least I was the one begging for a better face.

Beth visited us the month after the wedding as she stopped by our place in Florida on her way to shop at Worth Avenue in Palm Beach. She finally learned that a sculpture in one of her houses was sculpted by Robin and that Howard had forgotten to mention to her that he'd bought the piece. We talked all about her facelift, which was now a couple of years weathered. She had undergone more than one surgery, although Julie Sue was wrong about the ears being flattened. They still stuck out from her perfect face, but her dangling diamond earrings were so enormous that their extra weight pulled her ears closer. Her clinging hairstyle helped too. I assumed that a supplementary ear job was scheduled. The more invasive of Beth's procedures had been to correct her chin and jowls and another which involved moving her eyelids around. With some careful carving, they went from half mast to a new wide-eyed expression. Her surgeries had definitely enhanced her appearance and her alertness. Now everybody who spoke to Beth didn't have to be concerned that she was falling asleep. Her hazel irises beneath her contacts were now fully exposed, with nary a seam showing where there were some hidden stitches.

Mixed emotions haunted me after I saw Beth up close. I always thought she was a pretty woman prior to her surgery, and I felt ashamed that I looked for reasons to hate her for her good fortune. How could I be so petty when I wasn't exactly suffering from malnutrition or having to frequent thrift stores for my clothes and accessories? Also, Beth seemed anxious to please me. She chose her words carefully in suggesting she'd be happy to give me pointers about what was involved in a facelift operation..

"Marlene, dear," she always began, "do you have any interest in learning about how my surgeon performed my cosmetic rejuvenation?"

"I do, but Henry's against it for me, and nothing's changed. You had a great result, but I guess I'm not up to fighting with my husband when he keeps telling me I look like Elizabeth Taylor. Thanks anyway."

Of course, I was lying to Beth. Henry never told me that. He said that he thought I was a nice-looking mature woman. I didn't like the word "mature" the way he used it. He told me I had a sense of humor like the comedian Jerry Lewis.

"I should call you 'Jerry' because for a woman you're pretty good at telling jokes."

Henry was big with the term, "for a woman." It was his tricky way of putting me in my place. He figured it was harmless. It was. I never punched him out.

"Sure, call me anything you like. 'Jerry' is fine and dandy." I knew he was trying to soften me up. Once I shot back, "Yeah, when you call me 'Jerry,' you really mean "Jerry Atric." Gradually I was arriving at a decision to wait for the right moment to renew my plea. Then came Robbie's startling sex operation, an event which threw Henry and me into a pit of disarray and worry. After the wedding I was back in combat mode and was more determined than ever to have the facelift. I was going to get my hands on the money for the operation if I had to hide dollar bills in hidden Thermos jars.

36

"I've got "Post-Traumatic Wedding Stress Syndrome," I said to my bathroom mirror.

"Marlene, were you saying something? I thought you were talking to an inanimate object, and I didn't want to interrupt."

"Honey, I need something to perk me up that's healthy."

"Stop talking to mirrors and start exercising. We have all these ponds and sidewalks in our community, and you could do vigorous walking and then you'd get a chance to talk to your reflection in the water."

"I **was** thinking about exercise. You're so perceptive, dear. I'm thinking of taking up water aerobics with a group that works out in our community pool. I've heard it's good for the leg muscles."

"My impression of it was that it's for women who really want to gab and gossip. I saw a group of them one day in the pool. They were exercising their mouth muscles."

"It's not for just women -- it's open to all."

"Count me out. I used to do laps back and forth, but there's too much socializing in that pool. Remember that collision I had with that old woman a few years ago? She thought I was getting fresh."

"The one who was lying on her back on that blow-up Spiderman raft? I remember. That was embarrassing. Well, you don't have to worry about her any more. She moved into a retirement home."

I watched Henry's face for a reaction because he didn't like to hear about older people moving into those places. His strategy was to exercise and eat healthy until the day when he would have to be carried out bodily.

"Moving into a retirement home is good for some folks, but I know of too many people who died there because they stopped being active. It's not for me."

"Well, let's not talk about dying, then. I'm just getting started with my next career -- body building for septuagenarians. First I'll learn how it's done and then I'll teach it."

"You could use some limbering up."

"I've already signed onto those water aerobics sessions and I'm going to see if it works."

"Good for you. I'll even pay for a new bathing suit for your new shape if you like. What's the style now for women? Two piece or one piece?"

"Four."

"Sorry if I don't understand the new styles. You have to cover the tits, the bottom parts and what else?"

"One-piece suit, skirt, matching cover-up and accessories bag."

"I'll pay for just the part that covers your basics."

"Are you teasing me? You'll pay for the whole thing!"

"I was teasing. By the way, Robin left a message for you."

"I know. She wants to visit us. She's leaving the plant for good."

"When would she come?"

"Later this month. She's going to call and let us know."

"I've got a fishing trip coming up. Maybe It's better if I'm not around that whole time, at least while you two do your togetherness."

"Robin's had her hair styled by some classy outfit."

"Is she going to take a woman's bathing suit, I wonder?"

"Don't say 'woman's bathing suit,' like there's another kind for an adult female. Anyway, she is."

I heard Henry mutter under his breath something that sounded like, "Sure, she can now wear one of those tight-fitting woman's bathing suits with no nuts to worry about."

"Henry, I notice you're finally calling her a she."

He didn't answer. His unpacking was done, so he left the room while I probed for space in my closet for my new dresses. With my emotional attachment to every item of clothing I had ever worn and cherished, it was a painful experience. Finally, I seized on several shirt-waists and petite hemmed slacks which were purchased for a fatter woman. They had to go. I would find time to cry about my loss at a later time. What was harder? Getting rid of fat clothes or managing my feelings about Henry's avoidance of his feelings? The closet issue paled in importance when I thought about my own issues regarding Robin's visit. It was obvious that Henry wasn't amenable to being present, so we would be planning our own activities without him. Henry walked back into the bedroom. "Say, if you're into exercise, dear, why don't you go to the gym in our clubhouse? We're already paying the association dues, so it's free."

"I don't know. I'd have to look at all those lean muscular sweaty women wearing sports bras and skin-tight shorts and be embarrassed that I ever let myself get out of shape."

"Oh, sorry, I thought the people who go to the gym go because they think they are out of shape. My mistake. Anyway, you don't have to do pushups or lift barbells. Just start with the easy stuff. You're looking more and more like a young dish."

"I've lost twenty pounds and I still feel more like a soup tureen."

"Just keep up the good work. I know it's not easy. Say, what's in that bag over there in the corner?"

"My old stuff for the Salvation Army."

"Why honey, that's terrific. Tell you what -- let's go out to dinner tonight. How about that Chinese buffet you love?"

"That's an all-you-can-eat restaurant."

"So?"

"Well, they make you pay full price even if you eat less than you can."

"Would you rather go to a place that charges by the bite?"

"That's probably where Beth goes for lunch."

"I know what's on your mind, Marlene. You still want a facelift. Like your sister had."

"Maybe I do, Henry, maybe I don't. But when I do it, I'd like it to be my idea."

A relentless search of my dresser drawers proved fruitful. Tucked under two embarrassing fifties style one-piece swimsuits, which had to be held up with straps that tied around the neck, was a bathing suit ensemble that I had worn about five years ago. After about three minutes of wiggling, I got into it. Life wasn't so bad after all. Then I examined my face. My cheeks were less cheeky. My neck skin was worse and I noticed a few new lines and creases around my chin and became depressed again. I was ready to take extreme measures, like taking to my bed or hiding under it. I was too old to run away from home. Then I began to understand what was going on with me. My worries weren't about things I could control, like my weight, my fitness or any cosmetic surgery I might have. It was about Robin. It was about how unfair it was that a son of mine was born with something that made him unhappy about his birth sex. I couldn't stop regurgitating some old stuff still in my head:

Nothing is fair. Life is unfair. Being a short plump woman isn't fair, but I'm stuck with my height, so that's that. But Robbie was this handsome guy with the best physique in the world. If he had been puny or ordinary-looking, maybe I would have understood. Why on earth any man ever wants to live as a woman is still an enigma where I'm concerned. Wait till Robin really gets into dating! Will she be surprised! Wait till some guy tries to proposition her and force himself, like in a car on the way home! Well, the guy would have to be bigger than her, but there's always some giant clod out there! Two years of being a broad and she'll run back to the sex reassignment people and ask for her boy gonads to be sewed back on. Maybe she'll want her new tits changed back to her old hairy chest as soon as she realizes how quickly even the best brassieres wear out. Oh, and then, if she keeps her tits, when the sewed on boobs start to sag, because by nature, breasts get dragged downhill by the same ghoulish force that made that part of my neck underneath my chin droop, then Robin will see that having the surgery was a poor choice. Or was it? Maybe I'm still pissed off about my own female issues and my mood has nothing at all to do with Robin!

I suddenly felt hungry and it wasn't mealtime. Did I need comfort food or just comfort? What was a nearly seventy-one-year-old woman to do when issues were pressing in on her? What could another visit to the shrink do? Shrinks didn't know everything. I ran to my computer and clicked on my "Philosophical Cons" icon and began to write whatever popped into my head.

"Dear nobody: Henry isn't living in the world of the present -- he is living in the past. Sex reassignment surgery is here to stay. I've taken the time to read up on all the developments, even though I had to probe material that wasn't exactly mainstream. LGBT hard facts are no longer confined to focus groups. There's a lot of information out there on the Internet. Henry still doesn't believe in hormonal variations that have a major effect on gender. He never heard of the medical term "gender dysphoria." Until I got that earth-shaking first call from Robbie, I didn't understand any of this either. Henry and I are a microcosm of society's ongoing debate about choices people make when given the technology to choose. What did women do before we had effective birth control? We fucked around and worried ourselves to death. Now we fuck around and have new worries about diseases and unstable relationships, while the men feel gleeful when they're able to swallow erection pills when the moment is ripe. Technology really changes things, but are they good changes? Some are and some aren't. It's up to the individual. Robin is very brave. I want to be that brave."

I paused to read over my words and they made me feel dizzy. The rest of what I wrote was so extemporaneous, I could have adlibbed my way to becoming a ringleader of one of those 12-step groups. I'd name the group "Generation Gap Sufferers Anonymous." That title would include not only parents of people like Robin, but also wives of people like Henry who couldn't stomach the new lifestyles of their kids.

"Most women my age are enjoying their grandchildren's antics while I'm struggling with self-pity and denial. At least I'm making an attempt to rally. Exercising in a swimming pool would do me some good. Maybe I should also go to the gym. Let's see, where did I put that combination lock I used to have for a gym locker? Where did I put my fashionable Nike sweats I once worked out in? OK, so I only wore them twice. Tomorrow is another day. I'm going

to pretend I'm a beach blanket cutie and have fun. Say there, do I still need a shrink? I'm in heaven right where I am! Wow, did I just change my mood!"

I closed my new file in Philosophical Cons and shut the computer off. The phone rang in my cubbyhole. It was Robin telling me she was ready to flee Ohio's forecasted cooler than average late fall weather. When we spoke she seemed happy that she had earned enough money from her sculpture sales to pay back half of her loans from Linda and still have money in the bank to pay for the trip. I began to feel a lot better about how things were going with her new life. She seemed pretty upbeat when we spoke.

"Mom, I'm thinking of driving to Florida next weekend, and would you really like me to spend several days with you? Is it going to be a problem with Dad?"

"Uh, I'll have to check Henry's calendar. I know he's got a week-long fishing trip coming up. But I want you to come. We'd love it. Listen, just come when it's convenient. I'm going to be spending time in our community pool, so bring a bathing suit. Uh, did you buy girl clothes for that yet?"

"I've got everything -- even my man boxer shorts if I ever need to get out of those nylon things for a day or so. Oh, wait until you see my new car. It's an Audi. Now that I've left the job, I don't feel compelled to drive a GM model any more!"

"Sounds like a sort of a reverse perk."

"I'll let you know what time I'll be arriving. I'll get a motel halfway there."

"Oh Robin?"

"Yes?"

"How's your health?"

"You mean, how is my transition, don't you? Be straightforward. It's OK to ask me whether I still look like a man in a girl's bathing suit."

"Actually, I meant the healing of your last surgery."

"I'm in fairly good shape, with a few issues that should disappear over time. It's a shame that so much of the transition is about money."

"I really get that, Robin."

"Oh, here's some good news -- I just received two offers from major magazines."

"Which ones? And if they're like Cosmo or Hustler, don't do it!"

"I shouldn't mislead you like that, Mom. Sorry. No, it's two art magazines. To give them interviews about my sculptures."

"You had me going there, the way you said it. I thought some girlie rag wanted you to model a bikini!"

"I will probably be asked to do that too, eventually, but that's for somebody who's desperate to pay the rent. I'm finally over that crunch. These publications are interested in profiling my success story. I'm almost a celebrity."

"And I'm almost a mental case the way Henry's after me to exercise. But he's right this time."

"Do it for yourself -- not for what he thinks."

"I am doing it for myself. He'd have me hiking up mountains if I let him. Linda does mountains."

"Linda's a compulsive dieter and an exercise freak. Your pool exercise is better for you."

"Thanks, Robin. Listen, call me when you have the approximate time you'll get here so I can be at the house to let you in."

Well, and well, well, well! Robin was finally going to visit us as a complete woman. Let's see, besides shopping for clothes for both of us, maybe we could go to the Everglades. I could get exercise at a place like that. We could maybe take one of those bicycle rides past the alligators. Robin's never even seen a live alligator. A dead one, yes. It's covering one of her new purses.

37

I had been exercise averse for the last twenty years, or at least since my days of long distance running and bike-riding had turned into computer gazing and park bench gossiping. Oh well, how bad could it be? The water in the pool around my body would be all sloshing around, so most of my limbs could fake it if the challenge proved too tough. I was both nervous and excited that Robin was about to make her first extended visit to our home as a she. The timing of her arrival wasn't clear because she was driving, but she expected to be knocking on our door in the evening of the first day of my aerobics session. That would give me time to plan a few safe and private activities for the two of us.

I wondered if Henry was right about the aerobics participants being all women, so I asked him again why he thought that.

"You should do a brisk walk over to the pool area after you check the clubhouse schedule, honey. It's the equivalent of three blocks and will help loosen you up."

"Thanks, dear. But what I really wanted was a direct answer."

I was ready to do the aerobics and the day had arrived. Some of our residents had no qualms about walking over to the pool in swim attire, but they were usually in pairs or groups. Henry was busy in the bedroom packing for his fishing trip, so he wouldn't be able to hear the garage door creaking open. I drove over to the clubhouse in my bathing suit where the pool could be accessed through a secured gate. The accelerator and brake pedals felt funny on my bare right foot. There were available spaces in the parking lot, so I chose the closest one to the pool complex. It felt weird getting out of the car so scantily dressed. I had brought rubber beach clogs to shield my feet from the frying-pan-hot concrete. It was a challenge to put them on while behind the steering wheel, but I managed it. As I locked the car door and stuck the keys in my tote bag, I saw two maintenance men eyeing me. I didn't want any guys judging my shape just then, but I quickly discovered that the aerobics group included six ladies and one man. That man appeared to be over seventy, but even seventy-year-old dudes could be aggravating and judgmental. This one seemed strangely out of place. I thought, "What the hell is that bald overfed guy with the stupid Batman swim trunks doing here?" He was standing at the shallow end and I could tell by his paunch that he must have spent a great deal of time eating delicatessen food. The look of his puffy cheeks and the expression on his face went with a big fat cigar, but not even the lax pool manager would allow smoking in the water. All six women in the class seemed to be keeping their distance from him. It wasn't a good omen. His name was Sol and he had no sooner asked my name and introduced himself when I sensed that he was up to no good. My fears were confirmed when my back was turned toward the instructor. Suddenly I felt a pair of hands around my waist and a raspy male voice whispering: "You're the shortest lady here -- let me help you float a little higher."

I could feel his hands traveling upstairs but I wasn't about to allow this old geezer to get the thrill of a feel, so I quickly extricated myself and attempted to be tactful. "Uh, Sol, is it? No thanks. I can manage without help."

"I was just trying to give you a lift, honey."

"Save it for the nightclub dance contest, Sol. Please don't do that again." What I really wanted to say to him was, "If you try to put one hand on me after this, I'll put one of those little lizards in your shorts and see how you like it darting around your dick." I kept my mouth shut and aimed my most contemptuous expression at the jerk.

Sol seemed upset and swam to the deep end of the pool. I guessed he'd had enough water aerobics for the day. I turned my head to see if he was going to stay in place. The creep was holding onto the far edge of the pool, leering at me like I was his prey. The guy in the first Batman movie would have been less threatening. I swam over to the other ladies in the class and one of them seemed to know what was going on.

"That guy is not supposed to be in this group, but I guess they can't keep him out of the pool unless one of us complains. Did he try to touch you?"

"Oh yeah, he tried to feel me up right off the bat. Can't they do something?"

"As long as he stays on the other end, maybe leave him alone. We know his wife and she's a very nice person, and he's probably harmless if he's not encouraged."

"Thanks, I appreciate that. By the way, my name is Marlene, what's yours?"

"It's Sandy. After the class we all hang around those two tables with the blue umbrellas over in the corner there and have iced drinks. I hope you join us."

"I'd love to."

My pulse, which had been racing with anger and embarrassment, seemed to quiet down. Some women would have immediately complained to the pool manager, but I was new and Sol seemed likely to stay glued to his spot. I began to engage with the group and followed the water moves, but couldn't get the incident off my mind. I would have liked to kick the bastard in the groin, but realized it would have been almost impossible to do with any effect while in a swimming pool. After about ten minutes, while I attempted to perform the exercises, one of the other women said something to Sandy, and she edged over to me and told me that a very tall lady with dark hair was standing nearby next to the deck chairs and seemed to be gesturing toward me. I turned around to look too hastily and nearly swallowed a quart of chlorinated pool water. It took me but a fraction of a minute to recognize Robin, big as life and as frighteningly unexpected as a gorilla entering your sauna wearing pink sweats. The sight of her accelerated my heartbeat. Sandy thought I was choking and needed help, so I let her think that. She didn't need to know that I was having a near heart attack because Robin's unexpected arrival at the pool had caught me off guard. My statuesque daughter was wearing a two-piece black bathing suit with red, yellow and green neon colored stripes. The stripes glowed where the sunlight hit. Robin had determined to dress courageously. The bottom of the suit was skin-tight and the matching bra was fairly low cut, revealing a hint of cleavage. She looked fetching, but I worried about whether the electrolysis or whatever he had done had been thorough. Robbie had been quite hairy.

If any of the ladies had doubts about Robin's femininity, none were apparent. Sandy was very helpful and said, "Your friend seems to want to talk to you, Marlene. Maybe she'd like to join us. Why don't you greet her? There's only one more exercise and then we'll be gathering at that table next to that big pink hibiscus plant. See where we've stashed all our gear?"

"Thanks, I see it and we'll do that. That's my daughter. She's just arrived from out of town, and I didn't expect her until later this afternoon. I'll go over and talk to her. She might have made some arrangements for us."

I scrambled up the railed steps and walked over to Robin. She was smiling and seemed at ease, but I was worried. I couldn't help glancing at the crotch on her tight-fitting bathing suit bottom. It didn't have a bulge -- not even a hint of one where that package used to be. I didn't notice any indication on her chest that it had been hairy, but there was a redness that looked like a dry skin condition. *Dry skin on my child? Oh no, get the Vaseline! My kid has to have healthy skin! My memory of being a new mommy and coddling that cute little weenie and scrotum came back to me. If I had only known what that boy was about. And when he had it all removed, what did they do with it? We could have had it bronzed, like his baby shoes. I would have been the only mother in the country with a shelf that held a pair of metallic copper-toned shoes next to a matching metallic adult male organ. It could have really stood out among my collection of figurines. Now why am I going crazy again! I thought I had this thing handled!*

"Mom, are you happy to see me? I need you to be happy about how I look."

"I'm happy, dear, but I was nervous about seeing you in a bathing suit. You look good."

"The redness on my chest will go away. I have a really good cream for that. Is it real noticeable?"

"No, it's because I'm your mother. Mothers see things others don't. You look just fine. And I'm so excited about the sculpture! I'm not sure we can talk about it publicly. What do you think?"

"Let me be the judge of that, Mom. There are people who think I've exploited my sex-change operation, so I'm careful."

"Let me give you a big hug."

Robin hugged me and laughed at how short I looked next to her. She hadn't lost a single inch in height and was wearing wedgies.

"Robin, did you know I was in this class?"

"No, Dad was still there at the house and was getting ready to leave for his fishing trip. He just told me you were at the pool. I thought I'd do a few laps. And he was really nice. He apologized for the conflict in his schedule."

"I'm glad. He still needs time to adjust. Now, let's see, I wasn't sure you'd be comfortable being introduced to the girls."

"I'd be comfortable. Say, I think your friends want me to join them. I see them waving at us."

"Oh, tell them you can't -- that you just came for a sunbath or something."

"You're worried they'll figure something out. Don't worry. I promise you they'll never know. Let's both join them."

"Well, when you go in the pool, watch out for that guy at the far end -- see him? His name is Sol -- he's a sort of a sex maniac and a pain in the ass. He might put the make on you."

"That guy over there? I could deck him with one hand. He looks old and soft."

I called over to the ladies assembled at the tables. "Coming, people, my daughter will swim a few laps and then join us for a little while. I'll go get some lemonade for us."

My heart pounded with its usual nervous beat when I was unsure of myself. Robin was so much more relaxed than I was. I saw her talking to Sol for a bit and wondered about the content of their conversation. Suddenly I heard some shouting and saw splashing in the water. Sol's head was missing. Then I watched as he bobbed up and swam away. There was Robin, adjusting her top. Had Sol tried something? She swam over to the edge and then hoisted herself out of the water without needing to climb up the steps. Her athleticism was too much for me, but nobody seemed to notice anything strange. Robbie had always been good at chin-ups. Now I understood a lot more about her new self. Henry had warned me that she would still have male DNA attributes. Had he read the medical report? Something in it suggested that a newly transformed woman who had been athletic could still defend herself with a man's strength. My daughter was a tall shapely pretty woman with great hair and perhaps she might never have to be concerned about date rape.

While she was dragging over an empty chair to seat herself, two of the women did seem to glance at me and then back at her. I hoped it was because the difference in our heights was so dramatic.

"What's your name, Marlene's daughter?" That question was from a woman named Carolyn, who seemed impressed at how my Robin looked in a swim suit. I could tell by her expression that she was somewhat amazed at Robin's body proportions. Robin's breasts were perfect for her build. I wondered if it was right to use the term "build" for a girl -- maybe "figure" was better. I had to watch myself carefully because it was so easy to slip and use the wrong descriptive words. It was hard enough getting acclimated to the water moves. Talking about Robin's operation wasn't something I could stomach, especially among women I had just met. I felt my knees twitching and wondered if Robin sensed my discomfort, but she didn't seem to need my intervention as she responded to girl talk.

It was when Carolyn and Robin began to discuss where she had bought her bathing suit that I began to fidget in my chair. I concentrated on connecting my lips to the straw in my glass of lemonade. Robin spoke freely, in her strong baritone voice. "Do you know where I can visit a good dive shop? I need some snorkeling gear."

"Oh, just look on the Internet. They're all over this area."

"Thanks. Maybe my mother can drive over to a place where they have those wonderful reefs I've seen advertised. I'm crazy about the fish and sea creatures around here."

"Oh that's great that she'll do that for you. We've all just met your mother, and we're delighted she decided to join our aerobics class. Will you be staying for long?"

"About a week."

"You play Mah Jongh?"

"I do."

I was listening to the conversation and just then began to cough and was gasping for air. I had come very close to choking on a piece of lemon.

As we returned to the house in my car, Robin mentioned that she had to keep using a special defoliating cream, and that she had brought a whole bag of medications. She felt fairly certain that none of the women in the group suspected anything. "Mom, you're way too worried about me. I'm doing just fine. Didn't you hear one of the women ask me if I was planning to stay for a few days?"

"Sort of, but mainly I was just trying to keep from falling off that patio chair. I heard you tell her you played Mah Jongh. It really surprised me!"

"I learned while I was in the hospital. It's a very easy game."

"I also heard her ask you if you were married or going with somebody. And then another lady asked how I had borne such a tall daughter when I was so much shorter. She was the one who kept staring at your body and giving me hives. You gave just the right answer. Talked about Dad's side of the family. I don't think any of them figured you out, do you?"

"Probably not. I thought the woman who asked all the questions was envious of my designer swimsuit. I've noticed that older women are more likely to notice what another woman is wearing than wonder whether she's just had sex reassignment surgery."

"I never thought of that. What else have you learned? Like how do you fend off lascivious men, like that jerky guy, Sol? It looked like you two went at each other!"

"That asshole? He never stopped asking for my measurements, like it was everyday conversation. I would never go up to a woman I had just met and tell her I thought she was the most enticing D cup I had ever laid eyes on."

"You're not a D cup, are you?"

"No, a small C. Anyway, I told him to fuck off and dunked him. He got the message!"

"Did he try to lay a hand on you?"

"He tried. He must have known I was your daughter. Even after I told him to bug off, he said he didn't mind a mother and daughter act -- in fact it was his fantasy. He won't bother you again."

"Oh goody. Robin, you're wonderful."

"Today did go well, but I'm not out of the woods. I'm sure there will be some potholes ahead."

"Assholes, potholes, sinkholes, Florida has everything. What would you like for dinner?"

"What did you plan, Mom?"

"Would you like to go out or should I cook?"

"Either way. If we go out, let me treat. And how about that Chinese buffet you're always talking about?"

38

I circled around the perimeter of the rows of offerings at the Mandarin's Table. Despite my misgivings about my sensible eating resolve, Robin and I had arrived at the grandest and oiliest Asian buffet in the neighborhood. There were too many taste-tempting aromas and sizzling selections in plain sight for a weak person to handle. My stomach, my nose and my brain began having it out with each other. I knew I had to avoid the egg rolls, ribs, General Tzo's chicken, stuffed clams, fried rice, Buffalo wings and pizza for the American slobs, shrimp fritters and eighty percent of everything else in those steaming trays. That left the salad bar section and the steamed veggies for the tough-minded dieters, who probably had no business being in there. Hardly any of the patrons seemed to curb their appetites as they loaded fifteen or more samples of different varieties on their plates. The only folks who practiced restraint were the employees. I watched them scurrying around, getting serious exercise bringing in tray after tray from the kitchen. The young lady who worked our table had small hips, a tiny waist, miniscule feet and delicate hands. Surely she never indulged in anything from that buffet. I figured that her mother probably cooked her some broth, plain rice and seaweed for dinner before she came to work.

I'd agreed to having dinner at such a tempting place because I wanted to please Robin. At the same time, I forced myself to use some common sense. If the small-hipped server could live on seaweed and other vegetables and balance it with a couple of spoonfuls of rice, so could I.

My first and only entree plate would have astonished even my former Weight Watchers leader. I brought it to our table and never flinched as I watched Robin approach her seat. Her plate was stacked so high it was obscene. That moment was my ordeal by calories. Would I emerge victorious or slink away from this den of culinary iniquity with my self-esteem reduced to dark matter? I surveyed the population of customers and about half of them were overweight. The Asian customers were not among that half. If slimness was a cultural thing, it didn't explain my own family. I needed a new plan to replace the former plan, which would replace the plan before that. Maybe part of the fault was with the fork.

"Waitress? Miss?"

"Yes, Ma'am?"

"Please bring me a set of chopsticks."

Robin was amazed. "Mom, I've never seen you use chopsticks before."

"I think they'll slow me down. I eat too fast."

"You think it's the speed of your munching that puts on weight? That's a new one."

"Oh, thank you, Miss." I ripped off the paper and practiced using the chopsticks with a clump of spinach. Most of it fell back on the plate before it reached my mouth. I needed to work on my technique. While Robin finished eating everything on her plate, I was still working on the rice, grain by grain. Soon I was able to hold onto five or six grains and shovel them in.

"Mom, is that the way you're going to eat at home?"

"Maybe, that is, if I move to China."

"Look, it's not your nature to be that thin. I know what you're going through. It's tough!"

"Did I know what you were going through for all these years?"

"That's different."

"It's all a kind of suffering we do to manage our lives, Robin. There's no way to measure what each person's hell is compared to another's."

"That's good philosophy, Mom. How's your meal?"

"Very tasty. I especially liked that one little green morsel I manipulated."

"What was it?"

"It was a snow pea, singular. I couldn't manage the whole pod, so I cut it up to eat it one pea at a time."

"Mom, you shouldn't go from one extreme to the other. You don't have to starve yourself."

"Your father accuses me of eating like somebody's going to whisk my meal away."

"He's not right about everything. I'm proud of you."

"And I'm proud of you too, Robin. I had my doubts about your operation, but it seems you've acquired a lot of confidence. That certainly didn't come from me."

"Yes it did, Mom. You always stuck up for me."

"I only remember those years after you passed the six foot tall mark. I actually contacted my obstetrician to make sure he hadn't mixed up his deliveries. You're really my kid."

"Of course I am. I have your eyes and your chin shape."

"Yes, and now you also have my boobs and my ear lobes. Now we can go shopping together at the same departments."

As we were waiting for the check to arrive, Robin handed me a new surprise. "Mom, I'd enjoy playing Mah Jongh with those women. Don't you play?"

"A long time ago. I don't any more."

"I've always enjoyed games. While I was in the hospital I was in considerable pain for awhile, and the nurse told me that some of the recuperating ladies had gotten a couple of tables up and were looking for another player. So I watched them for awhile and spent some time checking the rules, and, voila, I was playing!"

"I can just see you with the bams and the cracks and the gossip!"

"I'll have to get used to the gossip. When I'm trying to win at a game, I work so hard the sweat pours off of me."

"My impression of the way typical women play games is that one part of the curiosity center of the brain works on the latest dirt to share while another part is moving tiles around. I'm not sure why they do that."

"To distract the opposition."

"I was so naive when I played, and I lost a lot. You're probably better at games."

"I don't know about that, but I was able to beat the women in the hospital without much trouble, once I got the hang of it. I noticed they did a lot of talking not related to the game, like who suffered the most with her hysterectomy. It drove me a little nuts, but after awhile I found myself getting more talkative. I think it could be catching."

"If that were true, then Henry would have already caught it after forty-nine years of marriage."

"You have a point. By the way, when I talk about what I did in the hospital, does it make you uncomfortable?"

"Oh, not much, as long as you don't discuss too many details of the operation."

"I have to get used to people saying to me: "Gee you do pushups really well, and for a woman! Did you do body building?"

"But Robbie, I mean, Robin, you did do body building! And don't you still do it?"

"Of course, but there's a few girls at my gym who have incredible muscular development. In fact, I finally got up the courage to discuss my surgery. I had to because in February, I was still wearing a man's gym outfit and then when I came back in June, I was wearing a sports bra with women's shorts."

"I'm almost afraid to ask you about your use of the locker room. I'd better not. But didn't you have to switch from the men's to the women's?"

"Of course."

"How did you, well, about those girls you knew at the gym before, you know, before -- how did they take it?"

"It wasn't so bad. One of the women who always began her workout hitting a punching bag came up to me and confessed that she's transgender and considering having the operation to become a complete male. She's scared, of course, but there's a lot of group support out there today and more doctors now who do that sort of thing."

"Robin, somehow talking to you is something like watching one of those new lifestyle movies."

"Lots of people think of it as science fiction. They can't believe it really works."

"Henry doesn't even want me to have a facelift."

"He's relieved he's gone away fishing because he's still very resistant. It's pretty obvious."

"Actually, I think he left because he didn't want to hear two women chatting rather than just one wife talking to herself."

"Sure, Dad doesn't like being outnumbered!"

"Give him time, give him time. Let's get back to the subject of what you'll talk about during Mah Jongh."

"Actually, I'd like to tell them about my sculpture, but then they'd know I had the sex change."

"Better let those older ladies who might be squeamish concentrate on their game."

"Okay, I'll be careful. Say, let's open our fortune cookies."

"Mine says, let's see, 'you have a wonderful story to tell.' What's yours?"

"It says, wow, listen to what mine says! It reads: 'You should always accept the way you are.'"

"Oh, we both have a "feel good" fortune. When was the last time anybody got a fortune that said: "You have big troubles ahead," or "Your days are numbered?"

The next morning Robin and I checked the event calendar before we made the decision to go in the pool again. We decided to visit a wetlands in the morning and swim in the afternoon. Luck was on our side because Sol wasn't there. Robin was a very strong swimmer. She had muscles like a male athlete -- maybe because she'd been a male athlete until recently. The fellow who had been maintaining the pool for years and knew everybody's business, including which family member was entitled to be there, was standing near the deep end watching her. I wondered what he was thinking, so I made my way over to him to extract some information.

"Hi, Dick, is it? Hi. Isn't my daughter some kind of swimmer!"

"Gee, that's your daughter? She looks so much like your son. Are they twins?"

"No, but everyone says that. He just couldn't get away this year."

"Oh. Well, all three of your children sure can swim!"

"You must have seen Linda when she was here. She used to win trophies when she was in college."

"I remember her. She was the one who was upset that the pool wasn't deep enough for a diving board. I told her where she could find a pool like that."

"You have an incredible memory. But how did you know that the swimmer over there was my daughter?"

"I'm the one who checks the clubhouse passes."

I waved goodbye to the maintenance guy before he could figure out that one and one didn't equal three. There had to be a way I could handle people's inquiries without having to dream up new lies. Anyway it was time for me to signal Robin that we needed to get back to the house if we were to enjoy one of my home-cooked meals. She hoisted herself out of the pool with the agility of one of those actors who played Tarzan.

"That was so refreshing, Mom. That quick swim really got my appetite stirred up. Say, mother dear, how about your chicken pie? I really miss your chicken pie. I know it's a lot of work, but I'll help you with the filling."

"Uh, of course, dear, what a nice offer."

"I wouldn't ask you to make it if it would tempt you too much."

"Oh, no, I still make it for Henry. It's no problem at all!" I felt obliged to please my daughter, but oh boy, did I feel like my whole dieting self was immersed in one desperate sacrifice after another. How was I going to resist having chicken pie, especially with that rich recipe I'd created some time ago? That's the trouble with being a mother, as well as a good cook. You have to keep feeding your kids the way they expect you to, and to top it off, you have to lie and go hungry or lie and eat secretly. I knew women who did both.

My next test was to deal with my discomfort sitting by the Mah Jongh foursome as a watcher. Robin's one slip during the game was when she took her eyes off her rack for a moment and scratched her crotch. One of the women noticed and looked embarrassed. I suffered a momentary nervous fit, but then relaxed. Why shouldn't a woman have an itch there? The Big Box drugstore had a whole shelf of anti-itch this and anti-itch that. I hardly knew these women, but their crotches had to itch once in awhile. It was the nature of the beast. As we returned to the house, I took care to be as tactful as possible.

"How can I say this, dear? Ladies don't scratch there in sight of others."

"It was a problem, Mom. I'm still not completely healed from my latest treatment."

"Maybe don't tell me about it. We're having dinner shortly."

39

Kids never stop needing a mommy, even the ones who have to switch locker rooms. Mommies aren't supposed to need their kids, even the mommies who did all the dirty work raising them. Robin and I had been getting acquainted with each other on her trip, but I still had issues.

"Robin, before you leave tomorrow, I have some pertinent questions I've been afraid to ask you about your life before your treatments and all the surgery."

"I think you want to know about why I made the big decision -- underlying reasons that weren't in the medical report."

"I do, but most of my ignorance on the subject of sex is because of the way I was brought up. In our day, if a person of marriageable age wasn't attracted to the opposite sex, our parents figured we just hadn't met the right person."

"I knew years ago that I didn't have an attraction to women the way I was supposed to."

"I always wondered when I was diapering you if I rubbed you the wrong way."

"Guilt, mother, guilt. Universal maternal guilt. They joke about Jewish Mother Guilt, but I've learned that most mothers in your generation thought they were doing things wrong. Mom, my problems weren't your fault! Dad was busy making a living. You tried to raise me the best you knew how."

"Wait a minute, if you're trying to psychoanalyze me, I want to lie down."

"Now you sound just like Dad."

"Nobody sounds just like Dad. We've been married nearly fifty years and I'm convinced he's the only one of his breed. They ought to put his brain in a jar, and figure out which portion of it has the attitude."

"Dad's a good man, but --"

"Don't you dare say he's set in his ways. I say he's set, but only like jello. If I shake him enough, he tends to fall apart, or even melt."

"What would he have been like around me if he hadn't gone fishing?"

"Less smelly, but he'd have found some project to work on, like paint the outside of the skeet shooting clubhouse or rip out a few old hedges and put in new ones. Oh, damn, I hear the phone ringing. Let me take it in the other room."

I needed to hear Robin's answer to why Robbie decided to go the full route and have the surgery. What I was hearing from him is something I already knew. He wasn't hot for girls, maybe never, maybe a little. I tried to think of my own girlhood fantasies. Maybe I once wanted to look at one of my girlfriends naked. Maybe everybody's a bit all cocked up when it comes to sex. Who on this earth knows how they are about intimacy until they start trying it out? I picked up the telephone in our bedroom and it was a wrong number. I needed to think before going back to twenty questions for Robin, so I kept holding the phone, like I was having a conversation. Then a lightning bolt hit me. The medical report that Robin had sent was incomplete. *Of course, it had to be incomplete, it was medical! I was no doctor! What I wanted to know was, what drove Robbie to decide he'd had enough of trying to live like a man?* I hung up the phone and returned to our tete a tete.

"Robin, It was one of my friends. Look, I'm trying to find out something basic. How did you know you were a woman in a man's body?"

"I didn't exactly know. I just knew that I was a miserable failure trying to be a man."

"Please, Robin, I'm trying to relate. Like all my life I've felt I've been a failure as a woman. I was attracted to boys, but I hated how they treated me. Then I got proposed to by Dad and he sounded like the best of all possible worlds. So guess what? He didn't treat me perfectly. I made do with what we had. Marriage with flaws. I still don't understand your misery versus my misery!

"I wasn't going to be happy ever pretending I was a man. I went to doctors, consultants, encounter sessions, psychologists specializing in alternative lifestyles, you name it!"

"Why didn't you just talk to me? Or Dad?"

"You forgot. I did."

"You didn't know all this when you moved out on your own?"

"Not really."

"When I try to understand you, I always go back to me. Maybe I'm not supposed to be an aging woman. I don't think like an old woman. But Henry doesn't want me to have a facelift. What the hell? If you can get yourself fixed up, why can't I?"

"You can. Do it, Mom."

Bam! Ding Dong! I remembered something! "Wait here, honey." I walked over to one of our drawers in the entertainment center and found an album in it which had an important picture of Robbie, when he was six years old. There was a date on the print. "Here, Robin, look at this photo!"

"Oh, I think I remember that one. I'm holding a Raggedy Andy doll, a boy doll you bought me because the Raggedy Ann one made the other kids laugh at me."

"Right. That's what you asked for as a Hanukah present!"

"Yeah, I liked dolls instead of guns. Dad bought me plastic guns before they were put on the endangered species list. You didn't believe me."

"I was embarrassed. I remember you wanted that Shopping Sheryl doll. Henry would have divorced me if I bought it for you."

"Mom, even if you weren't the Susan B. Anthony of the "Dolls For Boys" movement, I always thought you had the right instincts. And Dad was a typical husband, a good husband who loved you. You could have gotten him to do anything for you. You still can, dammit! You've got unused power!"

"Hey, who's the mother here? You're helping me more than I'm helping you!"

"Please don't keep score!"

"I like that power play idea. I'm going to use it! No more thinking my biggest leverage is the best way to wash the dishes. If Henry doesn't like the soap I buy, tough shit!"

Robin and I visited Lion Country Safari in Palm Beach County on the last day of her visit. Her favorite animals were the rhinos, but I preferred the chimps.

"Why are the chimps your favorite, Mom?"

"It's the way they do sex. Did you see the big one do the smaller one? The guy chimp and the girl chimp? Henry would have no qualms about describing how he could tell the difference between the boy and the girl. Then he makes a crack about the girl chimp never having a headache or it was too close to lunch or dinner." He got me to think I should act more like an animal."

"Chimps might have hands like people, Mom, but they don't become artists. Remember when I began to do pottery work? Dad thought my clay figure of Joan of Arc wouldn't sell. I took that as a command to forget about being an artist. Then later on, he would tell me to take my time about getting married. You would tell me that I should date a lot until I knew what I wanted."

"But did you know what you wanted?"

"Yes I did. I wanted to dress as a woman, have women as chums and not as sex partners. I wished I could live as a woman. I actually told that to Dad. He suggested I get a complete physical by one of his old fogey doctors, including a complete check of my head. I went to that doctor. He told me confidentially that I should go get laid by a prostitute. I tried it. It wasn't fun. She did all the work and I let her show me how to please her. But I couldn't get an erection. Should I draw you a diagram?

"I think you just did."

"Remember that girl, Karen? You kept telling me I should ask her out a second time."

"She was really cute. She really liked you!"

"Yeah, she tried to, uh, oh, she tried to undress me. I started to cry because I . . ."

"You don't have to go graphic. I get the picture. She was horny and you just needed a friend instead of a shtup. I figured you preferred a girl who was shy. Karen wasn't shy. She sent you love letters."

"You remember that? How did you know they were love letters?"

"The envelope had lipstick and lip marks on it."

"Oh, I didn't realize you were so involved!"

"I was interested! Look, you've inherited half of my, what, genes, chromosomes, whatever? You even look like me now, except for being skinnier! That's how I know I'm supposed to be thin. Something went haywire with my metabolism!"

"Your metabolism isn't haywire. Your cells know how to count calories and deduct for exertion. You eat for entertainment, or to soothe yourself, or something! You need to get out more and walk it off. Or be plump, who cares? Make a damned decision about what weight you like! Own it or lose it!"

"I now officially have a kid who's smarter than the parent. It makes me angry. I want to throw a pie in Henry's face sometimes! But not at you! I'm angry I hid some cheesecake in the corner of the fridge."

"Stop being angry at your weakness. I have a weakness too. I guess I'll always need Dad's approval. Not just his love."

Robin needed to get started on her long drive home. I could sense she was sorry she didn't try harder to talk about her problems with us years ago, and instead opted to enlist Linda's support. It was clear that she had become ripe and ready for having the operation. I listened as Robin refreshed me on the whole saga of her childhood again, the way that Henry took Robbie out in the woods to shoot squirrels and how Robbie started to cry because he loved the squirrels. He cried more than Linda ever did, and reminded me that Linda, who was five years younger, kept Robbie from being bullied. Everything Robin told me was helpful, but I would never have understood issues about a transgender child at that time.

Before she left, I gave her a homework assignment. I got her to promise she'd send me information about other trans people she knew or heard about and send them to me so I could feel wised up in my communications with Henry.

"Like stuff on the Internet, Mom, or magazine articles or TV spots?"

"Yes, keep me modernized, so I don't become like my ancestors or some of our socially backward friends."

"I will. I promise."

"I still know how to nag."

"Mom, I need to get back home. Let me go fix my makeup. I was crying a little while you were packing that "one for the road lunch" for me.

"You'd better call me when you get home safely! And don't forget that my kugel keeps. Put what you don't eat in the refrigerator. "

40

Thanksgiving weekend was approaching and I didn't feel like being thankful if I had to cook. Henry came to my rescue and said we would be invited out this year and I could put my holiday recipe cookbook back in the drawer. That book had an especially oily page dedicated to stuffing. Most of the other pages were oily also, but the ones that weren't oily were caked with frosting. The whole kitchen in our home contained evidence of heavy-duty use by a homemaker who conducted her meal preparation like a madwoman who didn't have time to wash her hands.

"Henry, where are you? I'd like to know who invited us! Henry??? Where the hell are you?"

I opened the front door to see if he had gone outside. In a few moments he appeared waving an envelope like it was a big refund check or one of his insurance company residuals. Neither was correct.

"Guess what?"

"I'm not in the mood to guess -- what's in that envelope?"

"An invitation. Here, you take it."

The envelope had been addressed to both of us in the style of script done by a professional calligrapher. Henry had already opened it and was smirking like he always did when he received written confirmation about his predictions.

"Marlene, did you read it?"

"Yes, it's a baby shower invitation from Beth and Julie Sue."

"Cissy had sex with Sherwin and it worked?"

"Most people celebrate the arrival of a child. You have a habit of celebrating the arrival of the dick inside the pussy."

"Did your visit with Robin teach you to talk like that?"

"No, I made it up myself. I got my ideas from the dirty old man I married."

"I'll be---- you surprise me! Anyway, you're going to be a great-aunt!"

"Doesn't it seem like they just returned from their honeymoon?"

"Are you kidding? She had to have conceived before she got fitted for her wedding gown. But nowadays, I hear it's the fashion. Nobody counts months any more. Don't leave the announcement on the pile of junk mail next to my fishing magazines. And let me know if you think you might want to actually go to the bash for the baby. It's in New York -- just a stone's throw plus thirteen hundred miles away."

"I'd like to go. Wait a minute. I just realized that the date of the shower is right around the time that Robin has a big gallery show in Soho. Oh, let's go to New York."

"I'm not going to any baby shower, especially one in New York."

"Why not?"

"Oh, the inconvenience. I hate flying. Et cetera."

"Well, what about Robin's big show? Wouldn't you want to go to that?"

"Let me think about it. If we're going to take a trip, I can think of other places I'd like to go."

"Come on Henry!" Men go to showers now."

"I said, I'll think about it."

"Henry, you're impossible."

"We're never going to be grandparents, I guess."

"No, but we have two successful children. Robin's sculpture income really took off last month."

"So I heard. There's a lot of well-heeled weirdoes out there, buying weirdo art."

"It was all because he had that "BoyIntoGirl" creature made into limited editions. The art-buying crowd bought them up like they were acquiring aphrodisiacs."

"I'll bet that some punk rockers with money brought those sculptures into their bedrooms and used them to jerk off to."

"You're disgusting, Henry. The sculptures are innovative. The original was not only titillating -- it was a knockout punch. Maybe she's the next Rodin or Michelangelo. Instead of one fig leaf to be put in place for the benefit of the modest set, it needs four."

"Uh, why four?"

"Dummy, the sculpture is a figure that is both a boy and a girl! Get it?"

"Oh, yeah, I get it. Say, I never knew that Robin had such enterprise in **her**. See, I only say 'her' now. At least all my financial training of HER paid off!"

"What training?"

"I tried to teach him the value of a dollar. He always seemed indifferent."

"That's when he was a guy who believed he was supposed to be a girl. Now that she's got the right physical attributes, she's been able to concentrate on essentials -- like being productive and making a good living. And that's not so terrible."

"At least I can take credit for it."

I ignored Henry's inference that I wasn't a good model for money management. "Sure -- and you still hardly speak to her."

"I spoke to her quite a bit when you didn't know about it. But go to New York? I don't know.

"Does your decision have anything to do with your dislike of Sherwin's family?"

Henry chose not to answer. He couldn't quite bring himself to admit he was intimidated by Sherwin's family wealth. "I'm going to get myself a snack. Maybe I'm getting just like you -- eating food when I really want to eat my heart out."

"I've stopped doing that."

"You look very nice. You're down at least twenty pounds? Or am I way off?"

"Like Cissy and her prematurely to be born child -- who's counting?"

41

I hated how high they installed microwave ovens in modern kitchens, especially when I had to clean ours.

"Don't builders and house designers realize that not all women are over five feet six? Henry? Did you hear me? Oh, where is that man? I thought he was standing by the dining room table."

The stepstool was awkward for me to use, but somehow I managed to avoid breaking my neck every time I mounted it, especially when my feet had to be on the higher step. Henry had a knack of being somewhere else when I needed him most. Didn't he realize that when I had to climb on something because I was so short, it was scary? What if I suffered from vertigo? Damn. And if I hadn't been so vertically challenged, I wouldn't have spilled spaghetti sauce all over that revolving tray. Double damn.

"Henry, can you come here and help me?"

I was screeching, but this was serious. I almost dropped the glass tray and now I was afraid I had twisted my ankle. No Henry came forth. Gingerly, I descended the stool, first one step, then the bottom one and, whoa, I was standing on the floor -- ready to lie down from exhaustion. The crick in my ankle, if real, disappeared amid my other complaints. I heard a faint call from the bedroom just as I cast a longing eye at the sofa.

"Marlene, can you come in here for a moment?"

"Coming, Henry." Hey, that sounded strange -- just like that old radio show, Henry Aldridge, who used to screech, "Coming, Mother!" I scurried over to the bedroom and found my husband half curled up on our Queen-sized bed, lying on his side. Henry never slept on his side. Was he sick or something?

"Marlene, please feel my forehead, honey."

"I can't believe this, you never let me check your head, do you think you have a fever?"

"Maybe. There's a thermometer in my medicine cabinet. Can you dig it out?"

"Well, the only one I know about is the old-fashioned kind. I would need alcohol."

"Don't give me a treatise, just bring it."

"OK." I darted into the bathroom and searched his medicine cabinet. It was neat, but where was the thermometer? Then I spotted it, its silver head exposed behind the Tylenol and the inhaler. It had to be at least fifteen years old or more. "Here it is, dear, but shouldn't I sterilize it?"

"Quiet, I'm going to insert it under my tongue and I won't be able to talk to you. Stop asking questions."

I clammed up while my health nut husband took his own temperature. It wasn't easy for me to refrain from touching him, like he was my sick child who wanted to go outside and play anyway. Oh, men were such terrible nuisances when they didn't feel well.

Henry pulled out the thermometer and handed it to me. "What does it say? I don't have my glasses on."

"I think it's below normal, but let me take it over to the lamp." My eyesight wasn't good at reading little numbers on little glass tube-like things. I needed my magnifying glass. "Wait one minute, be right back!" There was a magnifier in a drawer in my cubbyhole and I ran and grabbed it and slid the thing over the thermometer until I could discern the reading. Back in the bedroom, I gave Henry the news: "Your fever is very slight -- 99 and a half, but it is a low grade fever. Where does it hurt?"

"Everywhere. I think I have the flu."

"What can I get for you?"

"You can get yourself gone. Go for a walk or something. I don't want you hovering over me like I was two years old. I'll take something. Bye, bye!"

"I'm cleaning in the kitchen -- can't I finish?"

"OK, finish and then go for a nice stroll in the neighborhood. Lock the door and take your house key."

"Sure, I will, I hope you know what you're doing." How could Henry tell me to lock the door and then to take my house key? He was mixed up. If I was leaving and locking the door, I had to have my house key to do it. I was so pissed off with my husband, I left the bedroom, abandoned any idea of finishing the kitchen cleaning and grabbed my keys and my cellphone. My only pause was to run into the powder room to see what a mess I was, just in case I ran into a neighbor. How many husbands did I know who sent their wives packing when they were under the weather? Probably I had the only screwball spouse who did that. Just as I was walking outside with my key poised to lock the door, I heard a bellow:

"Marlene, don't go -- come here -- pronto! -- I need you!"

"Henry, I'm not gone yet -- I just heard you -- here I come!"

I ran back into the bedroom to find Henry sitting up, his shirt unbuttoned and twisted around his torso. "What's wrong?"

"Feel this -- on my left side -- under my arm -- no, Marlene, your other left! What do you feel?"

"Well, something is raised, like a-----"

"Say it, like a lump, say it!!!"

"OK, it does feel like a sort of lump. It's harder than a normal swelling. Does it hurt?"

"My whole stomach hurts, but what is this fucking lump?"

"I don't know. When did you discover it?"

"Last night I thought I felt something, but I fell asleep. It's here now and I feel lousy as hell."

"So what do you want me to do? Should I----?"

"Yeah, call my doctor. The number is in my book, in my office. When you get somebody's live voice on the phone, I'll pick up the call in here."

Two days later, after Henry had seen two doctors and taken some quick tests, it turned out that he didn't seem to have the flu, nor a virus, nor food poisoning. At least I was able to relax about one thing -- he hadn't eaten something I'd cooked which contained something awful. Why did I always blame myself for Henry's ills? Why did I think it was my fault that the twenty-year-old coffee maker died?

Henry's internist told him that she wasn't certain the lump was cancerous, but she didn't like the size of it. She sent him to an oncologist and an appointment was scheduled for the following day. We went there together. I hadn't seen Henry so frightened since the year he suddenly realized he had forgotten to make a mortgage payment. Fortunately, that omission was easily handled. This situation was more problematic. In the waiting room there were more women than men, but there was no way to tell who was the patient and who was the companion. Henry had brought his own macho magazine, but I saw that he was having difficulty concentrating. Then the waiting room door at the far end opened and a plump girl in whites came out with a file in her hand.

"Mr. Steinberg?"

Henry got up and walked toward her. "You mean Sternberg, right?"

She looked at her file. "Sorry, come this way, Mr. Steinberger."

"Nurse, should I come in with my husband?"

"Not unless he wants you to. Right now we're just going to have him fill out a form and take his pressure and some X-rays. It won't take long for the radiologist to examine the results. Why don't you wait back there, in the front of the waiting room where I can find you if I need to."

"OK, I'll be right here, in that chair over there." I sat in the only empty chair with arms and picked up a magazine from the table. It was from a year ago -- one of those malady-infested doctor subscriptions. "Your Health", I think it was. What I would have appreciated was an article about how to treat a man who was a miserable pain in the butt when it came to being under somebody else's care. My hands were shaking and I had a knot in my stomach. I stared at the TV screen for a half hour without knowing what I was watching.

It was Tuesday, so I knew Henry would not be missing his skeet shooting or one of the other weekend activities he enjoyed with his buddies. The oncologist had scheduled an operation for the following week. First there would be a routine biopsy, but Henry had to sign all the consent forms in case the lump was more serious. The oncologist called Henry himself and notified him that the biopsy was to take place with Henry actually admitted to the hospital. That didn't sit well with my fitness freak of a husband. He was white with fear when he heard this and I had to select my words carefully, not knowing how to be with him.

"Marlene, honey, come here and hold my hand."

"Come over to where you're sitting, dear?" Henry wasn't in his man chair -- he was seated next to the reading lamp on our sofa.

"Come here to the sofa -- sit next to me."

"Yes, yes, I'll sit there and, honey, just give me your hand."

"I want to tell you something you ought to know, Marlene."

Oh, oh, he's got a secret and he thinks he's going to be out of commission. I'd better steel myself for some sort of confession.

"Yes, dear, what is it?"

"Marlene, remember when you used to be bad with money?"

"Well, I wasn't that bad, but I certainly wasn't anywhere near as frugal as your mother. Why that woman could buy a whole week's groceries with pocket change!"

"OK, forget my mother. Listen to me. What I'm trying to say is, I know how you've done things in the past."

"Like what?"

"You know what I mean. You used to buy clothes and jewelry and stuff you didn't want me to know about. I figured you sometimes sneaked them into the house when you thought I wasn't paying attention."

"I didn't want to start a fist fight, so I kept us both healthy. I was concerned with safety."

"You wanted to avoid one of my lectures, which is closer to the truth."

"Well, you didn't like anything I bought, any time, like ever!"

"I liked things you bought. It wasn't about your good taste. It was the excess. You were accumulating an inventory, not purchasing a wardrobe. You had enough outfits to open a chain of boutiques."

"I couldn't fit into things when my weight changed."

"I knew that. But I also noticed you stopped doing it before you lost weight and even before I was ready to put my foot down. You began to get rid of stuff you didn't wear any more. I noticed."

"Why didn't you say something?"

"I was afraid you'd regress. I wanted to be sure it wasn't a temporary thing. You got better -- I mean, I can sort of trust you now."

"OK, so now I'm a whole lot more trustworthy. Now I'm more like your mother! You love me like you're my son. So what's the scoop? What do you want to tell me?"

Henry looked at the rug and wiggled a bit. He seemed jittery, so I knew it was a biggie, maybe a monster, probably something that would get me upset. I sat very still.

"Marlene, I've been holding back on you."

"It's about money, isn't it? You must have lost a bundle in the market and now that you're facing a minor operation, you can't keep it from me, am I right?"

"I don't know that I'm having a minor operation, and, no, it's the other way around."

"What?"

"Marlene, I've got another brokerage account you don't know about."

"Well, OK, I guess you still didn't trust me."

"I have to -- I'm, oh, how should I put this? I'm, oh shit, I'm mortal. I'm not going to live forever."

"Well, quickly, then, there's little time to lose! What's in this alleged brokerage account?"

"Like as of last week?"

"Like, yes, last week will do."

"Would you believe, oh God, you're going to kill me, it's close to two mill. A few of my investments went through the roof. I shouldn't have even had so much in an aggressive growth fund. I sold high because I got worried --"

"STOP TALKING!!! You're going too fast!! Two mill? Is that short for millage, millimeters, or what?" I tried to stay collected, but I could feel my heartbeat racing.

"Million, two million."

"Dollars, pesos, franks, yen, what, GodDammit?"

"Dollars -- stop swearing and stop playing with me!"

"You're pulling my cord, Henry. I'm not trying to play with you. I'm shocked so much I can't think straight!"

"Go take a look on my shelf -- the one over my computer -- there's a green binder there. Bring it in."

"Such melodrama. You've never asked me to go get something out of your sanctuary. OK. I'll go get it."

Later that evening, Henry took me through his hidden brokerage account. I almost went crazy. If ever I wanted to smash my husband over the head with one of his fishing rods, this was it.

"Henry, there are two accounts here. Why are there two accounts?"

"One of them is in joint tenancy for the two of us and the other is in your name alone. I was funding the marital deduction. Then the law changed, but I left it that way. And, well, last year the whole portfolio went way up in value."

"Is there some reason you didn't tell me about it? I would have liked to use some of this money." My head was going wild and any ability I had to think clearly had gone into the stratosphere, or wherever thoughts go when they take a ride.

"Years ago, I was afraid you wouldn't know how to manage it. I guess I just procrastinated. I'm sorry now, so there it is -- you have the whole story."

"So I'm supposed to understand why didn't you tell me before? That's not a way to treat a wife who loves you." I was on the verge of a crying jag.

"The truth is, I worried about a lot of things. I thought Robin might have been a gay man and was going to end up broke. And that made me think maybe I had directed too much to you and should have set aside money for him, that is, when I thought that way."

"I can't believe this. I thought you were shutting our children out. We knew Linda didn't need the money!"

"I didn't hate Robbie no matter what his private life was like. He didn't date women. It was upsetting and I was angry, but I guess it didn't go that deep. I wasn't going to shut him out."

"Well, so you shut me out!"

"Just the facts -- not the money! Well, I was wrong. Now I'm trying to make it right."

"OK, let's go over these investments. I'm not as stupid or as much of a spendthrift as you think. You've been a bad boy. A very bad boy."

I was glad I didn't hit Henry, although I had never been so close to a marital assault. It took me awhile to calm down. I retreated into our bedroom for an emotional release and locked the door. After about an hour, I unlocked the door. I could have unlocked it after ten minutes. I wasn't that upset. We were richer.

"Henry, show me everything I need to know about investments. You were wrong to leave me out and you have to make it right!"

Henry spent two hours teaching me about the difference between conservative and aggressive investments and how to track their values and also to diversify. I thought I might immediately take some of the money and have my facelift. But I was still a bit frightened of the procedures and realized my fears were real. The barrier I put in place about it not being affordable no longer held water.

I was absorbing quite a bit about financial management, but since Henry had opened himself up so much, I didn't want to waste any more time. I had to speak frankly.

"You really have doubts about your surviving this thing, don't you?"

"We'll all die some day."

"You mean, like soon?"

"No, I think the tumor will be benign. That's not why I'm showing you these investments. You've really gotten much better with money. Please forgive me. I know I was wrong. I should have told you about this stuff long ago. So you bought too many clothes you didn't need. I bought guns and fishing equipment. I'm not so tight as you thought."

"You've explained how you accumulated so much. If you were such a genius, why did you keep denying us certain expenditures? You dress like a hick and you've done nothing but complain about my trying to look nice."

"I hate show-offs."

"This isn't showing off I'm talking about. It's being a neurotic skinflint when it wasn't necessary."

"If I hadn't saved all this money, then how would we live if we had some real problems? If Robin had real problems? Robin is facing some tough issues health wise for the rest of her life."

"You know what, Henry? You kept too much information to yourself. We're married all these years! I actually thought you were shutting Robin out of your life. Now nothing makes sense. I'm so confused I don't know what to think."

"Did you think I was doing something illegal or harmful? Like one of my brothers?"

"I guess not. Say, did you ever do something illegal?"

"Yes, I took a deduction on our joint tax return for your therapy expense. That was probably borderline suspect. The IRS doesn't let you deduct stuff for your general well-being. I looked it up. You didn't need to see that shrink at all. But you used your own money, so I stayed out of it"

"Ha, ha, I have you there! I asked my therapist if the fees were deductible and he gave me a paper with the rules on them. They said to consult our tax advisor. I even called our accountant and he said it was legit."

"You talked to John? About our taxes?"

"Of course. I'm no damned innocent spouse. I'm a lot smarter than you give me credit for."

"I guess so."

"Also, if I were you, I'd dump the rest of that aggressive growth fund, or at least some of it. We're too old to put this much money in something that speculative."

The look on Henry's face told the story. I was stronger than he wanted to admit. Now he could go into his surgery with some relief that his secret was out in the open. But his expression conveyed a new kind of worry.

"Marlene, what if I become an invalid or worse and you turn out to be better at---"

"Shut up, Henry. Everything's going to be just fine. I'll forgive you in a few years. Just get well!"

"You know, Robin wondered how I could come up with the twenty thou so easily, so he, uh she, asked. I think the kids figure we're solvent -- maybe quite comfortable."

"You're still not in a good situation with Robin, you know. You've not forgiven her for having that drastic operation without telling you first, so you could talk him out of it."

I was very conscious now of Robin's timeline before and during the operation.

What a revelation! I had all this guilt for nothing! The reason Robin had kept his surgery a secret was mainly Henry's fault! Robin couldn't even talk to me about her operation in advance because she wasn't sure I could keep such a secret from Henry! Why don't the people in my family think I'm trustworthy? Why did Henry let me think he knew nothing about how I bought clothes? Is this or was this a man's view of a woman? Was Henry protecting me from myself? Even worse, was Robbie before the surgery protecting himself from me because I would have gotten Henry on his case? Did I have a habit of being careless with confidences? If I kept getting tripped up by my habits, what was it like for Henry, who still didn't believe a person could, or even should, really change everything about one's sex?

"Marlene, don't say anything about the money to the kids yet. Let me handle it. I'll probably give them a few details when I'm ready. Know what I mean?"

"I guess I do. Well, I think I'll fix myself some dinner."

"What's this 'myself' crap? Honey, know what I'd like? Can you rustle up that good old tuna casserole I used to love? I suppose you have to shop for the ingredients."

"Henry, my first instinct is, go make your own damned meal. But I'm going to try to forgive you. At least we're richer than I thought instead of poorer. If we were poorer and you kept it from me, I'd feed you nothing but potatoes and cereal."

"I like potatoes and cereal!"

"You're going to have surgery. At least you confessed, Mr. King Midas bastard. But nix on the tuna casserole. It's too fattening and I have to eat too! I'll go defrost some chicken we have in the freezer. You can grill it -- you're not too sick to do that! I'll put some green beans in the microwave. I got that thing as clean as the day it was installed. Just like your conscience is now scrubbed of all that old grime for treating your wife like a child. And here's another command, Private Sternberg: Go set the table!"

"Can you wait until I finish my newspaper?"

"Well, I waited, how many years for you to trust me about handling investments?"

"Oops."

"If I weren't such a good wife, I'd make you wait twenty-five years before I'd cook for you again, you weasel, you trickster, you CHAUVINIST, oh, I have other names. And don't look at me like that!"

"Marlene, I do love you, even if you're a bit nuts."

"Shut up, and oh yeah, here's another rule: For the following week you can sit on the sofa! I'm going to give your man chair a thorough cleaning, while I have a chance. Then, if you will, I'm going to hire us some cleaning help! And tomorrow I'm going shopping at Macy's. I really need some new underwear. My thinner boobs are falling out of my double D cups. Don't worry, I'll stay away from the jewelry. I've got enough bling and sparkly to wear for the next twenty years."

42

Henry's cancer scare rocked the two of us, as well as the kids, for a whole week. We moved around the house like zombies during that awful time. We were zombies getting dinner ready, zombies using the toilet, zombie-like watching TV (we avoided most of the movie channels and selected from our own collection of comedy films) and even spoke in a type of zombie-ish language of our own.

"Dinner?"

"Sure, chicken?"

"Steak. Rice. Salad."

"Freezer?"

"No, go to the grocery store. Need fresh."

"You?"

"No, us."

"Time?"

"Now. OK?"

"Affirmative."

"Marlene, why are we talking like this?"

"Henry, I'm speaking less because I want to keep my wrinkles at bay. Why are you speaking less?"

"I always talk this way."

"You do not -- you're closing in on less than ten syllables with each remark."

"Oh."

Somehow the week went by, one twenty-four-hour period at a time. We got to the hospital and the children had flown into town and were staying at a nearby motel to give us our space. Robin had been working day and night to get her sculptures ready for the New York gallery show, but she dropped everything to be with us. The biopsy would take a couple of hours. I brought four books to read to get my mind off the frightening period of waiting. My watch had the loudest ticking I had ever heard. At first I kept switching from one book to another. They all seemed so wrong for my mood. Finally, I turned to the science fiction thriller I had bought months before but had never read. I was easing into the hair-raising intro and the next rather compelling chapter when the surgeon suddenly tapped me on the shoulder. His face wasn't alien, but I was so into the creatures of another planet, that I nearly jumped out of the chair.

"Doctor, I didn't see you come in. Is my husband going to be okay?"

"The lump has been removed," Mrs. Sternberg. "Fortunately, it was benign -- a type of cyst that is not uncommon in these cases."

"Thank God. I'm ever so relieved. Whoosh! I need to breathe, give me a moment."

"Take your time. I'm not rushing away."

"Thanks. Doctor, can you tell my two daughters over there? See them by the table? Oh, can I see Henry -- where is he?"

"He's in recovery, just sleeping a bit until the anesthesia wears off. Also, it's routine, but we always send the tissue to the lab to confirm our findings. But we're confident -- your husband will be fine. Why don't you go talk to your daughters and I'll be here to answer any questions they have."

"Then I'm the first, uh, after the medical team, to know he's okay?"

"I think you mean, does your husband realize he's out of danger? I told him and he nodded. Let's you and I go tell your children that their father doesn't have cancer."

I looked at Linda and Robin, and gave them the high five sign, even though I didn't get up to make actual contact. It was too exhausting. I hadn't slept the night before. Henry's vital signs were so strong after his procedure that the decision was made to release him later that afternoon. Until then the three of us had time to get together for "coffee and" in the downstairs cafe. As we walked to the elevator, Robin pushed the down button and we stared at each other's faces with a new understanding. There would be no jockeying for petty self-serving attention this time. We were all in this together, each linked to the other by an undeniable family bond. The retreat to the cafe wasn't about thirst or hunger -- it was about sharing our feelings. But as soon as we walked into the somewhat noisy hospital guest-friendly buffet, I couldn't avoid the instinctive desire that hit me as soon as I smelled the aroma coming from the hot food area. Robin saw me glance in that direction and gave a little cough. It was a signal. No words were necessary. The cough was code for, "Mom, is this the time to ignore your calorie consumption? It's your call." These infants I had suckled knew everything about me. Instantly, my discipline returned. Wordlessly, we each gravitated to those sections displaying our respective food choices. Linda wouldn't let me pay for myself. "I'm in charge here, Mother, give me your food and go find a table."

I didn't mind being ordered around by the kid who understood business and finance ten times better than I did. She also treated her body with more respect. What did she order? A watercress and feta cheese sandwich on foccacia bread. Even during my worst fears about Henry's health, I'm not sure I could have looked at a selection like that without feeling like I was being punished by the High Commissioner of Food Intake. Robin selected a tuna fish salad on romaine lettuce, and I picked out a small package of whole wheat wafers -- not much of an "and." Any emotional joy I normally experienced in indulging my taste buds had been transformed, at least temporarily, in sharing my relief at Henry's outcome with my two youngsters. Such a contradiction in terms! None of us were young any more. We finished our snacks and returned to the waiting room. This time I sat next to my children.

"Mom, we knew it would turn out just fine," Robin said, as she squeezed my hand.

Linda put her arm around me. "Mom, I never doubted for a moment that Dad just had one of those pesky growths -- it isn't in our family history to succumb to, oh, I hate to even say it, cancer." Linda had read volumes on the subject of carcinoma, melanoma, and all the related types of undesirable cellular rampages. Always the scholar, my younger daughter consulted books and Internet compilations like some people used their spare time to go shopping or play golf. She was one of the few persons I knew who could pedal a stationary bike furiously while reading a 700-page book. I had to see it to believe it. "Linda, how can you read such small print while you're moving like that? I can't even manage a magazine, or even one of those large print booklets."

"It's just something I can do, Mother. I work at it. Time is precious to me -- I don't want to spend my life inspecting axles and company financial records -- I'm thinking of becoming a paramedic."

"Why not, you've done everything else? Why stop at super normal? Go for impossible!"

"I've probably gotten worse since Jimmy and I parted ways."

"Yes, I can understand that there's a bit of a gap in your life. Do you miss him?"

"A little. I've been dating this Roger fellow I told you about -- he's an engineer -- specializes in environmental restructuring. Not much of a great living there, but he makes out. We're maybe compatible."

"Maybe compatible? Is that like me getting accustomed to how to eat the latest dishes in restaurants? Sometimes only a few strands of pasta fall off the spoon while I'm trying to twirl it?"

"Oh no, you're almost hopeless. Can't I ever get you to understand my independence?"

"I do understand it. You seem somewhat fulfilled. I would be very lonely without my husband. I really had an epiphany about our relationship while we went through these last few trying days. You heard about my reaction to the financial confession, I suppose."

Robin had been quiet during our conversation. Now she leaned forward and turned her expressive eyes to me and spoke quietly. "When Dad sent me that twenty thousand dollar check I figured something was up. It was almost like penance on his part -- his guilt that he hadn't listened to all my years of complaining about my lack of interest in women, and my suspicion that I had been handed a different pattern of urges. He still doesn't really get it, maybe he never will."

"Robin, Henry loves you and cares about you. He's slow to deal with these generations of young people who think nothing of trying new kinds of sex, alternative this and that, technical innovation, the whole lot of it. He's conservative to his core and that is the way it is."

"But you, Mom, I know you get it -- why can't Dad?"

"I read all this stuff that is happening today, and I love what my children are all about. But would I do the things you do? Probably not. I don't think I would have been happy without my long marriage. And by marriage, I mean the kind where one man and one woman keep their vows and fight the good fight. I'm in my generation for keeps, even if I can somewhat understand all the new attitudes."

"Well, I hope Dad opens up a little bit. Linda and I could use more family togetherness."

Linda had been listening intently and now had to cut in. "Speak for yourself, Robin. You're in a unique situation -- not my problem. You've made your decision about having the big surgery and not everyone is on your side. You're a genuine pioneer, kid, a real front-runner, and pioneers don't get respected very easily. I think I've been there too, although my activities pale before yours. Sometimes those people who crash frontiers like you've done even die before they see what I call social approval. You'll have to live your life without needing all those pats on the back."

"I'm trying, Linda. I've gotten temporary notoriety with my art, but like everything else, the money, the fame, the feeling of acceptance in that way, it's fleeting. I'm putting away money in investments and making plans for a lot of rainy days."

"I'm glad, Robin, because you should never count on Mom or Dad for the, you know, the inheritance. Be your own security blanket. Take care of yourself. I can say this because that's how I live."

"Hey kids, let's go talk to Dad. I see the nurse waving to us that he's awake."

43

I never saw Henry act so humble as when he emerged from the recovery room and looked at me with sad puppy eyes, as though pleading for a biscuit. They had him sitting in a wheelchair until the effects of the anesthesia wore off. One of the staff nurses was standing by. She retreated to a nursing station to allow the family to visit. I had been ready to take over the wheelchair duty if needed and had several unanswered questions which would have to wait. I bent over slightly to talk to Henry at his eye level in order to lower my voice. My normal voice would have set off a siren in the quiet ward.

"How do you feel, Henry?"

"I'm all right, not too bad."

The children were up on their feet and went over to hug him. Linda hugged first. "Dad, I'm so glad you're fine," and "What a relief to find out you're well!" Then Robin gave him a leaning down hug because Henry was still too dizzy to sit up straight in the wheelchair: "Dad, it's so good that this worry is over!"

Henry looked at the three of us and tried to express himself, but his voice wasn't quite up to the task.

"Can I have some water please?"

I signaled to the nurse and she came over to help. I asked her if he could drink some water and she brought a plastic cup with a bendable straw.

"Here, Mr. Sternberg, sip very slowly, that's good."

Henry took a few sips and cleared his throat. "Hi, honey, I suppose you know the verdict. They think I'm a good patient. Treated me like a specimen. Everybody used gloves."

"It's a hospital, dear. It's standard procedure. Do you feel any pain?"

"Not just yet. I'm still a bit woosy, and, whatever they gave me, it's making me feel like I got a hangover from something. I have a bad taste in my mouth and it wasn't very much fun. Better to have a hangover from a beer blast."

"Oh, you sound real good, honey, real real good."

"I am good."

"Honey, the kids came all the way here and have to leave for home tonight. They just wanted to be here for the procedure and make sure you're fine, right, kids?"

Robin and Linda both nodded and were watching Henry to gauge his reaction.

"I wasn't that out of it, Marlene! I knew they had come. They waved to me before they put me under. My head's not that bad. But honey, what did the doc tell you about the biopsy?"

"Henry, they had to remove a piece from your arm-pit. About the size of a walnut. The nurse said you had a bandage over some dressing which will need to be changed a few times. They gave me instructions. Then you go visit your surgeon in a week to see that everything is healing, and then you can return to your usual routine."

"My father once accused me of having a hole in my head. Now I've got one under my arm. Wife, my love, you're so good to me, thank you. You've been putting up with me, and sometimes I know I've been such a putz. Oh, it's so nice, my family's here for old dad. Linda, and Rob -- Robin here, gee, kids, didn't we tell you guys you didn't have to travel all the way here -- you could have called on the phone."

Linda took her father's hand. "Listen, Dad, we didn't know how serious it might have been. We love you."

Robin gently placed her hand on Henry's back. "Of course we had to come. We only have one father, and we didn't know the extent of the medical problem or how it would come out."

Henry looked Robin square in the eye. "But Robin, when you had your operation, you didn't, uh, sorry, I have to cough up something. . ."

"Don't speak, Dad, just rest."

"No, I'm all right, what I'm trying to say is, you didn't have us there with you. You didn't even let us know beforehand. You never said how serious, oh, you know what I'm trying to spit out."

"I think you're still worried about a lot of things, Dad."

"We should have a nice talk as soon as I get out of this place and get back to normal again."

"We will, I promise, we will. Right now you need to let the anesthesia wear off."

"I think I'm all right, just a little dizzy. I won't feel like barking for awhile. Robin, you do the talking. I need you to tell me that the floor and the walls aren't crooked."

"That's what anesthesia feels like when it's wearing off, Dad."

"Yeah, but I sure wish somebody would straighten everything out."

"After my surgery I slept for more than twenty-four hours."

"Sure, sure, I can understand that. Oh my, you look nice, very nice. Forgive me if I still need to get used to seeing you different."

Robin leaned down again to whisper to Henry. "Still a jolt seeing me being a woman and dressing as a woman?"

"Yeah, takes a bit of adjusting. You're wearing slacks and a sort of blouse, and a jacket, a plaid jacket."

"It's cool in here."

"Sure. I understand. Well, now that I'm diagnosed with a non-malignant thing which grew almost overnight, I guess I'll have to find something new to worry about."

Linda had been holding her father's hand and she let gently let go of it, as though she trusted that he wasn't going to say anything hurtful.

"Daddy, you can worry about a lot of things, but worrying isn't a way to enjoy life."

Robin seemed like she wanted to say more, but Henry looked away from her, as though he needed to avoid further conversation with the person who was once his adored son. I noticed her pained expression, as though she'd been once again punctured by her father's rejection. The situation hinted at the underlying tension and I wanted to lessen it.

"Kids, Henry's got to rest today and you two have planes to catch this evening, right? Henry, as soon as the doc signs the release, we're coming back to the house and I have some snacks in the fridge I can dig up for dinner. I don't know if you have any appetite yet, but let's get going."

I knew that the kids were ready to cancel their flights if the outcome had been serious. After two more hours, with Henry being monitored and then assisted as he dressed in his street clothes, the discharge papers were handed to us. An aide accompanied us as we stopped at the front desk to check out. Henry couldn't stand up just yet and an attendant helped him get into my car. Robin and Linda followed in Robin's rental car and we all reached our house at about the same time. I took one look at my husband and saw that he was already half asleep. He threw a weak smile at Robin and Linda as they emerged from their parked car.

"I'm not going to be much company, kids. Thanks for being with me and I guess I'll be my old self in a day or two. Marlene, why don't you help me get to bed and then you can visit with the, uh, the kids. I should be myself by tomorrow. Marlene, call them later to see that they got home safely. Robin, can you help me out of the car and into the house? I need a big long nap."

Soon Henry was in his pajamas and within a few minutes his discernible snore could be heard. I didn't want to reveal my observation aloud, but I wondered if Robin had picked up Henry's stammer when he referred to "the kids." He couldn't quite bring himself to say "the girls," but in a normal family, wouldn't that be how a father described them? There was so much more to acceptance of a child's sex change than just the visual acknowledgment. I knew as a mother that the beloved individual who was my son for so many years, and now a daughter, still had my heart on a platter.

Henry's phone rang at 8:30 AM the next morning and I ran to answer it. Henry was still in bed. The caller was the surgeon's nursing assistant, and she was checking to see if he was able to sleep with a minimum of discomfort.

"Sure, he slept until 3 in the morning and then, I noticed he had gotten out of bed. I heard him rummaging in the kitchen for food. The doctor said he could eat anything he wanted, correct? And that all we have to be concerned with is the dressing on that wound?"

"Yes, Mrs. Sternberg. Just change it every day. Knowing your husband, he'll probably want to do it himself, but because it's in an awkward place to get to, you'll probably have to assist him."

"Better to have it in an awkward place than for him to be in the hospital with a malignancy."

I thanked the assistant and felt my pulse -- it was racing. Was it because I ran quickly out of our bedroom to get the phone in another room, or was there something else? Then I realized that I had been confining my emotions. Suddenly I needed to cry. Where was that box of tissues that always seemed to move around by itself? A hand towel would suffice. I ducked into the powder room and shut the door and had a good long sob session. My two post-operative loved ones were safe, although the younger one wasn't quite settled into her proper place in the family yet -- not quite. As my crying jag subsided, the writer-thinker in me emerged. What now? What was the best way to describe a husband you worried was seriously ill and then began to act like a pussycat until he knew the threat was over? Soon the pussycat would turn into a lynx and then the next beast up the line. The closest analogy I could come up with was how the personality of The Hulk showed up before he turned green again.

Until 10AM Henry remained in a deep sleep, snoring up a symphony of a Stravinsky-ish opus. I walked around the house in my robe, opening shades and checking the thermostat. Suddenly the symphony stopped. Instead of the clash of cymbals, I heard dresser drawers being opened and shut. The man of the house was back, doing his morning at his personal wall. He must have heard his own noise while lying in bed and had had enough. I wanted to give him an affectionate good morning, but hesitated, not certain of his mood. He was already sitting on the cedar chest and putting on his gym clothes. I saw two pillows which had been inside it on the floor.

"You're up, Henry. Feeling better?"

"I know I can't exercise today, but I feel like wearing what I would wear if I was going to lift weights and do Nautilus. I'm going to pretend that I'm working out."

"That's a good sign. What would you like for dinner?"

"Champagne. And maybe a takeout. Can you eat barbeque?"

"I can eat it if I don't make a pig of myself. I'll call in an order this afternoon. Say, Robin really looked good, didn't she?"

"I think she looks great, especially for a man with a makeover."

"You two didn't get much chance to talk. It just wasn't the time."

Henry sighed and looked at me. "What's on the damned TV? I'm going to have to suffer a really boring day. And maybe I'll -----------"

"What did you just say?"

"You interrupted me -- I didn't get to finish! I was starting to say that maybe I'll ignore the recovery instructions."

"And maybe you'll force me to go out of the house while you try to do your own bandage. If you ever do something like that again, I'm not coming back!"

"Sorry, I'm just mad that all the medical attention is over. While I was waiting to have the biopsy I was almost enjoying having everyone fawn over me."

"'I'm the worst fawner of all. That's the problem. I've spoiled you."

"Spoil me some more. Tell me I'm wonderful."

"OK, here it is: I've been forced by duress to tell you that you're wonderful."

"Oh hell, what's on the TV?"

"I have a surprise for you. I read the listings and they're just what the doctor ordered. Choice of two car chase movies or a brutal murder mystery. Or we can watch something I like."

"I'm not ready to make love yet, am I?"

"Well, if you're doing pretend weight and pretend Nautilus, you could do pretend sex."

"What time is the car chase movie?"

44

Two weeks had passed since Henry's operation. I was still Seventy, but pushing Seventy-One, that horrible milestone when a woman was supposed to review her Will and have certain new doctor visits for unspeakable conditions, like the big "A", for arthritis, and the shitty "D", for diabetes, or even worse, that maligned "C", for, fuhgeddaboudit. Crap and double crap! I had submerged any decisions about my facelift and what I'd have done about my neck except in my dreams. The worry about Robin and Henry's health scare had taken first place.

Last month when I tried to knock out a few short stories, I began to suffer something I thought I had outgrown years ago -- writers' block. Who could I punish for breaking my whirlwind of verbal promiscuity? Maybe I was depressed. I'd begun to lose my appetite without being sick. This couldn't be me who was staring at walls instead of digging into the fridge to see if I could cheat and wolf down a slab of cheese. We didn't even have cheese in the house any longer. Henry was watching his cholesterol. So where were my passions?

I wrote down some ideas about how to redecorate the living room and get rid of that ugly chair that Henry reigned from, but I didn't show my written plan to Henry. He would have balked at buying a new man chair. What to do? What to do? I was beginning to feel that our relationship was friendlier before Henry spilled the beans about his hidden stash. Then something occurred which woke me up. Henry was suggesting un-Henry-like suggestions, like how to spend our money before we began to get calls and e-mails from funeral directors and retirement home supervisors. I heard him say that we should be traveling somewhere special. It all started with an apology. . .

The day began as usual, neither of us speaking to each other until I asked Henry if he could pass the low-fat margarine across the table. He did it with his usual move -- a flick of his thumb accompanied by his being interrupted scowl. Henry hated to take his eyeballs off the specific line of his news article. Nothing was going to change, or was it? His eyes drifted a few inches and then he put down the paper and I saw his mouth begin to open. An important pronouncement, or even an edict, was about to occur. Such a gesture was surely a prelude to a conversation at the breakfast table. I gently laid my half-eaten breakfast bread slice on my plate, waiting for the big moment. Henry's stern expression was defrosting -- going from growly to soft and droopy. The needy puppy dog had returned.

"Wife, I've probably done you a great wrong by hiding so much money and making you feel poorer than we were."

"Please continue."

"Of course, even with my tight hold of the budget, you still managed to buy enough clothes to fill several racks at both Dillard's and Macy's."

"I was buying myself extra love."

"You had an orgasm from wearing more slacks? Does that Cosmo rag know about that one?"

"**How many times have I explained to you that sex isn't love**!!"

"I lost count. Don't beat me up when I'm trying to be nice."

"All right, but you should have simply had a talk with me long ago about how to manage money. Did you think I wouldn't understand our finances? I seem to be able to balance a checkbook."

"It's complicated. I've always been worried about being poor again. I think about my family and those brothers and sisters of mine that aren't with us any more. My brother, Louie? He was only 47 when he had a heart attack. And Pete, the kid who wasn't quite right? Dead at age 25. Gladys was born with a defective heart, so when she passed in her teens, it was a tragedy, but nobody expected her to survive childhood at all. I remember when only my father was working and earning barely enough to feed us. I sold newspapers. Manny ran errands for people for dimes. Ah, it's all in the past. Forget it."

"We have fairly good health, honey. We should travel while we still can."

"OK, you're on my wave-length. I've already decided to go somewhere -- you pick the destination. Maybe restrict it to the Western Hemisphere for now. Then later we'll see about a tour to the South Seas, or some damned island that's the latest place where fools go. What do you think?"

"I still want to go to New York. I had told Cissy I wouldn't be going to the shower and I also gave our regrets for Robin's big New York opening. So you say it's up to me? Well, we're going to New York. You don't have to go to the baby shower, but I want you with me for Robin's opening."

"Oh, oh, I think I've just walked into it."

"Henry, you just said I should pick the destination. I just picked a destination. It's New York -- take it or leave it!"

"Me and my big mouth."

"Forget it, then. Let's just stay in Florida. We can go see Disney World or sit here on the sofa and watch soap operas. Orlando's a good vacation place -- we could buy a fun package. You can shriek on one of the roller-coasters and probably find some pink shirts with Mickey on them."

"Marlene, I expected you to say you wanted to go to Alaska, or Hawaii, or maybe the Cayman Islands or another exotic getaway. I wasn't thinking about New York."

"Make up your mind."

"We'll go to New York."

"OK, and after the gallery show and the shower, I want to visit with my sister Beth and then Julie Sue."

"It's winter -- maybe Julie Sue will be around, but after the shower where will Beth be?"

"I think she'll stay in town until the baby arrives. But I'm not sure -- knowing Beth, she might take a spin over to Rio or the Riviera. Maybe after the gallery show, we should go find a convenient island somewhere."

"Yee-gads, woman, I give you an inch and you take a yard! OK, we'll go to New York and then the Cayman Islands! I'll make all the arrangements for the flights, the car rental, and then a week on Grand Cayman."

"I really deserved Alaska, but it's the wrong time of year and we've been there already. Grand Cayman, it is."

"You had this gallery visit planned, didn't you? How did you know I'd be amenable?"

"I'm a writer. I can read you like a book. Your plot line was showing."

"Well, don't just stand there -- we don't have control over the dates. Draw up an itinerary, including when we have to leave and stop driving me nuts. Oh, and I don't want to depart on a Friday and miss the skeet shooting. Any date after a Sunday. Oh, I guess if I miss a week or two of shooting, I don't care all that much."

"I'll plan it so we get to the gallery show opening. I'm so excited I could skip dinner!"

"We're eating out with George and Carol."

"I'll skip it some other time."

45

Henry had a plan of what to do while I went to Cissy's shower. He had never been to the Empire State Building or seen that area of Manhattan, so we drew up a schedule so that both of us could do our separate things. I was glad to let Beth know that I'd be at Cissy's happy event after all. Of course, there were a number of issues I had to deal with. I'd have to act nice to both Beth and Julie Sue, who were no doubt going gaga over the prospect of the first grandchild in the clan. And what had I to brag about? My daughter, the used-to-be-son, had become a celebrated artist in the community of uninhibited sex sculpture buyers. My kids had both been invited, but each had to decline for business reasons. Robin's work, now displayed in multiple galleries, was becoming one of the biggest draws of the year. Critics wrote in columns that she was one of the best of the crop of emerging sculpture artists. I had so much wanted to be an emerging writer, but had always settled for being pre-emergent. I knew a bit about art, so I had some perspective.

Take Mapplethorpe, they thought his stuff was erotic? Why next to Robin's sculptures, they're quite timid. Those well-known photos by the maestro of male nudity are not only yesterday's wow, the collections have gone mainstream, now relegated to the rooms that display Richard Avedon's celebrities -- almost all of whom are of people with their clothes on. Sissy pictures. Nobody but my Robin has dared to sculpt (is it 'sculp' or 'sculpt?') a four foot tall marble man/woman with boobs plus a hint of what was once a well-hung groin area with a new pussy. Oh, that's not all, she's also preparing to do some major work in bronze! No more auto plant work for my transgendered daughter. He was assembling this collection at least two years before the surgeries and keeping the whole thing under wraps until afterwards! That locked bedroom of his held more than just some blueprints and tools! I don't think there are many people on the planet with this transgender problem who could overcome it the way my child did. But I always knew Robbie was a great talent. I just didn't get the whole picture. And Henry still doesn't get it.

Was this notoriety happening to me and the child I had given life to, even if he was nearly born in a grocery store?

Oh, God, I can't believe what the world of acceptability has come to -- does anything go today? Has everyone in society given up boundaries and morals? What do the rabbis think? Do they have a new description of a reformed reform rabbi? Will they now ordain a rabbi who chants with explicit details? Where is it all headed? Can a gay out-of-the-closet woman now discuss her sex life, like whether she wears a strap-on, and not be wondered about? Should I go to one of those adult superstores and give them my autograph for being the mother of the most beautiful girl in the transgender world? Nothing is sacred any longer except the dollar bill, which is now worth thirty cents. Next thing you know someone will marry his pet Doberman.

I began to feel aggravated once again because, while I respected Robin's choice about gender surgery, I still didn't respect myself. My face still looked wrinkly and Seventyish and I needed to lose another ten pounds. My mood became more and more somber until I read the newspaper the next morning. Some crackpot bozo had gone to his preacher with a petition in his hand -- it seemed he was intent on tying the knot with his French poodle and already had a following. I had always wondered about certain women who seemed highly attached to their large dogs, but a guy? How would a man consummate a marriage with a poodle?

I knew that Linda was unable to attend the shower, but I had to find out if my sisters had any concern about Robin's attendance. Wouldn't Beth worry about my new daughter stealing the show? It was unthinkable that

I ask her this question, so I phoned Linda in her Cleveland office and got her secretary. She knew my voice very well.

"Hello, Mrs. Sternberg, if you're looking for Linda, you'll have to call San Francisco. Is there anything I can help you with?"

"Oh, Dana, you must know about Cissy Duberstein's baby shower -- the one Linda couldn't attend."

"I know about it. Linda is sorry she couldn't be there. And I heard that Robin dropped off a gift and left a nice note. She's completely overwhelmed with the finishing touches on her show in New York."

"Dana, did you read my mind? That's sort of what I was calling Linda for! I didn't want to call my sister Beth and ask her how she felt about the possibility Robin would be there! It's good you're so informed."

"Is there any message I can leave with Linda when she phones in?"

"Yes, tell her that her Mother, the pre-emergent writer, mother of two prominent children, a bus company CEO and a famous sculptor, is coming out of her shell. Tell her I'm not waiting until I'm Seventy-Five Years Old to get my face lifted!"

I arrived at the shower in a bad mood because Henry could have come with me. There were several men in attendance. Beth greeted me warmly and I melted a little.

"Hello, Beth, you're looking well, and how wonderful for the family."

She was wearing a scarlet ribbon over her ivory lace mini-dress. The ribbon reminded me of an old song by Jo Stafford. I could see Beth's older lady skinny legs without a hint of cellulite and, when she bent over to kiss a couple of her pals' kiddies, her pink underwear showed. She wasn't that much younger than me and she could dress like a chorus girl! My envy had reached a breaking point. I told myself to stop being resentful just because my rich female sibling could pass for a fifty-year-old. What if she was three inches taller than me? Who cared if a taller person needed more food? And as for Beth's intake? She ate diddly-squat for lunch and diddly-squat lite for dinner. Who but Beth would turn borderline anorexia into an art form! Was I as jealous as a turkey eye-ing a peacock? I had to watch what I said, so I kept my clenched fists in the pockets of my flashy new dress slacks. Nobody uttered a single word about the weight I had lost. I looked around for any approving eye I could spot, but the attention was all on Cissy or the luncheon menu. Then my kid sister, Julie Sue, came up to me and whispered in my ear:

"Marlene, you look wonderful. You've not only kept your weight down, you've lost even more! How did you do it?"

"Julie girl, I just love you. You're the only one who noticed."

"It's not true -- it's just that Cissy has a knack for hogging the attention. Did you catch sight of that new Rock of Gibraltar on her right hand?"

"That green stone? The one that nearly blinded me when I got up close?"

"Emerald, from Winston, no less. Sherwin gave it to her for getting knocked up."

"Well, that makes sense. A rock for a knock. How come when I conceived my first child, all I got from Henry was a new cookbook and a pair of slippers from Penney's?"

"Henry's a good husband, Marlene. He's been faithful and I know he loves you."

"Isn't Paul, uh, the same way?"

"Truthfully, I'm not so sure."

"Oh no."

"Oh yes. Paul goes out of town a lot. He comes home with a pile of money and a pile of excuses for why I can't always reach him."

"Julie, he's a businessman. Maybe he's a little thoughtless, but --"

"He does love me, but I think he has a friend in New Jersey."

"A woman?"

"I'm not totally sure about that."

"Don't say another word. Where's the bar? I need a refreshing gulp of a Martini."

"You should revere your man. Emeralds aren't everything. If I had to choose between a roving husband with bucks or a straight-laced home-at-night man who pays the bills and keeps his marital vows, well, I'd rather have fidelity. Of course, that's simply my common sense talking. You know I love Phil."

"I do and you're right. Maybe I take Henry for granted. But it really bothers me that Howard cheats on Beth with more than one woman. I find it hard to fathom how a man can be so disrespecting of a devoted wife."

"I'm not sure, although he certainly doesn't spend much time with her. And then at the wedding? I know something was going on between them."

I knew where the conversation was headed and didn't want to go any further, so I played dumb. "Really? Do you have any clues about what it was?"

"There was a bit of gossip that one of the female guests was more than just one of his secretaries."

"Oh no, and Beth found out about it?"

"I'm really not sure, but I did notice that she seemed very upset right after the ceremony."

"Then I wasn't dreaming things after all."

"If so, then we both had the same dream."

I was becoming quite uncomfortable with the direction our gossip was taking. It was up to Beth whether to discuss her private marital issues, even with her sisters. "Julie, let's go see what the well-wishers have brought with them. Cissy's going to open the loot now."

"Marlene, I admire you for being thoughtful of Robin's situation. You're a good person. What Robbie did was a huge shock to all of us."

"Julie, sometimes I feel like an old bag, but at least I feel like a likeable old bag with standards."

"We're all facing our golden years, sister -- sooner or later we'll see our youth so far in the rear view mirror that we won't even remember it. By the way, remember Shelly Mintz, my pal from my high school?"

"Sure, what about her?"

"She's in a nursing home."

"Wait, Shelly's your age -- not even sixty yet."

"She just turned sixty. She's not herself any longer -- doesn't even recognize her children. It's awful."

"That's terrible. Poor Shelly, and poor Shelly's family. Well, we have to be thankful for what we've got, Julie. At least I recognize my children, the one who was born a girl and still is one, and the other one."

"Linda is a good daughter. Robin is a good person."

"You can't say it, can you? Robin is a woman."

"She's the most beautiful transgender woman I've ever laid eyes on. Not that I've seen more than one or two. And Robin has become a success in the art world. Without your loving encouragement, Marlene, could that person you raised with all your heart have accomplished all that?"

"What did I do? Robin did it all by herself. I don't think I deserve credit for the artistic success -- maybe a bit for trying to be understanding. Oh, oh."

"What's oh, oh?"

"I think my new bra has come undone. Julie, I've had more doggoned problems with underwear this year, I can't believe it! I can't even go to my niece's shower without a wardrobe crash."

"Wardrobe crash? That's a new way to describe it!"

"I sit at a computer a lot, so some of the jargon gets in my everyday talk."

"I think they're about to open the presents."

I took a taxi over to our hotel and Henry was already settled in the room, waiting for me.

"The shower was a real success, dear. There were about seven or eight men there. You could have attended."

"I had a good time. I got a little dizzy looking out of the window on the top floor of the Empire State Building, but the view was really worth it. I'm fine now. Tell me about all the gossip -- I know you have gossip."

"Well, everyone oohed and ahed and took pictures of the beautifully wrapped gifts and got seasick from all the shrimp, lobster, crabmeat and

Chilean sea bass that was served at the lunch. Cissy seemed ecstatic. She was sporting a new emerald ring big as one of the Irish isles. We joked about how she would handle her newborn child with that new ring in the way. Maybe she'll get one of those king-sized treasure chests to put it in, along with her massive pearls and the rest of her jewels."

"Do you want a ring like that?"

"Not really, but I'm not finished with my demands."

"I know. You still want the face lift."

"We'll talk about it later. Right now I need to wash my face, as well as dig the makeup out of my neck creases, and a few other aging lady things, and then rest."

I walked into the bathroom and looked at my image. I was going to do it. I was ready. Some sadness about Shelly Mintz showed up for me, and also my being a bit rocked by Julie Sue's disclosure about some husbands not being saints -- like Beth's, and perhaps Julie Sue's also. Ugh! I had gotten a serious lesson in down-home values at Cissy's shower.

As I gazed straight in the mirror that evening, I tried to love the face I had and appreciate the rest of my existence. I didn't want to derive my feeling of self-worth from the approval of others. At the baby shower I held my head high in the presence of at least thirty or forty exceedingly rich and well-groomed women. I was definitely in the minority -- a nearly Seventy-One-Year-Old long-married female who had never been divorced, cheated on or treated for removal of cellulite.

46

The sign said, "SCULPTURE BY STERNBERG." I wasn't dreaming or fantasizing. I knew we were in Soho because there was no place to park and the roots of regularly spaced trees had been forced to grow through concrete squares.

Henry said it was a mistake to come so early. "Wanna cup of coffee? I saw a deli a few blocks down that didn't have its burglar resistant folding gate closed. I think it had parking."

"So you're gonna tell me it was silly to arrive at 8AM?"

"What time does the show open? No, tell me this: What time does the gallery open?"

"Robin told me the setup was to be at 9AM because they have to get all the pedestals arranged, the prices put in place, the floor cleaned, the catalogs laid out, the----"

"Will you stop spewing out their detailed work schedule and just tell me when the damned gallery opens the damned doors?"

"You said you weren't going to swear at me any more!"

"You promised me you'd learn how to answer a question without attaching an atlas!"

"Oh. Well, I'm not sure. I really don't know. The public isn't invited until 7PM. That's when they'll have the caterer bring the wine and cheese and grapes and, I don't know, tofu, whatever. But Robin will be here all day."

"You're going to be in the way. This was silly."

"You're right. I have an idea. Let's go shopping! Macy's still has their flagship store on 34th Street!"

"Marlene, I'm not driving around Manhattan for anything. Please? Come on, coffee at a deli, or we go back to the Hilton? I'll pay the guy his hundred bucks and he can find an illegal parking space or whatever."

"Coffee. And let's get some flowers or plants for Robin and she can say they're from a rich art collector."

"Fine. We'll cruise around Soho and there's sure to be a florist somewhere. So they charge double here in New York, so what?"

"You're still edgy, like you're going to run out of money. Relax."

"Honey, this is about as relaxed as I'll ever get until they lower me down about six feet."

Henry still had two chips on his shoulder, but it was down from about four or five. We were making progress. I couldn't believe he would give in and be a guest at Robin's show. He hadn't even wanted to come. I asked him why he changed his mind. He told me he wanted to please me even though he thought he'd feel uncomfortable and could I please not give him a cold look just because he was expressing his feelings.

"Henry, I'm not giving you a cold look. It's impossible for a woman with my loose wrinkly skin to look cold."

"So if you get your face lifted, then you'll be giving me one of those icy stares?"

"Let's see, will an icy stare get me what I want?"

"That depends on the rest of your body language."

The attendance at Robin's gallery show was huge and Henry behaved well. Would this garishly attired flock buy anything? Did the owner take credit cards issued from offshore banks? Once again I was the designated conversationalist. I introduced Henry to folks he could only relate to because he had seen a few cult movies. At one point he whispered in my ear that he thought we were on the set of "Midnight Cowboy." I was prepared for the variety of dress styles worn by the art lovers as they filed in. Most of the colors were shades of black, differentiated by material. Real leather had that rubbed look. Plastic was shinier and reflected the track lighting better. Flashy jewelry was everywhere, even on the women. I thought of a great name for a new off-Broadway clothing boutique chain -- "Skinny and Statuesque." We were mingling in a world of dubious sexual orientation. Robin seemed quite relaxed, but I couldn't believe she wasn't wound up tight as a drum, hoping to be appreciated for the daring and skill her work required. I tried observing the expressions on the visitors. Did the few mainstream folks who snaked their way among the anti-homophobic movers and shakers know the whole truth? Were the people who knew Robin "before and after" wonder whether they should hug her, slap her back or shake her hand? My worries were as useless as my extraneous chatter. Robin was simply spectacular.

I was careful not to use the word "gorgeous" in describing her looks or her outfit. I knew it had been purchased at Bergdorf Goodman and that she had spent hours shopping for the two piece ensemble that would de-emphasize her height and shoulders and highlight her calves and hips. The material itself was a beaded black creation studded with splashes of large floral designs in the most vivid raspberry over mauve I had ever seen. I would never have been able to wear a dress like that in my wildest dreams. The back of the tunic was low-cut and Robin could now safely wear that style. Her bare back seemed as smooth and soft-looking as the day he was enrolled in a special after-school program I discovered while driving around a neighborhood in Milwaukee . . .

Was there something about that ceramics learning center that might have influenced the boy? It was just an impulsive idea of mine. Instead of engaging in a rough game of hockey, couldn't Robbie be just as content with a craft hobby? He was such a bright ten-year-old. I thought he might enjoy working with clay. The students who displayed an aptitude for design with their early attempts using an easy coil method were taught how to work a potter's wheel. When my son came home with some bowls he had made for his mother, I put them on a shelf in our living room. He wasn't much interested in hockey, but he loved track and swimming and tennis. And now she was a woman who could earn a living selling these unusual figures. There was a surreal beauty about them, as though Robin had embedded her deepest fears and strengths right in the marble. The two bronze prototypes were compelling also, but I thought that the marble had a special purity about it.

"Marlene, you're just standing there staring. Am I interrupting something?"

"No, I was just looking at this one standing piece."

"It's bigger in scale than the others. The pussy part is right above my nose. If it was any closer and had hair, I could probably smell it. Look at the price on the sticker."

"One Hundred Fifty Thousand Dollars."

"Hard to believe for a new artist. Do they get bargained down?"

"I don't know. I'm a little overwhelmed also. Robbie had all this in him and now this person, the child I bore like a field hand, is a beautiful and successful woman. I'm feeling a bit sad, actually."

"Why?"

"Because most, if not nearly all, transgender people, well, they just can't do this. Or maybe they can with financial support and emotional help, but if you read stuff or check the Internet to see how they're doing, it's mostly sad news."

"The opening's almost over. I'll wish Robin good luck with the rest of the show. I guess it lasts a month or so."

"You want to leave, don't you?"

"Don't you?"

"I want to go to an all-you-can-eat buffet."

"You told me you pigged out only when you were needy."

"I'm needy right now."

"I'll never understand women."

"Look, Henry, that character -- see that guy over there in the silky suit -- looks like something a mafia member would wear -- he's about to plunk down cold cash, probably a bank note, for the $150,000 new marble piece."

"Proves my point. All men love pussy, even when it's on a fucking statue. How much does Robin get to keep of that money?"

"I heard it was either thirty or forty percent. The gallery owner gets most of the money and a share goes to the association or something. Publicity is pooled. But Robin has other pieces which are selling. Look at the pedestals and when you see the red dots, that's a sale."

"Gee, I can't believe these bozos are paying all that bread. Where do these people get all their dough?"

"They hide it from their wives, I guess."

"OK, OK, let up on those digs. And where do they keep these obelisk monstrosities?"

"I don't know, in their Park Avenue apartments -- maybe on Sutton Place or mansions outside of the city. Some of the people here are just gaping, but others have real wealth. See that fellow over there who looks like he weighs over three hundred pounds?"

"OK, I see him."

"I know who he is. He was the CEO of a Fortune 500 Company until he retired a few years ago. He's a very well-known art collector."

"Marlene, don't you think it's stuffy in here? We were about to leave."

"It is. So why don't you go congratulate Robin and tell her something nice and we'll start to wrap it up."

"I'll be quick. It's almost impossible to believe that an offspring of mine would be mixing with all these, oh, I'm afraid somebody will hear me, you know what I mean."

"I know exactly what you mean. And keep your voice down. There are people like Robin here who haven't had the operation because they can't afford it. Also, not everyone looks that good afterward."

"Robin does look very good."

"So are you glad about the operation?"

Henry looked at me and motioned for me to walk toward a corner where we wouldn't be overheard. "Marlene, I don't know if I'll ever be glad about it. Maybe in a few years it won't bother me. But right now, I still want to know what the hell happened to the son I brought up."

"Guess what, dear? Our son might still be a disgruntled grunt in an auto plant. Our daughter is raking it in and taking a chance at a real life. Please get my coat, Henry. Where's the car?"

"I gave it to a fourteen-year-old girl -- she handed me a ticket. I think she gave the keys to a seventeen-year-old. I didn't want to know where they parked it."

"Good idea. Just make sure the radio and the CD collection are still there."

"Hey, you still want to go to a play tonight?"

"Only if we can get good tickets for a great play. If not, let's go back to the Hilton. We've got one more day. Let's go to the Metropolitan Museum tomorrow. I want to look at their marble statue exhibit."

It was time to leave Manhattan Island. I couldn't help sympathizing with those short-sighted natives who gave up their rights for a few baubles or whatever they got. Henry would have advised them to hold onto it for the long term. We left the Hilton and arranged for our rental car to be returned. I knew that famous skyline, now getting smaller and smaller in the rear view mirror of our taxi, would show up for me once again. I was going to have my facelift operation at a hospital in the Bronx. The same surgeon who had performed the surgeries for Beth would now be plying his art on the older sister -- ME! I couldn't quite feel that money was no object, because of all those years I had felt guilty spending on myself, but in reality, the money was there and I was ready to be indulged. My latest fantasy was a scene where Henry saw my new face and thought I was one of those society women from Palm Beach.

47

I cringed as usual as I emerged from the parking lot. Too many balky back muscles reminded me that I hadn't quite managed to throw the arrow of time into reverse. My saunter was still evident, but it seemed a bit slower. I didn't care. So what if I walked like a lady about to celebrate her Seventy-Second birthday?

"I need to show myself who I really am," I explained to my legs, as I very slowly made my way toward the Macy's mall entrance. There were always two benches there, one placed on each side of the row of automatic doors. I normally avoided sitting on either of these benches because the bugs who lived on the leaves of the plants lining the long pavements seemed attracted to something about my post-Sassoon cropped haircut. Who needed a swarm of them following me into the store?

I was only five pounds overweight now. My loss of twenty-seven pounds the past year and a half represented twenty pounds of hardy fat tissue and, by my reckoning, seven pounds of cosmetically removed and re-sewn skin, cellulite, moles, unwanted hair follicles and miscellaneous body garbage. And, thanks to the skillful hands of two New York surgeons, I could still smile like the cute person I was meant to be! Only one little thing about my surgery annoyed me, and only occasionally at that: I still looked so very much older than my sister Beth. Poor Beth, speaking matrimonially, of course. Howard was never going to change his habits about occasional romps with thirty-somethings. Divorce was out of the question. The scandal and disruption were not components of my sister's idea of life after public humiliation. Her cup of tea was to continue to enjoy the pleasures of the country club while taking up rug hooking and digital photography classes. A few of her best friends were in the same predicament, and they all shared similar philosophies. I didn't have that problem.

After I had completely recovered from the work on my face and dolled up for an intimate apparel fashion show with only Henry present, he grudgingly told me I looked beautiful. He was so moved by the change in me, he switched barbers.

The week after I returned from New York where the surgery was performed, Beth visited us in South Florida. I had a few bandages on my chin that would remain for awhile. We went to a lovely park and had one of our franker discussions. She was much more enlightened about her situation than I realized, as she revealed her attitude toward her marriage and her husband.

"You can't change a man's tendencies no matter how hard you try, Marlene. Howard is Howard, and, well, Henry is the old guard conservative loyal tough bird. You're fortunate that you two are compatible."

"I could never go to bed with a man who might have just secretly washed perfume off his shirt, and it wasn't my perfume."

"Howard has a maid to deal with that. I don't want to know what brand it is, or even what nation, French or domestic, it's not my affair. At least he's not a politician. I don't think I could handle what those wives go through."

"Beth, you could handle anything. You're as tough as my daughter Linda."

"I thought you might say as tough as Robin."

"Now, that's really tough. She's like a rock, although a very porous rock, something like, oh, here's a crazy comparison! She's tough, as in 'tuff!' The softest rock in the world. Yes, Robin has problems, but at least she has friends and sympathizers."

"I heard he's made quite a bit of money, I mean she. It's amazing."

"And just think of it, Beth. You have one of those sculptures right in your foyer in, I forgot which house."

"Oh, the Duchess County one. Wanna know the latest? Howard commissioned two more of them -- both for the Hampton place. Wouldn't tell me what he paid. I didn't mind. At least the money will remain in the family, sort of."

"I admire Howard's taste in art."

"Your face looks good, the part I can see. I think my surgeon did a better job on you then on me. It should last you at least ten years."

"Yeah, and they'd better be thin years. I still go nuts for cheesecake."

"That's an expression describing the inside of a woman's thighs."

"Can we change the subject? How's the grandchild? We saw her on Skype. She looks like one of those kids on the Pampers for newborns."

"She is one of them. Cissy offered her up as an infant model and they hired her."

"Nothing like starting early to build a portfolio."

"You're now so well-versed in investments, Marlene. I stay away from that page of the newspaper. I, uh, saw that you started Cissy on Barron's."

"She seemed interested. Beth, our kids are smarter than we are. Howard quipped that you take the financial section of the Wall Street Journal and use it to wrap up the doggie doo doo."

"He told me he cussed Henry out for treating you like you guys were poor. Hell, you weren't poor -- your surgery cost a mint!"

"Beth, the word 'poor' doesn't describe a woman who can't afford cosmetic surgery. It describes a woman who can't afford cosmetics."

"I know that. We donated a great deal of money last year to a foundation to help the impoverished."

Good old Beth -- showing her guilt once again. At least I didn't flaunt my thousands the way she flaunted her millions. After our visit I sent a check for Two Hundred whole dollars to a fledgling local foundation supporting new artists. I went on the Internet to find the right vehicle, thinking it would be easy, but most of the links were those seeking financial sources posted **by** artists. I probably needed to refine my search skills, but I was too busy cleaning out my closet and the dried up nail polish and make-up still stored in the vanity under my sink. Henry had been needling me about it -- saying it dated from the time of the Crusades.

What a great party the girls had given me for my Seventy-Second. My two daughters were there but Henry wasn't. He had gone to visit his two surviving sisters in Wisconsin. I was happy that he decided not to be so reclusive and that he had made plans to pick them up on the outskirts of Milwaukee and then drive up to Door County and have a nice week-end at one of the resorts on the peninsula. Wonderful Henry, the man I had just joined with, only Fifty-One Years prior, still finding excuses for not being around Robin too much. Oh, it was better than a year ago, but still not easy.

Let's see, what had actually occurred and what could still occur?

I was doing my reflection again, sitting on a cast iron two-seater bench in our back yard. It had nice scroll work and Henry thought it was dumb to buy a bench that nobody would use. His attitude caused me to purposely sit on it as much as possible, even in the hottest days of summer. We had a small pond in the yard and I had placed the bench near it where I could look at myself in the water. Suddenly I felt a teeny jab on my arm, no two jabs. I tried to crush the intruding insect with a folded section of The Wall Street Journal, which I now read regularly. As usual the insect escaped and I chalked up another loss. Sometimes I hated warm moist weather, but not enough to move back to Milwaukee.

48

It was winter according to the calendar. I had read somewhere that we lived in Temperature Zone Nine or Ten. Most of the Midwest was zoned Four or Five. People in our zones regarded winter as the time to cover the outdoor orchids with a protective covering, but only when a frost was forecast. People in the Midwest didn't have outdoor orchids unless they put a florist's potted orchid plant on the cold ground or stuck it in the snow. It would stay nice for a half hour. From the talk on the Weather Channel, it had been an especially grueling snow season in the Midwest. I wanted to visit Robin at a grand opening she was having in Cincinnati. Henry wanted to go to a gun show in Fort Lauderdale that same weekend. Publicity describing Robin's show had just arrived in our mailbox and it was spectacular. We got an invitation that had been scented with roses.

"What'll it be, Henry, guns or roses?"

"I don't want to be a spoil sport, honey, but wouldn't you like to see me sell a couple of the shotguns I don't need any more?"

"For real money?"

"No, the buyers will give me a gift card for a lifetime membership in the NRA."

"You're kidding, of course?"

"Yes, I'm kidding. Let's see, a lifetime membership for me would be worth about five hundred bucks, maybe even six hundred."

"Oh, have you planned the year of your demise?" Henry didn't answer. "Read what Robin wrote on the note that came with the invitation, please?" I watched Henry's face for any sign of emotion or pride, as he read the handwritten words on his note:

> "Mom, while I don't expect you and Dad to attend this event, my fondest dream is that I make this debut of my exciting new series with you two by my side."

Henry finished reading and sighed. "You should go, honey. I'll pay for the whole trip. Get on the computer and find a convenient flight. It's a good time for me to spiff up the garage. I'll buy some paint and hardware and finally clean out the junk and fix up the generator for the next hurricane season. Of course, I'll root for Robin's success."

"All right, I'll do that. I'll put the trip details on your desk. You'll drive me to and from the airport?"

"If I can, otherwise take a cab. Take some money out of the household account."

The plane trip was turbulent. I could measure the relative intensity of the bumpiness by the body language of the passengers around me. As we approached the landing strip I could see lightning flashes off to the West, but they seemed to be retreating. The tops of nearby buildings got closer and closer. As soon as I felt and heard that reassuring thud indicating wheels were hitting terra firma, I felt my regular heartbeat returning. My courage when flying had become stronger in the past few years with my increasing sense of becoming a sophisticated frequent flyer. I once hated having to use the lavatory on a plane, but now I used it a lot because I liked what I saw when I washed my hands and looked in the mirror. It made up for what I suspected was a bit of arthritis in my fingers. My published articles were fewer, but my wardrobe was richer. I had been doing quite well with some of my own investments lately, thanks to Suzie Orman.

I struggled with my one carry-on, the lightest I had ever packed, and rented a car at the airport in Cincinnati because it was cheaper than paying taxi fares. The rental place had a sweet little metallic teal blue Ford sub SUV just for me. It was the most feminine car they could find, although I had requested a pink Cadillac. The foreign-born rental car clerk didn't get the joke. As I reached the gate where people exiting had to show their papers, I asked the attendant: "Hey, can you tell me how I turn on the wipers? I forgot to ask the guy inside." I had expected people to be accommodating to older ladies, but now that I had this younger face, did I detect some subtle arrogance on the part of the man who helped me? The creep might as well have been wearing a large campaign-style button on his shirt that read: "Female airheads direct stupid questions here." I jerked on the drive transmission handle and eased the car over the toothed metal device that warned the driver not to back up. Whoopee, I was in Cincinnati and I had a GPS and it was bitter cold and I had been so smart as to have my new luxurious winter wool coat handy. I was this wardrobe wizard and gloated the entire way to the part of town where I could check into the motel. Robin would be proud of how I knew how to get around.

When I arrived at the fairly impressive gallery in the heart of Cincinnati's artsy section, I saw a guy who had the look of a valet standing by the front door. He noticed my rental car and knocked on the driver's side window. "Are you Robin's Mom?"

"Yes, how did you know?"

"She told me to look for a beautiful woman driving a rental car who wouldn't know where to park."

I looked around the area to pretend that such a description had to be somebody else. "Oh, well, while you're trying to find her, can you help me?"

"That's what I'm here for -- you can get out and I'll take over. I have a claim ticket for you. Robin's inside and she's excited to see you."

"Thanks, oh, what's your name?"

"George. Just call me G.S."

"Initials? What do they stand for?"

"George, Silly, everyone here uses initials because it's cool."

"I'm all for being cool."

As I walked into Robin's one woman show I was amazed at how professional and upscale everything had been handled. I was greeted by a chic lady of about thirty, who would have shopped at my mythical chain of boutiques with the name "Skinny and Statuesque." She smiled so broadly as she offered her hand, that I wondered if she had mistaken me for someone else. Women who dressed as though they had just been furnished with attire for a lunchtime fashion show at Neiman Marcus didn't normally smile at me. Sometimes they accidentally bumped into me, murmuring they were sorry, but didn't see me walking nearby.

"Hello, and you're---"

"I'm Valerie Jean, I'm the owner. Your daughter is one of the greatest sculptresses we've shown, and I'm expecting a huge crowd in about an hour. Are you hungry?"

"Well, I, uh---"

"There are refreshments in a room at the back for the V.I.P.'s. It's over there at the end of that corridor and help yourself."

"Sure, thanks, I'll do that. And is Robin busy right now?"

"Not for you, Mrs. Sternberg. You're our guest of honor."

"Me? I didn't do anything to teach Robin how to create art -- I'm just the doting mother."

"That's not what I've been told. Robin never stops talking about you." Valerie Jean leaned down to me and whispered something that made me catch my breath. "We know what Robin has been through and that without you, she'd have been a troubled man with no hope and no chance to pioneer this kind of work. Never sell yourself short, Ma'am. We all love what she says about you and you're wonderful to make this trip."

"Oh, Ms. Jean?"

"Call me Valerie."

"Valerie, I don't know how to accept all the credit you're giving me, but I'll try to digest these compliments. And really, I have always loved art and artists and it's a thrill for me to be here."

"It's a thrill that you came all the way here from Florida for this show."

"One other question I have."

"Yes?"

"Those five inch heels you're wearing? I tried wearing four inchers similar to that and I felt that my toes were going to go black. Is there some trick to it?"

"Mrs. Sternberg, let me confess something to you -- my feet are killing me!"

My two hours spent with Robin the next day were the happiest moments of my whole year. That was even counting the excitement I had felt after seeing that my face didn't turn out like a roadmap, with broad lines for major highways. Henry's benign diagnosis the year before was up there also. The best thing about my making the trip to Cincinnati was when Robin and I talked about how I might help her bridge the stubborn gulf between her and Henry.

"Mother, don't push him -- he's got to let the thing cook in his head and then let it gel. If he loves me, and I think he does, he'll come around. But know this, Mom -- it might take several years. I think we'll all be given the time by some miracle to work this out."

"I've learned something about miracles, Robin. A miracle is that I left your father back at the house without prostrating myself to have him help me carry my suitcase. I helped that miracle along by boarding a plane without an escort, getting off the plane, renting a car, finding this gallery and seeing you look happy. Now that's what I call a miracle!"

"I think what you're suggesting is that when a person lets go of a certain stubbornness and rethinks an attitude that has stuck for an eternity, then that's the definition of a miracle."

"I've been seeing psychologists for more years than this gallery owner lady has been alive. Henry always thought my spending money on it was asinine. He still does. I thought that the shrink would teach me to hate cake and creamed foods. He didn't. I still love them. So here's the miracle: I stay away from those foods because I happen to like how it feels to never get tempted to put on a breath-constricting girdle again."

"I think Dad's having his own kind of miracle. His miracle just takes a little longer."

"Maybe you're right. He doesn't like to talk about anything inside his head! He doesn't like Picasso, but he likes Chagall! He hates creamed spinach, but he loves tuna fish, plain and on a plate with the salt shaker handy. He gets on the scale and worries if he gains a half ounce. He is who he is! Right now he's home painting a garage that doesn't need painting. What can I say? He's an enigma! I've been married to him for fifty-one years and I still can't predict his next move!"

"I guess there's no exact science as to how a human being makes decisions, then."

"Like the mystique about how you decided to have the operation?"

"I went to several doctors and told each of them I was feeling lost and depressed all the time and that I thought I should have been a woman. Finally, one of them understood. Remember what I wrote in that covering letter I enclosed with the medical stuff?"

"I did, but it took me a long time to really get it."

"You're wrong, Mom. Sometimes I think you got it a long time ago."

"So has the operation solved a lot of your problems?"

"Most but not all. At least now, I have better problems."

"What's a better problem?"

"Like now I transform my feelings by expressing them through material -- metal, rock, maybe glass, which I'm taking classes for -- and at least have a passionate objective to keep me going. Most people still think I'm a freak, but things are changing. I might live long enough to be understood."

"How did you conquer your embarrassment?"

"I didn't."

"Well, Robin, let me tell you something. I think you've just opened up a clearing in my mind when it comes to Henry! He loves you as a parent loves a child and he's just embarrassed to show it because of, uh, because of, whatever. Society! Manliness! Guy Stuff! What's the difference?"

"My Uncle Howard bought three of my sculptures! He's got the first one in his front hall and will soon have two more at the other house! Rich tycoons see them and ask where they can get one!"

"Your talk of Howard and his art and his several homes? It just reminded me of something my mother told me before I married Henry."

"What?"

"It's about any gainfully employed man. She would say, "He makes a living? Don't knock it!"

"When you get home, Mom, maybe use some psychology. When Dad asks you questions, don't even answer, except with one word or a syllable. I think you call it your brevity system. The quieter you are, the more curious he'll be. And he'll have to make the first move. Just be yourself, but don't even think of nagging him."

"Nagging never did anything with your father, you know that."

"Of course. If he asks technical questions about my procedures, I'm going to give you a new book which you should take with you. Don't even tell him you have this book. Leave it lying around somewhere, like where you toss books you're reading. He'll see it and he probably won't want to read it at first, but he might want to crack it open when you're not around or maybe when you are, as long as you don't make a fuss about it. Who knows?"

"Maybe that medium that Beth used to go to knows."

"I love you, Mom. You've been terrific. And don't think I don't recall that first conversation we had. Actually, your sense of humor is what I remember. Don't you know that humor cures a lot of rifts in relationships?"

"Well, your Dad and I goof around a lot. After we have a fight and want to practically kill each other, one of us says something nutty and then we start laughing!"

"It's a known fact that you can't always laugh at something when it's like a fresh wound, but after it starts to heal, well, that's how it works! For example, we all loved your saggy neck even if you didn't. I couldn't say to you, Mother, do you know your neck is so wrinkled and ugly, we thought you were spending too much time in the water? But once you get over the fact that your body did what bodies do, sag with age, well, you might as well joke about it."

"So here's my lead-in to my joke, Robin, are you ready?"

"Go for it!"

"What did the mother ask her transwoman artist daughter?"

"I dunno. What did she ask?"

"Sweetie, about that new naked sculpture over there on that pedestal?"

"Oh, oh, here it comes. . ."

"What inspired you to make that male member part so fucking long?"

"I don't know exactly, Mom, it just came out of me!"

Before I made my gracious exit from the gallery, I took pains to offer a few helpful suggestions for Valerie Jean about where to re-position a few of the pedestals. I left Robin's very successful show feeling high-spirited. Some habits just don't disappear easily. I couldn't refrain from reminding her as if she were still a little kid, to take all the vitamins recommended by her primary physician and not to lose the list. But Robin had a comeback -- she asked me if I had gotten rid of all my plump lady clothes. That almost got me upset. Maybe because I had been experiencing abandoned clothes syndrome and had temporarily stashed them in a bag in a corner of the garage, just in case I couldn't deal with the final parting of the ways.

49

"Marlene, I don't think that Robin is very happy, not even now, with his, dammit, HER, new wealth and better face."

"Henry, you've hardly spoken to Robin these last few weeks. You're still the father of our daughter. Why don't you take her out to lunch? Just the two of you. She's coming here for a visit next week."

"I know. You're suggesting it's time to offer a peace pipe."

"She doesn't smoke. Linda's the one who resorts to an occasional joint."

"Don't I have to understand why Robin had to have that operation in order to feel better about herself? Because I still just don't get it."

"It would be very helpful."

"What's your shrink's phone number?"

"You're kidding, of course."

"I'm not kidding."

"Maybe you don't need the shrink. You read that medical stuff Robin sent. Did you understand the procedures and the prognosis regarding the patient's mental health?"

"No, and that's one of the reasons I want the shrink's number. I need somebody other than you to explain the whole thing. But I need that report. Where did you put it?"

"In my file drawer -- under "R" for Robbie. I never changed the name on the folder."

"OK. I'll get it and read it again. And I have a surprise for you. I lied just now. I already got hold of your phone number book and made an appointment with the psychologist. It's tomorrow. I knew that Robin was coming. I'll blow the whole visit unless I get some coaching."

"I don't believe it."

"And here's another thing: You can't come with me when I see the shrink, but if you have a problem with my boundaries, maybe you should see him separately."

Despite my curiosity, Henry refused to discuss his session with my psychologist. He told me it was private and none of my business.

"All right, Henry, but what about your having a long talk with Robin over lunch?"

"It's on. I just firmed up the date. It's the day after tomorrow."

"That's great, dear. Well, I have a hairdresser appointment at that time. But you two don't need me."

"I need you. The shrink thought we should both be there. Forget about keeping that appointment, please. Wear your hairpiece if you have to."

"I'm afraid I'll hog the conversation."

"I'll take some duct tape if your mouth goes off in an untimely manner."

"If you can see a psychologist when all your life you thought they were quacks, then I guess I can keep quiet for a prolonged period during our lunch. At least for an hour or so."

"I still think they're quacks, but this quack wasn't so bad. And he suggested that I should manage the conversation during our lunch."

"It's worth my missing my hairdresser. Anyway, I can reschedule the appointment. Where are we lunching?"

"The Breakers."

"Wow, you're really having a rush of insight and energy. Did you swallow some of that multi-hour caffeine-laden pomegranate liquid?"

"No, I just had some of your power water in that orange plastic bottle."

"Did you like it?"

"Not particularly."

Something had changed about Henry's attitude. He seemed perkier than usual. I would have expected him to be apprehensive about being seen in a public place with Robin. Even at a fine dining destination like the Breakers, we might unexpectedly bump into someone who knew us and our kids. While Henry was grooming his face and hair, I asked him if he was at all worried or still confused about the sex change.

"Not so much any more, dear."

"So what made you soften up, Henry? And by the way, I'm waiting for you to finish combing, er, arranging your appearance. I hope you hurry a little."

"I think there was a question there somewhere. Well, I'm still hard-assed about certain things. Remember the day you made me wear that damned yellow shirt with the blue palm trees on it?"

"I do."

"Well, I'm not going completely squishy. I've already put that shirt in the garage so I can use it when I change the motor oil."

"You can still wear it. That pattern is so busy, nobody will notice any grease spots on it."

"If you thought that shirt was so busy, why did you buy it for me?"

"I bought a matching one for me. I thought we'd both wear those shirts at some couples' event. Anyway, I only wear mine when I go to the gym."

"By my calculations, that's at least twice a year."

"I'm up to once a month."

"We all have to wise up, sooner or later. I have a favor, no, a demand, I must make on you."

"Yeah?"

"When we return from our lunch today, don't analyze me."

"Yes, dear. I mean, I won't dear."

"Robin, you sit up here in the passenger seat."

"OK, Dad. But I have to get the seat way way back. I can't stretch my legs out otherwise."

"The lever's to your----"

"Dad, I have it. I helped build this car."

"Right. Marlene, are you OK in the back?"

"Mmmm."

"Mother's not talking to you?"

"She promised not to butt in."

"That'll be the highlight of the afternoon."

"The only reason I stay with her is because she's so cute."

"Cute with my new arm, cheek, neck, thigh and butt adaptations?"

"Mom, don't talk!"

The waiter had just placed some concoction of artichokes with a gooey reddish sauce in the center of the table where we could all dive in. I eyed the offering with misgivings.

"Who ordered that?"

"Marlene, I thought you liked artichokes."

"Henry, I'm certain I told you several times that I liked the idea of artichokes suffering repeated crop failures."

"Oh, sorry, dear. We'll eat them and you can order what you like."

"Thanks, I'll pass."

I kicked myself under the table. Already I was breaking my vow of silence, and ruining my whole plan. Robin flashed a smile at me, as though she knew what was going on. It helped, and I was able to concentrate on playing with my napkin, while they studied their menus. It was such a large napkin I was able to make a butterfly out of it. I asked the server for two toothpicks and some green olives so I could do the antennae. Henry ordered salmon croquettes with escalloped potatoes, a female's kind of lunch. Robin chose lamb stew and curried shrimp chowder. I choked up as soon as I read the choices. All the entrees were either fattening or about as appealing to me as rabbit food. I wanted so much to concentrate on my agenda, which was to keep my mouth shut and my ears open. Robin's agenda appeared to be one of honesty and openness and good-hearted resolve. Henry had an agenda as well, but all I perceived was a nervous man fighting discomfort and humility. I loved seeing my arrogant husband that way. He would be on his guard and rustle up his best self. As for me, the state of remaining quiet and demure at lunch wasn't so difficult, so long as I listened intently. Although I refrained from furtively jotting down comments, I knew that as soon as this test was over, I could go home and write a short story summarizing the whole conversational happening, complete with analysis and footnotes.

Henry broached the philosophical query of his moment. "Robin, I want to ask you something, and it's hard for me."

"Dad, if you want to talk about what's hard, try to understand what I've been going through, not just recently, but most of my life."

"Sure, Robin, uh, yes. Well, it's like this: Now that you've settled into your lifestyle, so to speak, are you really happy? Or maybe just answer if you're a little happier than before the treatments and the operation."

"I'm somewhat happier, Dad. There are times I get low. I have a habit of turning to my art for comfort and getting me back up when I'm down. It keeps me going. Then, when I have a really good piece of work in process, I get excited. It's like being lost in a garden paradise, I don't know how else to describe it. I feel my hands working with what I see with my heart."

"But what about your social life?"

"It's better than before. My few dates with guys have been casual and tentative. Nothing at all serious. I still face a lot of humiliating distrust. There's terrible material on the social media, but some is supportive. I'm still shy about my body. I hear my friends telling me I look great. I'm trying --"

"Sorry to interrupt, Robin, but do you want a refill on your soda? The waiter is coming with a pitcher."

"Please, yes. OK, where was I? Oh, how happy I feel? Well, I'm trying to get used to my new self, but I keep getting tripped up by the past. Let's see, I used to hate my body years ago when everyone kept telling me I was handsome and I wanted to be different -- anything but handsome, like a stud. I wanted to be appealing. I was afraid to use the word 'attractive,' so I kept going to therapy. I needed a lot of help."

Henry was paying attention to Robin's words like he was following a script. His lines came next. "You know I've always discounted the value of therapy."

"It's helpful, even amazing for some, Dad. Not everybody benefits equally. I benefited a great deal. It probably saved my life."

Hearing my beloved husband and my beloved child talk about therapy was nearly impossible for me to hear without chipping in with my views. I wiggled in my chair, thinking of writing a story about a woman who woke up one morning and had lost the power of speech during the night. Then I noticed that Henry was wiggling in his chair also. His wiggle was more noticeable than mine because Robin was staring at her father's movements and glancing around the room, as if she wondered if our table was getting any special attention.

"Dad, is there something wrong with your chair?"

"No, it's not the chair. I need to excuse myself. I'll be right back."

As Henry got up from the table, I saw him reach into his pocket. I remembered that it was where he kept his inhaler. Robin and I smiled at each other as Henry walked toward the rest room. There was something to smile about. The father's shell was being pried wide open, like everyone knew there was a pearl inside. Neither of us spoke, and I made an effort to become involved with my chicken Caesar salad. I really wasn't able to enjoy it very much. All I was entitled to was plain chicken on plain lettuce, so I piled the croutons up on my bread plate where they were further from my fingers and tongue.

Henry returned from his visit to the rest room with a scowl on his face. "I seem to have lost my inhaler."

"Was it in your pocket, Dad?"

"It was. But the only thing in that side pocket right now is a quarter-size hole. I should have had Marlene mend these slacks, but I tried to do it myself. I'm no seamstress -- that's certain."

"Dad, there are folks you can hire to do cleaning and mending for you. I have reason to believe you can afford to get a little outside assistance with certain chores."

"It's time I bought some new clothes, Robin. Joseph A. Banks has a great sale on."

"I know you didn't lose your wallet. Father, please take back that hundred dollar bill you threw on the table. I'm treating. But maybe don't put that bill back in that side pocket."

"Good idea! OK, you can treat, but only because you called me 'Father.' See, I don't have to control all the family money!"

"You're hot, Dad, very hot."

"OK, so I get that you're somewhat happier, and maybe it's because you're a good artist, but I'll probably always wonder if I tried to steer you into the wrong business."

"You tried to be a good parent. You were a good parent. I'm not blaming you. I'm not blaming anyone."

"Nobody is that forgiving. At least nobody I hang around with."

"I'm not forgiving. I'm just trying to save my energy. I need it to get through, like, the rest of my life."

At this exchange, I couldn't keep still. "Robin, are you still, like, using the 'likes?' Haven't I taught you to speak without, like, every other sentence, like, don't say 'like?'"

"Mom, be quiet just a few more minutes. I was having a chat with your husband without you butting in."

I closed my lips again. Also, I was done eating with my appetite submerged, so I got two things accomplished.

Henry was back in charge. He always did treasure being center stage. "Robin, can you do one little thing for me, like right now?"

"Sure, Dad, what is it?"

"Give me a daughter-to-father kiss. I don't care who's watching."

Robin had to get up from her seat and went over to Henry and gave him a hug and a kiss. When she returned to her chair she lost it altogether. She took out her lace handkerchief and began to drench it with more tears than I had ever seen come from Robbie, even going back to when he was little. I saw her dabbing at her eyes and knew in my gut that a man couldn't act like that. My God, what kind of stuff did they put in those hormone treatments? If they made guys feel like crying like women, mightn't Henry benefit from a little dose? At that moment my unemotional husband looked extremely uncomfortable. He hated it if I cried even one teardrop. I sat on my hands because it helped me remain silent. Henry looked at me for assistance, and I shook my head. This was his party.

Henry caught on quickly. It was his turn to improvise with his lines. "Um, Robin, are you OK? I'm not sure what's going on. I get nervous when Marlene cries. What's wrong, Robin?"

"I'm just, oh, just, oh shit, I've got this 'boys don't cry' thing, but I'm not a boy any more. Please, give me time, oh, I can't talk right now."

This sudden outpouring couldn't have been all about our family reunion. It seemed to me as though Robin was crying about the past. How many years of catching up would she need? I also remembered right at that moment that Linda hardly ever cried. Certainly she didn't do it in front of us. These things were much too complicated for me to figure out.

I surveyed the room to see if anyone was watching. More of the lunch crowd seemed to be older people. They were very smartly dressed. I tried to smooth a wrinkle in the skirt of my cotton outfit, but it stayed wrinkled. I'd always be self-conscious about my appearance. Henry and Robin were taking care of the tab, although I knew Robin wanted to treat. I guessed she let Henry handle the tip after all.

"Dad, we need to leave now. There are lines of people waiting for our table. Thanks for being with me."

"Oh, it was my pleasure, daughter. And I appreciate your picking up the check. Here, you're a lady now, let me help you with your chair. Keep your mother company while I get the car, please."

Robin stayed at our place for two more days and then left in her treasured Audi. She seemed so much more relaxed than she did on her prior visit. But all wasn't roses with Henry. During our heartfelt goodbyes, he had anguish written all over his readable face. As we trudged back into the living room, I knew better than to ask him what was wrong. If my calculations were on target, he would soon spill everything out in the open, according to his own timetable. Ignoring his presence, I proceeded to dust the top of the picture frames, humming a ditty which I had heard during St. Patrick's Day.

"Day, de doo, day, de do, la, le le, ooh, le, lay ----"

"Will you cut that out?"

"You don't like my singing?"

"I don't like it when you don't ask why I look perturbed."

"Oh, do you look perturbed? I guess I missed it."

"Drat, woman, you were supposed to ask about my feelings!"

"Henry, tell me about your feelings."

"I feel really bad. I don't like it that I had a hole in my slacks. I need some new clothes. Will you come with me to pick out some new duds?"

"OK. But I have to confess something to you."

"If it's about your own impulsive purchases, I already know you bought some new expensive underwear. You left the price tags on."

"I thought I hid those bags from Bloomingdales!"

"I saw the bags in your closet when I went in there to get some hangers. Is that your confession?"

"Part of it."

"What's the rest?"

"I ordered some slacks for you from L.L. Bean. I knew your size."

"Why are we so fixated on clothes when we've just had this heavy-duty lunch with our daughter? Shouldn't we be dwelling on how well it went?"

"You can dwell, Henry. You begin."

"I feel really good about it. I think I'm getting used to having two daughters instead of a son and a daughter."

"Henry, I applaud you for turning the other cheek and accepting Robin into the family. I won't even say 'it's about time,' but it's about time."

"Well, that kid's life still isn't exactly a fairy tale, you know."

"Don't use that expression."

"I mean, uh, she still has a lot to deal with."

"Yes, she does. And so do we, but, DARLING, isn't it nice? Remember those conditions I made you agree to when we got engaged?"

"No, what conditions?"

"Henry, I told you that I wouldn't marry you unless you agreed to have a boy and two girls."

"So, we didn't fulfill the conditions, I guess."

"Oh no? Well, answer me, Henry, and be truthful. Did we have a boy and two girls or didn't we?"

"Smart-ass woman. You have to have the last word, don't you?"

"No, but I'm going to feel happy about one thing when my time comes to check out."

"What?"

"I'm going to revel in the fact that I finally gave birth to a sister for Linda!"

THE END

38555071R00166

Made in the USA
Lexington, KY
14 January 2015